FACTORS INFLUENCE CONSUMER BEHAVIOR

JOHN LOK

Contents

Preface

Prepare

I write this book aim to explain how and why whether artificial intelligence (big data gathering tool) is better method to compare economic or statistics or psychological methods to predict consumer behavior. If future artificial intelligent technology can be developed to apply to predict consumer behavior, what requirements does it need to achieve consumer psychological prediction function?

In future, organizations to consider how to raise staff efficiency and performance in order to raise productivity. I shall give opinions to explain how to attempt to apply (AI) technology to make psychological analysis to assist any organizations to make more accurate raising performance and efficient methods.

In my this book part five, I shall explain future how to attempt to apply (AI) technological method to give psychological recommendation to any organizations to assist them to raise staff efficiency. I shall attempt to indicate how to apply (AI) psychological recommendation technology to give any efficient performance opinions to let these organizations to learn, such as marketing consultant organization, basketball team organization, interior decorating organization, bank organization, hotel organization, university organization, film organization, nuclear factory organization ,electronic assemblies factory organization, medical organization and television organization.

This book aims to explain why and how future artificial intelligent technology (big data gathering method) can be applied to assist businesses to predict why and when and how consumer behavior changes. I shall explain why traditional psychological and statistic and marketing methods are applied to predict consumer behaviors, human's judgement and analytical effort will be worse to compare AI machine's judgement and analytical effort. Also, I shall indicate different business organizations why they apply AI big data gathering method to help them to design any questionnaires (surveys) questions which will be more valid and useful to conclude human's questionnaires (surveys) design questions method.

This book has these two research questions need to be answered?

(1) Can apply (AI) learning machine predict consumer behaviors?

(2) Can (AI) learning machine replace human marketing research method, e.g. survey or human psychological and micro and macro economic methods to predict consumer behaviors more accurate?

Nowadays, many businessmen or marketing research professional hope to apply different methods to predict consumer behaviors in order to know what will be future market activities and market changes to help them to choose to implement what kinds of marketing strategies more accurately. The methods include economic environmental change prediction method, consumer individual psychological change prediction method, micro or macro behavioral economic environmental change prediction method, marketing environmental change prediction method etc. different kinds of methods which can be applied to predict how consumer behavioral changes to influence whose behavioral consumption to the manufacturer products sale within one to two years short term or three to five years middle term, even above five years long term business plans.

Hence, if the product manufacturers can apply the most suitable consumer behavioral prediction method to predict how consumers' choice will be changed to influence their products sale easily. It will have more beneficial intangible and tangible advantages to achieve the their product easier sale aim to ensure their businesses' future market share to be increased more easier to their countries' choice target sale markets. Otherwise, if they applied the inaccurate consumer behavioral prediction methods to predict how their consumers' behavioral changes wrongly. Then, it will influence their market shares to be same level, even it will decrease their market shares, when their consumer behavioral prediction inaccurately.

In my this book first part, I concentrate on indicate whether any artificial intelligence (AI) tools will be one kind of good consumer behavioral prediction method to be choose to apply to predict consumer behaviors. I shall indicate some examples, cases to give reasonable evidences to analyze whether (AI) tools will be one kind suitable tool to be applied to predict when and how consumer behavioral changes. If (AI) can be one kind tool to attempt to be applied to predict when and how consumer behavioral changes. Will it replace other kinds of methods to predict consumer behaviors? Does it have weaknesses to be applied to predict consumer behaviors, instead of strengths? Can it be applied to predict consumer behaviors depending on any situations of only some situation? Finally, I believe that any readers can find answers to answer above these questions in this book.

In my this book second part, I shall explain why and how human can possible apply (AI) tool to predict consumer individual emotion. I shall indicate case studies to explain how consumer individual better or worse emotion how to influence whose consumption behavior in different situation. Finally, I shall indicate evidences to conclude how and why (AI) tool that can be used to predict consumer individual emotion and it will have direct relationship to influence consumption behavior, as well as how (AI) tool can assist businessmen to judge whether what reasons case the customer does not choose to buy its product, it is possible because the product high price factor, poor product quality or poor staff service performance or attitude etc. different factors to influence the consumer decides to choose to buy the other product consequently, when the (AI) tool can confirm consumer has good or bad emotion to judge what factors are the causes his decision making at the moment.

Readers can understand why and how (AI) tool can be attempt to be applied to predict customer emotion and it can influence positive or negative consumption behavior to the product clearly in this part.

This book third part has these two research questions need to be answered?

(1) Can apply (AI) learning machine as well as micro and macro economic methods predict consumer behavioral changing?

(2) Can (AI) learning machine replace human marketing research method, e.g. survey or human psychological and micro and macro economic methods to predict consumer behaviors more accurate?

The part indicates whether micro and macro economic methods can be attempted to apply to predict when, how and why consumer behavioral changing for every kind of different business. The second part indicates whether artificial intelligence can be attempted to apply to predict when, how and why consumer behavioral changing for every kind of different business.

Nowadays, many businessmen or marketing research professional hope to apply different methods to predict consumer behaviors in order to know what will be future market activities and market changes to help them to choose to implement what kinds of marketing strategies more accurately.

The methods include economic environmental change prediction method, consumer individual psychological change prediction method, micro or macro behavioral economic environmental change prediction method, marketing environmental change prediction method etc. different kinds of methods which can be applied to predict how consumer behavioral changes to influence whose behavioral consumption to the manufacturer products sale within one to two years short term or three to five years middle term, even above five years long term business plans.

Hence, if the product manufacturers can apply the most suitable consumer behavioral prediction method to predict how consumers' choice will be changed to influence their products sale easily. It will have more beneficial intangible and tangible advantages to achieve the their product easier sale aim to ensure their businesses' future market share to be increased more easier to their countries' choice target sale markets. Otherwise, if they applied the inaccurate consumer behavioral prediction methods to predict how their consumers' behavioral changes wrongly. Then, it will influence their market shares to be same level, even it will decrease their market shares, when their consumer behavioral prediction inaccurately.

Whether can businessmen apply micro and macro-economic methods to assist them to analyze how marketing will change, what marketing trend will develop next month or next half year, even more than one year marketing development trend in possible?

In my this book final part, I shall considerate on businessmen and customers both beneficial view point to explain how to apply behavioral economic concept to predict how their specific industries marketing development trend or consumer behavioral changing trend in these micro economic (individual consumer psychological shopping change trend) and macro-economic (global every specific industry marketing changing trend) environment.

This third part researches this two questions:

(1) Has it relationship between macro and micro economic environment change factors to influence marketing development change trend?

(2) Can businessmen apply macro and micro economic methods to predict future marketing development change trend in their specific industries?

I shall indicate some specific cases industry to attempt to explain whether it has really relationship between macro and micro economic environment change factors to influence marketing development change trend as well as whether businessmen can apply micro and macro-economic methods to predict future marketing development change trend in these specific industries.

In my this part, I concentrate on indicate whether any artificial intelligence (AI) tools will be one kind of good consumer behavioral prediction method to be choose to apply to predict consumer behaviors. I shall indicate some examples, cases to give reasonable evidences to analyze whether (AI) tools will be one kind suitable tool to be applied to predict when and how consumer behavioral changes. If (AI) can be one kind tool to attempt to be applied to predict when and how consumer behavioral changes. Will it replace other kinds of methods to predict consumer behaviors? Does it have weaknesses to be applied to predict consumer behaviors, instead of strengths? Can it be applied to predict consumer behaviors depending on any situations of only some situation? Finally, I believe that any readers can find answers to answer above these questions in this book.

In my analysis, I conclude marketing development or marketing change trend will be influenced by consumer behavioral change model or attitude factor. Finally, I hope my readers can give opinions to make judgement to evaluate my opinions whether is right or wrong in this research topic.In part four, I shall indicate sample case study to judge whether it is possible to apply (AI) tool to attempt to help businesses to predict consumer behaviors in different business environment.

Prologue

Table of contents

AI prediction consumer behavior tool

CHAPTER ONE

AI prediction consumer behavior tool

1.1 How can artificial intelligent tools predict consumer behavior in vehicle market

What is (AI) consumer behavioral prediction tool? How any why will (AI) tool assist manufactures to attempt to predict consumer behavior before and after consumption occurrence? First, I shall indicate how to apply (AI) tool to predict vehicle product consumer behavior case example.

Nowadays, many vehicle manufacturers hope their vehicles can attract to vehicle buyers to choose to buy their vehicles. However, there are many different brands of vehicles to provide to them to choose, so the vehicle market competition is very serious.

How to judge their different kinds of vehicle price which is reasonable acceptance to attract vehicle buyers to choose to buy the brand of vehicle manufacturers' any kinds of vehicles, e.g. fast speed sport style vehicles, comfortable and slow speed common cars, for four passengers common small size or more than four passengers common large car size? How to evaluate the vehicle prices issue is important factor to influence vehicle buyers' choices. Either if the brand of vehicle price is too high to compare brands, it will influence many vehicle buyers choose to buy other brands' vehicles or if the brand of vehicle price is too low, it will influence vehicle buyers feel this brand's vehicle's quality is worse to compare to other vehicle brands' similar vehicle products.

Thus, if the brand of vehicle manufacturers can predict how to design vehicles which can attract many vehicle buyers to choose to buy whose any vehicle products. What are future vehicle buyers' favorable vehicle styles? Then, the vehicle manufacturer can concentrate on manufacturing the kind style of vehicle products to sell already. It will reduce its vehicle manufacturing investment risk.

How to apply (AI) tools to predict vehicle buyers' behavioral consumption model? Whether artificial intelligent tools can predict automotive buyers' behavioral consumption model and predict future trend. In fact, automotive brands and dealerships are facing an increasingly competition when attempting to manually gathering the vast quantities of data required to create customer focused programs that increase retention, ultimately new sales and service automotive business. Building a based on that client's intrinsic needs and interests to any kinds of automotive vehicles at any given time. This is especially true in the automotive industry where the time span between purchases is measured in years. Because vehicle buyers would not like often to change their old vehicle to another new one. So, their decisions to buying another new vehicle, the time is usually after one year, even longer time. Hence, it seems any vehicles won't be frequent consumption products to the owned at least one vehicle family consumers (vehicle buyers).

Hence, how to predict vehicle consumers' taste or preferable which styles of vehicle choices issues is very important. If the vehicle manufacturers can not manufacture any attractive vehicles to sell easily in this year. Then, it will lose time, money in this year because it won't know when the owned least one vehicle users or non-owned any vehicle users who will decide to buy one new vehicle or change another new vehicle ensure. The different brand vehicle dealers will possible wait more than one year to attract them to buy their vehicles if their styles are not attractive to compare other brands of vehicle competitors.

However, artificial intelligence and machine learning can help any vehicle manufacturers to find solution to solve patterns in highly to solve patterns in highly complex data-sets that are beyond the capability of a human brain, and then building and automatically acting on the customer insights it generates.

Given the automotive customer need for individualized communications, this technology is positioned to become a critical component of any successful vehicle retailer's domestic or/and overseas vehicle markets. How can vehicle manufacturers and retailers use (AI) to enhance their vehicle marketing campaigns? How will (AI) affect their vehicle sale marketing strategy? What criteria would they use when selecting on (AI) solution?

Vehicle consumers today are able to quickly access different brands of vehicle information, research vehicle products and reviews, negotiate prices and compare one vehicle brand or retailer to another resulting of the brands of vehicle customers. At the same time, the rise of " big -data mining", wearable devices that track user's every move and preference and greater contextualization in advertising and social media has resulted in consumer expectations of individualized. Thus, it seems that (AI) tools can be used to gather " big-data" and then they can make human's mind to analyze how to design kinds of vehicles to satisfy vehicle buyers' needs.

As automotive vehicle marketers can apply (AI) tools to achieve messaging strategies to meet the needs of this new generation of informed vehicle consumers, using data from a variety of sources to move from a variety of sources to move from mass- messaging to more personalized messages aimed at particular vehicle buyer segments, e.g. fast speed sport vehicle buyer segment, slow speed comfortable small size or large size of buyer segment. However, when 90% of vehicle marketers believe having a single vehicle buyer view is important, only 6% have achieved it.

However, one of the main issues vehicle marketers facing is the lack of capacity to efficiently sift through and analyze the massive vehicle buyer amounts of data required to create vehicle buyer individualized vehicle customer experiences easily. This is especially difficult for automotive dealers, the long periods between purchase cycles, and the highly considered nature of the vehicle purchase means that each vehicle dealer needs to not only track a large number of potential vehicle customers for an extremely long period of time, but each of those vehicle customers will generate a huge amount of different kinds of vehicle behavioral consumption data as they research their next vehicle purchase. However, by choosing the right (AI) technological tools and programs , vehicle dealers can solve this big data gathering challenge into a major advantage.

For Forrester vehicle brand example, vehicle consumers have more power over the Forrester vehicle brand's reputation than ever before. Mayne, L. (2014) indicated that Forrester calls this new (AI) tools is the " age of the vehicle customer", a 20 year business cycle in which the most successful vehicle enterprises will reinvent themselves to systematically understand and serve increasingly powerful vehicle consumers. To win in this new age, Forrester declares companies must become vehicle customer obsessed and the only sustainable competitive advantage is knowledge and engagement with customers, such as (AI) gathering data knowledge.

Thus, the biggest challenge vehicle businesses currently face is not the collection of a large quantity of vehicle consumer data, but what to do with that data once they have it. Even at a large vehicle data research firm, the data sets are often too big for a single analyze, or even a team of analysts to sort through and draw conclusion from. However, enter artificial intelligence and machine learning , an efficient technology solution that can continuously find patterns in highly complex data sets that are way beyond the capacity of a human brain and then automatic drive action based on the customer insights is generated.

What is (AI) machine learning tool? Machine learning is a type of (AI) that learns from data and is not explicitly program. Think Amazon, face book. Machine learning serves up relevant content based on an individual vehicle purchase behavior and experiences. More simply, machine learning is a computer program that can learn relationships between data, subject those learnings to errors functions, and then learn from its errors. The program in effect, trains itself.

Lee, T. (2016) explained that "Thus, (AI) tools can learn deep a more advanced branch of machine learning inspired by how our brain's nervous function, has also been found to be especial effective in identifying patterns from data."

When this way sound is complicated from a vehicle dealer perspective, the implementation of a marketing program driven by artificial intelligence can take care of these tasks in an automatic vehicle fashion with little to no manual intervention required from the staff at time vehicle stores.

In practice at a vehicle dealership, the program will continue track vehicle customer behavior online, merging that data with any offline source (like CRM or DMS data) and then analyze this aggregated vehicle buyer data set to predict what vehicle customer may be shopping for and what information they might like to relevance from different kinds style of vehicle design photos.

1.1 Why can (AI) be applied to predict consumer behaviors?

Artificial intelligence refers to complex in vehicle market, machine learning that posses the same characteristics of human intelligence and that have all our sense, all our reason and think just like human do. Besides, machine learning is the practice of using algorithms to collect and examine data, learn from it, and then make a determination or prediction about something in the world.

The machine is " trained" using large amounts of data and algorithms that give it the ability to learn how to automatically perform a task with increasing accuracy. Otherwise, deep learning is primarily based on artificial neural networks inspired by our understanding of the biology of human's brains.

Deep learning breaks down tasks in ways that enables machines to assist us with increasingly complex tasks, driverless cars, better preventive healthcare and more accurate product recommendation (including vehicle recommendations). So, such as why (AI) technology can be applied to predict how vehicle consumer behavior changes to bring to judge whether vehicle consumer will like what kinds of vehicle styles next year. Then, vehicle manufacturers can gather overall vehicle consumer data to analyze and conclude the more accurate vehicle design direction for next year any new design vehicle manufacturing products.

Thus, (AI) machine learning can help vehicle manufacturers to solve how to design any new vehicle products challenge. A vehicle is both one of the most important and carefully considered purchases the majority of people will ever make in their lifetime. It is also a purchase that tends to be fundamentally tied to a person's identify and view of themselves. As the same time, vehicle consumers changing lifestyles result in changing vehicle needs, e.g. the young sport car enthusiast matures into the family driver.

Automotive dealers need to remember that vehicle customers and prospects are individual human beings with risk, complex and ever-changing lives factors, these factors will influence every vehicle consumer why who feels has vehicle purchase need, and how who choose to buy the first vehicle if who decided to buy the first vehicle.

The (AI) technological customer behavioral prediction tool seems to be the best vehicle salespeople in the world are those that know every one of their vehicle customers. Their likes and dislikes which style of vehicle design, preferences and changing tastes to vehicle choices. The capacity of the human brain, however, limits us from achieving this type of vehicle sales and frequent turnover at vehicle dealerships often results in the further loss of vehicle salespeople along with their vehicle customer relationships and knowledge. In this competitive vehicle environment, machine learning enables platforms to assist the vehicle sales team by tracking the vehicle consumer behaviors of each vehicle customer, learning and memorizing their preferences and predicting their future vehicle purchase needs.

Finally, I recommend that for a vehicle dealerships marketing platform to make their customer engagement efficient and fully-functional, I should be able to: applying (AI) tools to track every vehicle customer behavior across the web, connecting to a society of data sources, CRM, DMS, third-party, web vehicle brands, social email, click etc., aggregating and accurately cross-reference data from a variety of sources, leveraging this data to drive insights on a mass scale, as well as on an individualized basis, driving actions and automatically direct customer engagement via multiple channels based on where each customer is in their individual lifecycle.

1.2 How can (AI) provide businesses with better-informed decisions

I shall explain how (AI) technology can provide businesses with better-informed decisions to drive top-line growth, deliver meaningful experience for customers and smooth their path along the consumer journey. The widely understood definition of (AI) involves the ability of machines or computers to learn human thinking, reasoning and decision-making abilities.

A Narrative science study in 2015 year identified that (AI) was being used primarily in voice recognition, machine learning virtual assistants and decision support. This study also highlighted the many branches of (AI) and that techniques and their definition are used interchangeably. It is possible that (AI) can be used to gather big data , then to analyze to help businesses to predict consumer behaviors. For example, one of the most common techniques is machine learning, where algorithms are used to perform tasks by learning from historical data. Another growth branch of (AI) is natural language procession.

However, during 2017 year, search engines will begin to factor additional behavioral data into prediction of customer behavioral results, such as the user's history of searches and locations and previously captures conservations. Artificial intelligence will use this information to power predictive search results, e.g. predictive future consumer's choice behavioral processing for any kinds of businesses.

Predictive search will improve the quality of search results, and provide new insights into consumers' behavior and the moments which matter to them. Search will give recommendation into tailored how consumer individual choice in consumption process. Several of the largest online platforms already use machine learning to improve predictive consumer behavioral search results.

For example, Google's rank brain technology adds research by understanding the context in which the consumer has entered it. Over time, rank brain will learn further from user behaviors Amazon's DSSTNE (pronouned destiny) learns from shoppers' purchasing habits and consumption behavior to offer better product recommend actions, which Amazon can offer before a consumer has entered anything into the search bar. However, this technology is not independent of human input. For example, Google engineers will periodically retain the rank brain system to improve the models it uses. For another example, in 2016 year , Apple computer revamped its photos app to allow consumers to search for specific items in the phots, they want to find, not just dates and locations. Each photo that an intelligent phone or intelligent pad user takes goes through 11 billion computations, so that photos can understand exactly what is the photography.

It seems that in future, (AI) machine learning will allow search to evolve even further. Search engineers will deliver refined recommendations to their business users and use less human input to predict consumers' needs. For IBM computer example, it indicated 90% of the data that exists today has been created in the last two years. This huge explosion of data gives brands the opportunity to quickly spot and react to the latest trends, fashion and fads among its clients and potential clients. This will allow companies to better engage with younger consumers, who gain influence access to the latest trends, and use the brands. They associate with to help define who they are as individuals. Thus, brands have to identify and make use of them before consumers move on, but the vast quantity of data available makes. This a resource-intensive task. For next example, Lesara, a based online clothes store, uses this machine learning to inform its product decision often gathering information from internal and external sources. When its trends -spotting shoes. Lesara has a range of over 20 styles and sells hundreds of pairs a day. It focus on giving consumers, the very latest trends allow Lesara to develop on average of 50,000 new items each year. It compared to 11,000 old items each year. Thus, (AI) brain seems to human brain to own analytical ability to predict consumer behaviors.

For another example, Lesara is one online clothes store, uses machine learning decisions after gathering information from internal and external sources. One of its most popular products, shoes with LED started life when its trend spotting software flagged up a blogger wearing similar shoes. Now Lesara has a range of over 20 styles and sells hundreds of pairs a day. Its focus on giving consumers the very latest trends allows Lesara to develop an average of 50,000 new items each year, compared to 11,000 for its competitor Lara. it seems (AI) machine learning can help Lesara business to predict what kinds of shoes design or style that shoe consumers will prefer choose to buy in future shoe market trend. Thus, Lesara can predict shoe consumers' taste successfully and it can manufacture many attractive style of shoes. (AI) machine learning can gather global past shoe consumer's shoe shopping experiences, then analyzes to make conclusion to give lesara recommendation successfully. This will make the experience more enjoyable for shoe consumers and allow Lesara to advert whose different new style or design of shoes to deliver them move relevant messages by understanding the context of the experience.

However, (AI) machine learning will have this risk who manufacturers need to concern if they applied this technology to predict consumer behavior. It is on sample consumers' privacy issue, in order to avoid complaint chance occurrence. However, machine learning can tie this data together to identify which f the billions of devices are being used by individual consumers. This helps brands understand how consumer engagement and actions can be attributed to different messages in different contexts and at different time. So, machine learning can help brands to build confidence to promote their products by any advertisement channels. When, this new (AI) machine learning technology can conclude how to design their products to be the most attractive, due to it has more accurate to predict consumer behaviors to compare human themselves prediction judgement effort. It seems that (AI) machine judgement effort is more accurate to compare to human judgment effort.

For example, google is moving away from cookies and using logged in data to track and make to users. It plans to expand the scope of the brand lift tool from online video. Thus, consumers are responded will to shippable context, finding it persuasive and easy to navigate by (AI) machine learning decision. For example, fashion brands can aggregate their You tub videos and blogs into a mobile context marketing experience, such as brand centric context into a personal shopping activity gives the shopper an experience, who are likely to remember and tell their friends about any new style of products design promotion from these internet advertisement channels after (AI) machine learning tools' styles of product design recommendation.

CHAPTER TWO

What is (AI) deep learning techniques to forecast environment behavioral consumption

The (AI) deep-learning technology leads to performance enhancement and generalization of artificial intelligent technology. It influences the global leader in the field of information technology has declared its intention to utilize the deep-learning technology to solve environmental problems, such as climate change. So, it will help agriculture farming businesses can raise any plant food: vegetable, fruit, rice which grow up very easily if farmers can apply (AI) deep-learning technology to solve environment problems to influence their plant food grow. If the whole year seasonal change is very good and it is suitable for any plant food to grow in farming land easily, e.g. rain is enough and soil is enough for any plant food to grow in the farm lands. Then, fruit, rice, vegetable etc. agriculture businesses will have much beneficial attribution to global farmers.

The question is how to use deep-learning technologies in the environmental field to predict the status of pro-environmental consumption. We predicted the pro-environmental consumption index based on Google search query data, using a recurrent neural network (RNN model). To certify the accuracy of the index, we compared the prediction accuracy of the RNN model with that of the ordinary least square and artificial necessary network models. For example, the RNN model predicts the pro-environmental consumption index better than any other model. we expect the RNN model to perform still better in a big data environment because the deep-learning technologies would be increasingly as the volume of data grows. So, deep-learning technologies could be useful in environmental forecasting to prevent damage caused by climate change to influence any rice, vegetable, tomato, potato, fruit etc. different plant food grow in any countries' farming land easily.

For South Korea example, over 800 government agencies spent 2.2 trillion Korea won on eco-products in 2014 year. However, green products are rarely purchased outside these agencies. This phenomenon occurs because there is a gap between consumer attitudes and behavior , that is environmental attitude is a major factor in decision making vis-a-vis the consumption of " green" food and services (Jorea Ministry of Environment, 2015). Therefore, it is necessary to understand those consumer attitude, that will lead to sustainability-conductive behavior and consumption.

2.1 Environmental consumption prediction

Recently, many researchers have studied pro-environmental consumption and household indexes as well as suicide rate predictions using messages posted by internet users on Google trend, Tweets etc. channel. Whether can environmental consumption be predicted by (AI) deep-learning technological internet channel? How can impact the pro-environmental consumption attitudes of green policies? Korea scientists estimated pro-environmental attitudes using search query data provided by Google trend and confirmed through regression analysis, that pro-environmental attitude has a positive correlation with the pro-environmental attitude index. They also explained that environment-friendly attitude of residents plan an important role in policy making. In the past, most household consumption indexed were calculated through surveys, but (AI) deep-learning technological tool " big data" have recently gained research attention (Lee et al. 2016).

It seems that (AI) deep-learning technology can help agricultural export countries' farmers , e.g. US, UK, Canada, New Zealand, Australia, Japan, China, India etc. they can predict environmental behavioral consumption to any rice, tomato, potato , fruit, vegetable etc. plant food consumers. The beneficial advantages to them include as below:

(a) Assuming they know their countries' weather, when it has less rain to cause drought or when it has more rain in any seasonal time in the year. They can choose not to grow any kinds of above these plant food to avoid loss.

(b) They can make any kinds of above these plant food price raising after their prediction of these bad seasonal time to cause their plant food shortage supply challenge. Because these plant food consumers' demand number is more, but the supply of these above plant food supply number is less. However, due to they had predicted when the bad seasonal time can not allow them to grow these above plant food before. So, they have enough time to grow many these above plant food number in predictive good seasonal time to prepare to supply to their plant food import countries' plant food consumers to eat. Thus, these predictive environmental consumption plant food export countries can raise their plant food price to sell to them. When, the other non-pre-predictive environmental consumption plant food export countries can not supply any one of those plant food to them to eat, due to the bad climate to cause them can't grow any one of these plant food to export to sell.

Thus, (AI) deep-learning technology can be applied to predict how to raise the plant food supply number in order to raise price to the import plant food countries consumers to eat, due to they feel difficult to buy these plant food to eat in the bad climate seasonal time in whole year.

(c) (AI) deep-learning technology can help climate scientists to find what reasons cause their countries; rain sudden increases or cause their countries' rain sudden decreases. After its gathering data analysis, it can assist climate scientists to find solution methods to attempt to control the rain level can be right falling down level to let agricultural export farmers who can grow their plant food to sell to agricultural import countries in whole year.

(d) The agricultural export countries' farmers can apply (AI) deep-learning technology to help them to choose whether growing which kinds of plant food in that whether climate time to earn more plant food consumption number more easily.

Due to the agricultural countries climate will often change, for example, tomato, potato, rice, fruit etc. plant food can be adapt to grow in more rain time, but vegetable can not be adapt to grow in more rain time. If farmers can apply this technology to predict when it will have move rain or when it will have less rain to fall down in their countries. Then, they can choose to grow which kinds of plant food number more, in the suitable seasonal climate time in order to raise plant food growing number productivities to supply to sell to satisfy any agricultural food import countries' demand effectively.

(e) (AI) deep-learning technology can help agricultural import countries to solve agricultural food shortage challenge in long term. When this technology can be popular to base applied by the agricultural plant food export countries. It will solve global agricultural food shortage challenge. For example, when one agricultural export countries‘ farmers can popular accept to apply this technology to predict when to grow which kinds of plant food more to rise number productivities to sell. e.g. vegetable, fruit, rice Besides another agricultural export countries' farmers can also accept to apply this technology to predict when to grow plant food, e.g. potato, tomato to raise number productivities to sell. Then, they can concentrate on growing the specific kinds of plant food in order to raise the specific plant food number productivities in every seasonal change time every month. Then, global agricultural plant food supply must be raised, due to these predictive environmental change farmers can know who ought grow which kinds of plant food to sell to raise number productivities.

2.2 How can apply (AI) digital channel to predict consumer behaviors?

(AI) digital channel can be applied to help businesses to evaluate whether how much the product price is the most attractive to persuade consumers feel it is the most reasonable price to sell. It helps consumers to feel which brands of products which ought change the price to let consumers to choose to buy the brand of product. It can be applied to predict whether how many consumer numbers can be increased or decreased when the brand of product's price is variable. It aims to give opinions to help any brand of product manufacturers or sellers to judge whether which price is the most reasonable to let consumers to accept to choose to buy the brand of product in popular.

Thus, (AI) price measurement technology can be preference to be applied online communication ecommerce and mobile phone internet platform aspect. As businesses can enter their past products prices data and past customer number data into computer or mobile. Then, (AI) price measurement technology can gather these data to analyze these product prices and past customer number to compare their prices variable changing range level to find their price variable difference to measure to make conclusion about every product's price variable changing will influence how many customer number increase or decrease changing to choose to sell their different kinds of products more accurate. Then, (AI) price measurement software will help them to analyze all past price variable changing data to compare whether which price range can let customers to feel it is more reasonable and attractive to influence them to choose to buy the product among different brands of product choice.

Because any product's price is one important factor to influence consumers to choose to buy the product, instead of quality, durability, shape, appearance, color, brand familiarity etc. factors. Any online businesses with a focus on

Asia should considerate (AI) customer care, and virtual shopping experience, whereas is Europe and North America still value face-to-face and/or real human interaction over (AI) or virtual worlds.

For example, Amazon publish has applied (AI) price measurement technology to help authors to decide how much every different topic of e-book or paper book price, it can attract the largest number of readers to buy. Any one author only needs to type whose book name to Amazon publish author himself/herself Amazon website. Amazon publish (AI) price measurement learning machine will help them to auto-calculate and judge how much e-book or paper book price is the most attractive and the most reasonable in order to increase reader number to buy their e-books or paper books to read. So, (AI) online price measurement machine will gather past similar book names and past every similar book readers‘ reading times and the number of readers to give opinions to let every author to judge whether his/her very new e-book or paper book ought charge how much price to the e-book or paper book which can attract many readers to choose to buy. Although, it is not ensure that the e-book or paper book price must let readers to feel it is the most reasonable price to choose to buy in reader's view point. However, it has other factors to influence readers' choice to buy the e-book or paper book, e.g. whether the book content is attractive to public, the author's familiarity, the book's page is enough or not to satisfy readers to read etc. factors. But, instead of all these extra factors to influence readers to choose to buy the book to read. (AI) price measurement learning machine can real give opinions to every author to let them to judge the e-book or paper book different price range whether is too high to influence readers to choose to buy to read or tool low to influence readers feel it is possible poor content book to compare other similar content books. Thus, (AI) price measurement machine can help authors to predict every reader's reading behaviors or reading experience and reading habit from online channel in short time easily. The author only enter the book name to let Amazon publish price measurement machine to check, it will follow past reader's reading habit and reading experience to judge whether the similar all book topic sale record to judge how much price is the reasonable price to attract many readers to buy the book.

Hence, (AI) can be applied to digital channel to help businesses to predict consumer behavior in the future. In the future, mobile/smartphone, laptop, desktop will be most frequent used ecommerce channels to develop online business. So, (AI) can be also applied to these platforms to gather data to make analysis to help businesses to predict consumer purchase behaviors popularly. Due to , ecommerce is popular to global, so digital online and instore channels can be one good channel to let (AI) learning machine to make platform to gather past every online consumer purchase (buying) experience data to help businesses to build brand personality and having a responsible, positive impact on society.

To apply (AI) learning machine technology to understand customer online purchase behavior, it will raise business e-commerce successful chance: For example, (AI) learning machine can help businesses to gather data to analyze to determine whether short-term or long-term signals in the online consumer behavior that indicate higher purchase intents to let every online business to know. (AI) learning machine can find that online users with long-term purchasing intent tend to save and click through on more content.

However, as online users approach the time of purchase their activity becomes more topically focused and actions shift from saves to searches from online consumption channel. Then, (AI) learning machine will further find that the brand product purchase signals in online behavior can exist weakness before an online purchase is made and can also be traced across different online purchase categories. Finally, (AI) learning machine synthesize these insights in predictive models of online user purchasing intent to the brand of product. Taken together, it's work identifies a set of general principles and signals that can be used to model online user purchasing intent across many online content discovery applications. Thus, (AI) learning machine can help online businesses to gather any online users‘ click online behaviors data to judge whether there are how many online users will choose to find their online business websites to make final decisions to buy their products from online channels. Then, it will give opinions to help the online businesses to let it to judge whether what are the important website factors will help its online business to attract many online consumers, e.g. designing unattractive website issue, online unattractive product photos issue, unclear website color issue, unclear website advertisement message, contents and words impressions issue, lacking image movement frequent attractive seeing issue etc. different website factors. Thus, online digital channel will be one good choice to apply (AI) learning machine to help businesses to predict consumer behaviors.

2.3 Can apply artificial intelligent learning machine " big data" gathering method to predict manufacturers' behavioral performance ?

In consumer view point, can they apply (AI) learning machine to predict manufacturers‘ behavioral performance to judge whether whose products are value to buy. Nowadays, (AI) and big data are reshaping the risk in consumer privacy. For example, consumers want to hide their willingness to pay just as firms want to hide their real marginal cost, and buyers have less favorable information, say a low credit shore, prefer to withhold it just as sellers want to conceal poor product quality. So, it implies that it is possible (AI) learning machine can help customers to gather any manufacturers' past sale performance, e.g. how many complaints or appreciation from clients, product quality etc. sale data to let consumers to make judgement whether it is value to buy to compare other competitors. So, it has risk to the poor product quality of manufacturers. Otherwise, it has benefits to the good product quality of manufacturers. It also implies all manufacturers‘ privacy is not protected or secret when (AI) learning machine is popular to be used to predict manufacturers' behaviors by consumers.

Information economists suggest that both buyers and sells have an incentive to hide or reveal private information, and these incentives are crucial for market efficiency. Data technology that reveals consumers type could facilitate a better match between product and consumer type, and data technology that helps buyers to assess product quality could encourage high quality production.

Thus, (AI) big data technology can also assist consumers to gather different manufacturers‘ data to compare what their advantages and disadvantages of their products are. Then, consumers can make comparison to choose which brand of product is the suitable to whom to buy in these more choice consumption market. (AI) learning machine will gather similar brand their products' data to analyze to make conclusion to let consumers know or feel to make final judge to find what advantages or disadvantages of these sample brands of similar products‘ comparison from internet. On the other hand, it means that manufacturers can gather consumers' past purchase behaviors or purchase experience from (AI) big data gathering method to record and analyze to give opinions to let manufacturers to know what reasons or factors influence consumers choose not to buy their products from internet.

(AI) big data gathering consumer behavior prediction method can give these benefits to manufacturers and consumers both, such as: New concerns arise because (AI) technological advance which have enables reducing cost of collecting, storing, processing and using data in mass quantities extend information beyond a single transaction. These advances are often summarized by the big data, it means charge volume of transaction-level data that could identify individual consumers by itself or in combination with the datasets.

The popular (AI) takes big data as in input in order to understand, predict and influence consumer behavior. Modern (AI) is used by legitimate companies, could improve management efficiency motivate innovations and better match demand and supply. But (AI) in the wrong hand, also allows the mass production of fraud and deception. Since , data can be stored, traded and used long after the transaction. Future data use is likely to grow with data processing technology, such as (AI) big data gathering consumer and manufacturer behavioral prediction method from internet channel.

Thus, future (AI) big data learning machine can also help consumers to choose the best brand of manufacturer's products among different brands of manufacturers products choice to compare their past sale performance from internet. They can apply (AI) big data statistic method to gather all different manufacturers' similar products past sale data to compare their advantages and disadvantages to make the best decision to choose to buy which brand of product is the most suitable to them to buy to use. It seems (AI) big data can also help consumers to predict any manufacturers' manufacturing behaviors or manufacturing performance whether they are improving their product quality or are deteriorating their product quality. Thus, (AI) big data tool is also important to help customers to predict future the different brands of manufacturer performance will have improvement in possible.

Thus, I believe that artificial intelligent "big data" gathering method can be suggested to be applied to attempt to predict consumer behavioral changes in global business environment, the reasons are as below:

On the consumer's beneficial hand, Consumers can apply this method to attempt to gather any global manufacturers data to be analyzed by this artificial intelligent learning system. Then, it analyzed all the different brands of specific similar product manufacturer' data to compare what are the range of the best past manufacturing history and sale data to the group of best manufacturers, and what are the range of the better past manufacturing history and sale data, and what are the range of the good past manufacturing history and sale data, and what are the range of the common past manufacturing history and sale data. Finally, the (AI) learning system will compare all the specific similar product, e.g. mobile phone or computer, television, car etc. different kinds of specific products of global manufacturers to conclude the result is such as whether which brands will be the best manufacturers to let the consumer to buy the television or mobile phone or computer or car etc. different kinds of products. It can make more accurate judgement to compare general human's phone or questionnaire surveys investigation method, newspapers, television, radios, internet searches etc. different manufacturing news or data gathering channels to find which brands are the most worth confidence to consumers to choose to buy the specific product in the global consumption market.

On the manufacturers' beneficial hand, manufacturers can apply (AI) data gathering method to predict consumer emotion and buying behavioral changes more accurate. For example, the vehicle manufacturer, it plans to gather data to predict potential driving fast speed sport vehicle consumers' preferences trends in order to make the accurate judgement how to design its sport vehicles to attract many sport vehicle buyers who will choose to buy it's brand of any driving fast speed sport vehicles. It can attempt to apply (AI) intelligent learning system to gather global different brands of sport vehicle data concerns that all past driving fast speed sport vehicle buyer's preference of sport vehicle design. Then, the (AI) intelligent learning system gather global different brands of driving fast speed sport vehicle which had ever been purchased by the different country's driving fast speed sport vehicles consumers. After, it can compare divide the range of similar driving fast speed sport vehicle design and similar price to be different groups. The (AI) intelligent learning system can attempt to follow the past number of different brands of driving fast speed sport vehicle buyers to calculate how many driving fast speed sport vehicle buyers who choose to buy the brand of driving fast speed sport vehicle as well as it will analyze and make judgement to find whether the cheaper price reason attracts the different countries sport vehicle buyers choose to buy the brand of driving fast speed sport vehicle or the attractive design reason attracts the different countries sport vehicle buyers choose to buy the brand of sport vehicle or fast speed reason attracts the sport vehicle buyers choose to buy the brand of sport vehicle.

For example, although some brands of driving fast speed sport vehicle manufacturers' prices are very high, but they can still attract global many sport vehicle consumers to buy. Whether all sport vehicle's attractive design is the main factor to influence them to buy or whether it's fast speed is the main factor to influence them to buy or whether it's safe confidence it the main factor to influence them to buy or it's familiarity brand is the main factor to influence them to buy. (AI) intelligent learning system will attempt to make judgement and analysis to conclude whether the attractive design factor is the main factor to influence many sport vehicle consumers to choose to buy the brand of sport vehicles.

Otherwise, for another example, although some brands of driving fast speed sport vehicle manufacturer's prices are low, but they can not still attract many global many sport vehicle consumers to buy. Whether all vehicle's unattractive design is the main factor to influence them choose not to buy their fast speed driving sport vehicles or whether the unsafe factor is the main factor to influence them choose not to buy their fast speed driving sport vehicles or whether unfamiliarity brand is the main factor to influence many consumers choose not to buy their fast speeding sport vehicles.

Thus, when (AI) learning system had helped the fast speed sport vehicles manufacturer to gather all different brands of fast speed driving sport vehicle's past sale data and price data, design of different sport vehicle, e.g. color choice, method of style, comfortable chair styles and chair sizes and what kinds of steel material to manufacture the sport vehicles data and driving safe and accident occurrence data and the data concerns what reasons of the past complaint to brand of sport vehicle manufacturer from its sport vehicle buyers. Then, it can make more conclusion to give more accurate opinions whether which brands of fast speed driving sport vehicle manufacturer(s) whose sport vehicle design is the main factor to attract consumers choose to buy its any driving fast speed sport vehicle products really. Thus, it seems that it can make more accurate judgement to compare television survey, questionnaire survey to gather data concerns how to design the fast speed sport vehicle to attract consumers to choose to buy the sport vehicle manufacturer's planning sport vehicle products. I believe that (AI) learning system can help the sport vehicle manufacturer to make more accurate conclusion or judgement how to design its fast speed driving sport vehicles to attract it's consumers more easily.

AI predicts customer emotion

CHAPTER THREE

(AI) tool predicts consumer immediate and expected emotion how to influence consumption decision

If (AI) tool can be confirmed to apply to predict consumer behavior, then I can conclude that it can be attempted to apply to predict what the factor(s) of the product itself can cause the consumer has positive or negative emotion, so the manufacturer can attempt to avoid the bad factors cause to bring negative emotion to influence the consumer chooses not to buy the product more easily, such as vehicle product case.

Economists refer to the consumption desirability is as " utility" and the product or service consumption decision making is arose

influenced by maximizing utility only. However, they neglect consumer individual immediate emotion change will also influence the consumer individual consumption decision consequently. Expected emotions are those that are anticipated to occur as a result of the outcomes associated

with different possible courses of action. For example, if a potential investor, were deciding whether to purchase a stock, who might imagine the disappointment who would feel if who ought it and it reduced its price. Otherwise, whose emotion would experience , such as regret if it increased in price, but who does not buy it before the stock rise its price. However, I believe nowadays technology, in the future one day, (AI) tool can be attempted to assist consumer psychology profession or marketing research profession to assist them to find what are the bad factors to influence consumers choose not to buy any manufacturers‘ products. Then, when the manufacturer

can discover what are the bad factor(S) cause(S) consumers who do not choose to buy their products, then the manufacturer can raise whose product of consumption desirability or " utility" to raise whose product's consumption decision making is influenced by maximizing utility. Hence, (AI) tool will be possible to find what the bad factor(S) to cause consumers do not choose to buy the manufacturer's product in order to raise the product's utility to bring consumer positive emotion to choose to buy its product in possible. SO, (AI) tool will be one consumer psychological

emotion prediction tool to assist any manufacturers
to help their products to build positive emotion to any consumers in possible.
The key feature of expected emotions is that they are experienced when the outcomes of a decision materialize, but not at the moment of choice, at the moment of choice, they are only feel about future emotion. Such as consumption case, if the consumer chose to buy the product or consume the service before it's price is increased. Then, the consumer will feel happy and it is worth to purchase or consumer the service as well as the consumer's expected emotion is positive before who decides to buy the product or consume the service, because who believes or feels the product or service's price will be raised in short term, e.g. after one month, one week. Thus, it means that if the consumer does not believe or
feel or predict the product or service's price either it will increase or decrease in short term, whose emotion will be negative, those negative emotion will influence who does not decide to buy the product or service, it is possible that who feel it is not worth to buy the product or consume the service immediately. He She will choose to consume the service or buy the product to wait it's price is decreased later. it seems that the consumer's positive or negative emotion will influence who decides to buy the product or consume the service later or earlier. Thus, it has close relationship between the consumer individual immediate purchase or consumption decision and positive emotion or negative emotion (either expected emotion or immediate emotion influences).
Consequently, if (AI) tool can help any manufacturers
to predict when its product price ought to be increased or decreased in order to attract consumer to choose to buy its product. Then, it can help any manufacturers to build positive expected emotion to attract consumers to choose to buy its product more easily. For example, when the (AI) tool can predict when the consumer expects the product price will fall down, then it can give ideas to the manufacturer to raise up the product price in the month, then it predicts many consumers expect the product price will fall down after six months. So, the product price will not be fall down after six months. So, many consumers will feel disappointment and they will choose to buy the product if the manufacturer
decided to raise the product price after six months. Then, the higher product price will cause many consumers worry about the product price will continue rise up, so they will prefer to choose to buy the product immediately after six months because they afraid the product price will continue to rise up in the year. Then, I assume that (AI) tool has effort to predict when consumers feel the product will rise up or fall down, then it can give ideas to the manufacturer when to rise up or fall down the product price in order to attract or persuade many consumers choose to buy the product in different period in the year.

1.1 What does (AI) tool predict immediate emotion mean?

Psychologists indicate that immediate emotions, by contrast, are experienced at the moment of choice and fall into one of two categories. Integral emotion, like expected emotions, arise from thinking about the consequences of one's decision, but " integral emotion", unlike expected emotions are experienced at the moment of choice. Such as purchase stock case, the share buyer might experience immediate fear at the thought of the stock's losing value. " Incidental emotions" are also experienced at the moment of choice, such as a consumer predicts the product or service price whether it will be risen up or fallen down. If he/she feels the product or service price will fall down after next month and he/she will choose to buy the product or consume the service. But consequently, after next month, the product or service's price won't fall down absolutely.

Then, he/she will have incidental emotion to influence whom to choose whether he/she ought buy the product or consume the service, due to the product or service price is not still fall down. Otherwise, he/she is fear the product or service will not fall down in short term. Even, it will increase price later. Hence, whose incidental emotion will have possible to influence whom to choose to buy the product or consume the service after one month, if the product or service's price is still not increased absolutely. So, (AI) tool can be attempted to apply to predict when the product price ought need to be raised or fallen down in order to attract consumers to choose to buy the manufacturers' product in different period.

Economists indicate utility an individual consumption with an outcome might arise from a prediction of emotion: For example, a dinner eater might choose a higher utility to an Italian restaurant dinner than a French restaurant dinner because who anticipates being happier at the former, even the former's dinner price is higher than the French restaurant.

So, such as this restaurant dinner case, if one (AI) tool can assist the French restaurant owner to find what factor(S) cause(S) the dinner consumers do not choose to go to its restaurant to eat its food, e.g. high price factor, bad taste factor, bad wait service performance factor, bad cooker's cooking skill factor, poor advertisement promotion factor, poor familiar factor, poor location or poor eating environment etc. different factors. Then, the French restaurant owner can find methods to avoid the bad factor(S) cause(S) many dinner consumers do not choose to go to whose French restaurant to eat dinner more easily.

The question is that whether the positive emotion factor can influence the consumer changes whose mind to choose to consume the more expensive service or buy the more expensive product. To answer this question. it depends on whether the consumer has an imperfect understanding of whose own tastes or the consumer has a perfect understanding of whose own tastes to the product or the service.

It means the consumer will choose to buy the product or consume the service, even it's price is higher than other general similar products or services if who has a perfect understanding of whose own tastes to the product or service. Otherwise, who won't choose to buy the product or consume the service, due to it's price is higher than other general similar products or services if who has an imperfect understanding of whose own tastes to the product or service. So, it seems that the consumer's negative or positive emotion arise will be influenced by whose perfect or imperfect understanding of whose own tastes to the product or service factor.

It concludes that whether how much degree of the consumer's utility to the product or service. It is not the only one important factor to influence the consumer to choose to buy the product or consume the service. Otherwise, the consumer's imperfect or perfect understanding own tastes to the product or service factor will influence the consumer to arise positive or negative emotion to make final purchase or consumption decision immediately. It will be one more consumption influential factor to lead the consumer to make the final consumption decision making immediately. So, future (AI) tool ought to be innovate to own how to judge good taste or bad taste for any food in order to predict food consumers to choose to buy the food manufacturer's any foods more attractively.

Chapter Two

(AI) tool technical innovation in cruise tourism immediate positive emotion influence to cruise travelling consumers

Can apply (AI) tool to cause positive emotion to cruise tourism consumers? Cruise tourism industry is the most influential emotion industry example to influence cruise travelling consumers' travelling entertainment choice. I shall indicate some evidences how it's innovation will influence cruise travelling consumers' emotion to be changed to positive from negative immediately as well as to prove how the cruise traveler higher utility feeling to the cruise tourism provider is not the main factor to influence whom to choose the cruise provider to consume whose cruise journey service arrangement.

Nowadays, cruising has become one of the fastest growing sectors within tourism, cruise service providers need have themselves unique different entertainment service arrangement to satisfy every cruise travelling consumer individual needs in order to attract every one to choose whose cruise arrangement easily, e.g. meals, activities, entertainment and varied destinations create one-stop holiday shop, reasonable competitive ticket fare. Hence, it seems it is one exciting emotion industry. If the cruise service provider can bring positive emotion to influence many cruise travelling consumers immediately. The, even it change higher service fare to compare other similar cruise service providers. I believe it won't influence them to choose other similar cruise service providers if it can often bring immediate positive emotion to its cruise clients during they are staying in its cruises or during they have left its cruises, but they will often remember or won't forget to enjoy their cruise service provider's happing time forever. Hence, if (AI) tool can be attempted to help cruise entertainment providers to arrange different cruise journeys for varied destinations , to arrange different entertainment facilities, to arrange the different taste food to satisfy different countries age cruise consumers' needs. Then, the (AI) tool will assist the cruise providers to bring positive emotion to let every different countries age cruise consumers to feel satisfactory in order to choose to the cruise providers' cruise entertainment service more attractively.

2.1 How can apply (AI) tool to predict cruise service providers bring positive emotion to their clients?

Future, (AI) tool can help any cruise providers to design these kinds of any one entertainment service arrangement to satisfy the cruise provider's customers' needs.

There are different special interests cruising , such as wellness at sea, freighter cruises, river cruises. It has increased the attractiveness of cruising: Romance is for lover cruise traveler target, luxury is for rich cruise traveler target, exotica is for enjoyment exciting feeling traveler target. So, every kind of cruise traveler target will have different kind of cruise entertainment service to satisfy their needs. If the cruise service provider can provide the right and attractive cruise entertainment service to satisfy the specific cruise target. Then, it will bring the positive emotion to the specific cruise target consumers more easily.

Cruise travel was shaped for mass tourism. Prices have been very differently segmented. There are basically four types of markets (Biederman, 2008):

● Contemporary market: On board fun and amenities are playing important role and destinations have secondary importance.

● Premium market: This category is more expensive than the contemporary category and where the destination has same importance as on board amenities.

● Luxury market: It was once dominant type of cruise tourism, but now it has only a small portion of the industry. Generally, it is the most expensive cruise category and usually it takes longer than average cruise days.

● Adventure/exploration: It refers relatively long cruises with special and exotic places where the destination is the main purpose of the trip.

● European cruise travel: Duration takes more five days than worth American travel duration. There is a tendency on European market during the years that duration of travel is getting shorter. This short demand of is explained with the strong demand of customers (Hensen, 2003). Beside this, it is most likely that cruise companies try to convince tourists with short haul travels instead of long term cruise trips for more expenditure.

Thus, I believe that even, the cruise service provider charges higher ticket which won't influence cruise consumers who do not choose its entertainment service on its cruises. If it can arrange the attractive cruise entertainment facilities and destination journey arrangement, staying days arrangement to satisfy different specific cruise target market needs absolutely in order to bring whose emotion to be positive to it's service provision. Then, the cruise service provider will attract many potential cruise clients to choose its cruise service absolutely. Otherwise, if it only bring negative emotion to its cruise clients, it will not attract many potential cruise clients to choose it or loses its old cruise clients, even, its cruise ticket price is needed to decreased in order to raise competitive effort.

In conclusion, I believe that future (AI) tools need to learn how to bring cruise consumers to arise individual immediate or expected positive emotion, this positive emotion consideration is more important to compare to how to reduce cruise ticket price in order to attract cruise clients in global cruise competitive cruise industry.

2.2 Differentiation through the characteristics of cruising route method from (AI) tool route judgement

Future, (AI) tool can attempt to help any cruise entertainment service providers to judge how to design different route to attract different countries age cruise clients' choices to satisfy their cruise journey entertainment needs. The determinants of the cruising route's characteristics (functional, social, and emotion) is important factor to influence the cruise service provider's success. Cruising product is no longer selected primarily for the cruising service, but for the content of cruising route. So, the cruising route will influence the cruise consumer individual emotion, because it is the main service need for every cruise consumer.

The approach called the " land sea cruising in product development" is increasingly becoming an area of interest, e.g. determining the direction of the effects of the individual cruising route characteristics on service value's perception , and providing an evaluation model of the route's perception , and indicating significance variables of attraction.

The questions that cruise planners need to know: How does each of the identified determinants affect the overall perceived value of the cruise route? How the overall perceived value of the cruise route affects customer behavior intentions?

Because different routes factor will influence cruise consumer individual emotion changing seriously. It means the ship has become only a tool, when the offered route whose attractiveness highly influences the impression of the guests has become crucial.

Consumer behavior in cruising segment includes all the activities and influences in the selection of the specific cruise route. There activities result in decisions and actions related to a defined price, selection and reselection of cruising company (Cannot, Brink and Brijball, 2006).

2.3 How to apply (AI) tool to arrange cruise route planning have close relationship to influence cruise consumer emotion?

Firstly, use value of cruising routes is based on the subjective experience, and shows how individuals assess the route during, or immediately after sailing. It is affiliated with the benefits that cruising guest realize by choosing a route , and it is subjective because it depends on the individual assessment (photo taken on the route for one guest presents just a family souvenir, and for professional photographers are embodied financial capital).

Secondly, the utilitarian value is also subjective-oriented and is tied on the point where the inner and us ability of cruising routes are compared with the sacrifice of the client (money and time). Finally, the value is considered as the outcome of the comparison of scarifies and personal benefits, which is resulted in essentially utilitarian nature.

Hence, route design is the main value of cruising tourism and it is primarily determined and analyzed from the aspect of observed customers. Otherwise, the cruise is only one tool to be caught for the cruise passengers, whether the cruise can let whom to sleep comfortable , providing what kind of food to them to eat, what kind of entertainment facilities are provided to them to play, these issues are not more important to compare how to design route to bring them to travel to anywhere to enjoy in this cruise journey factor. Because how to design the route factor can bring each cruise passenger to influence them to feel either negative or positive emotion directly. The whole route journey planning is the most influential factor to influence the cruise passengers to feel whether they ought choose it's service again or not in the future.

CHAPTER FOUR

(AI) tool judges the difference between utility factor and emotion to influence consumer decision making

In economic utility or immediate (expected) emotion aspects, whether which is more influential to excite consumption. To analyze whether it is economic utility or immediate (expected) emotion more influential to excite consumption. It depends on the consumer individual consumption choice is in which situations. For example, if the industry's general consumer individual consumption decision is concentrate on emotion influential aspect, such as cruise entertainment industry, hospital care service industry, theme park entertainment industry, movie watching entertainment industry etc. Above all these industries have same nature, it is service. So, it seems that service industry's main influential factor is immediate (expected) emotion influence, it is not economic utility influence. Otherwise, product sale industry's main influential factor is utility.

3.1 (AI) judges consumer utility factor

For this toy choice situation example, parent choose to buy one toy to give whose child to play. They usually considerate which kind of toy is attractive to their child whom like to play. In many different kinds of toys choice, if the child likes to choose the kind of toy to play. After the child's parents had purchased the kind of toy to let whose child to play one period time, e.g. six month. Then, when the child feel that who has need to buy another new toy to play, due to he/she feels bored to play this toy. So, it seems that the child feels this toy has less utility or it's utility is decreased. So, he/she expects whose parent can buy another new kind of toy to let whom to play. It also implies that it is not emotion factor to influence the child to feel boredom and unfunny to play this kind of old toy after six months. It is the product's utility factor which can not attract the child to play it any more. So, this old toy's utility is decreased when this child spends six months to play it. This toy's value is only six month utility to this child to play. Otherwise, if this kind of toy is bought by another parent. It is possible that the another child like to play this kind of toy one year or more. So, it's utility to another child is one year or more period. So, product's utility period is difference, it depends on how long time of the user's satisfactory time.

As this toy case, the child's decision will influence whose parent choose which kind of toy to buy to whom to play. Usually toy price is not difference too much. Parent won't consider when the toy price will be increase or will be decreased to influence their emotion to decide not to buy the toy immediately. So, when the child like to play the kind of toy, even the product's price is more than other kind of toys, and the parent feel it is possible that the kind of toy's price will be fallen down later. They will still choose to buy the kind of toy to let their child to play, they won't be influenced not to buy this kind product by later cheap price factor. So, immediate emotion is not the main factor to influence this parent does not choose buy this toy at this moment. Otherwise, utility factor will influence when the parent will buy another new kind of toy to provide to this child to play. If the child enjoy to play it only three months, after he/she will feel bore and he/she will tell whose parent to buy another new kind of toy to let whom play when the fourth month is beginning. So, it implies that if the kind of toy product can have more attractive utility time, then it can attract many parent to choose to buy it among different kind of toys. Thus, when this kind of toy's utility time is longer time. Then, it is possible that it can influence many parents choose to buy it's different style or design of similar kind of toys to let their children to play. In general, when many parents accept to buy this kind of different style or design of similar toys to give their children to play. Due to it's popular long time utility factor, it will influence children like to play it longer time to compare other kind of toys. Consequently, it will influence parents do not need often spend too much money to buy other kinds of toys to give their children to play. So, longer time utility factor to the product can attract many consumers to choose to buy the kind of product to compare lesser time utility factor to the product. Hence, it proves the explanation why utility factor is the main influential factor to influence the consumer choose to buy the product.

3.2 (AI) judgement tool of Medical care and utility case

Medical care is an input in producing health, it is subject to law of diminishing marginal productivity. Health yields utility to the consumer. It is subject to law of diminishing marginal utility. It bring this question: Does either the patient's emotion or the medical care service or medical care product utility which one can influence the patient's hospital choice more?

To answer this question: We need to know medical care is one kind of nursing care service in hospitals or clinics and medical care product is one kind of medical care product sale from merchants, e.g. medicine or medical equipment. So, in medical industry which has different kind of medical care services to provide to patients in hospitals or clinics as well as which has different kind of medical care products sale, e.g. medicine or wheelchairs, heart health measurement equipment etc. different medical care products in medical health industry.

In medical care aspect, it is one kind of any medical care service to patients from hospitals or clinics. So, medical care is an input in producing health service to patients from hospitals or clinics. When the patient is admitting to hospital or clinic, who needs to see doctor and the doctor need to give the right medicine to the patient to eat to ill whose illness. Even, if the doctor feels the patient whom needs to live hospital for one time period. Then, the hospital nurses must need to take care the patient during he/she is living in the hospital period. Consequently, if the patent can be health in short time, e.g. within one week leaving time, then he/she will be shortened time to leave the hospital in next weak. Otherwise, if the patent can not be health in short time, e.g. within on week, then he/she needs to live the hospital more than one week, even, one month, three months or more. So, the staying hospital time will influence the patent's emotion to feel whether the doctor's effort. If he/she needs to live the hospital long time, he/she will bring negative emotion to feel the doctor's medical effort is not good. The doctor's medical effort can not achieve or satisfy whose expected emotion during whose staying hospital time.

Thus, medical care is an input service in producing health, it is subject to law of diminishing marginal productivity. When the patient does not need to live the hospital longer time, the patient will feel more satisfactory to the hospital's doctor and nurses' care effort as well as the patient can give less money to spend the expenditure to live the hospital. So, the law of diminishing marginal health productivity will explain the hospital will shorten time to the staying days of the hospital to the patent as well as the patient's care expenditure will be decreased when he/she only needs to live to the hospital in short time. Otherwise, the patient needs to live longer time in the hospital, it means that the diminishing marginal health productivity to the hospital, the patient's staying hospital days will be increased and the patient's medical expenditure to the hospital will also be increased. It will bring negative emotion to patient and why this negative emotion factor will influence the patient would choose another hospital to live or find other doctors to see if he/she felt illness in future one day.

In medical care product aspect, health yields utility to the consumer. It is subject to law of diminishing marginal utility. Because patient needs to buy different kind of medical equipment to use or medicine to eat to attempt to cure whose illnesses. So, if the patent can choose the right medicine to eat from the doctor's recommendation or if the patent can choose the right medical equipment to use from the doctor's recommendation. When the patient buy less number of medicine to eat, then he/she can be health or when he/she buy the medical equipment to use, then he/she can be health. Then, he/she will spend less money to buy medicine to eat or medical equipment to use and he/she can be health in short time. Then, the medical consumer will feel the medicine or medical equipment has good utility to satisfy whose medical needs. So, good medicine and good medical equipment can only need short time and less money to let the medical patient to be health.

3.3 Immediate (expected) emotion factor

As cruise entertainment case, every cruise journey must provide fixed stay days on the cruise to let every cruise passenger to play to every cruise journey. So, cruise passenger can not change or extend whose fixed stay day choice in every cruise journey, when they had caught the cruise to go to sea on the day. Is implies that cruise entertainment has none longer time utility factor which can influence each cruise passenger's choice to each different design of cruise journey arrangement.

If the cruise passenger feels very satisfactory and enjoyable to the last time of specific cruise journey arrangement, e.g. five days and four nights New Zealand and Australia cruise journey. Due to this cruise journey can bring positive emotion to let the cruise passenger to let whom feel that he/she can not forget or remember this happy cruise journey forever.

It is possible that this time happy five days and four nights New Zealand and Australia cruise journey will bring positive emotion to influence this cruise passenger to choose to find this cruise service provider to help whom to arrange this same cruise journey or another similar cruise journey again after one month, or three month, or six month or one year or more. Due to this cruse passenger felt this cruise service providers' cruise journey design arrangement can satisfy whose needs and it can achieve whose expected emotion to be positive. So, this cruise entertainment industry must be immediate (expected) emotion influential factor more than time utility factor to influence the cruise consumer's cruise service provider and cruise journey choices.

In conclusion, it is not only utility factor can influence consumption decision. It is emotion factor can also influence consumption decision. It depends on situations whether the consumer is choosing to buy one product or consume one service. If the consumer is choosing to buy one product, how long time of the product's utility factor which will influence the consumer choose to buy which product. If the consumer feels the product can give longer utility time among other similar products, then he/she will have more chance to choose to buy the product. Otherwise, if the consumer feels the product can give lesser utility time among other similar products, then he/she will have less chance to choose to buy the product. If the consumer is choosing to consume one service, emotion factor will influence the consumer choose to find which service provider to consume the same service or similar service. If the service provider can provide excellent service to the consumer, then it will bring positive immediate or expected emotion to whom and it can attract the consumer to choose the service provider again. Otherwise, if the service provider can not provide excellent service to the consumer, then will bring negative immediate or expected emotion to whom and it can not attract the consumer to choose the service provider again.

Why and how (AI) judgement tool can judgement what utility factors are to influence consumer emotion

In emotion and utility both aspects, they include these situations. I shall explain how and why emotion and utility factors can influence consumption behaviors in these different situations as below:

(1) In the first situation is brand factor, the brand image, product quality, product knowledge , attitude and

(2) brand loyalty intangible factor will attract the consumer individual purchase.

For example, luxury

products, e.g. luxury fashion brands of clothing. Brands like Zara from Spain and H&M from Seweden began to produce catwalk-style fashion at low cost offering consumers of luxury fashion alternatives at low prices.

Nowadays, the luxury fashion sector is the fourth largest revenue generator in France, and one of the most remarkable sectors in Italy, Spain , the USA and the potential markets of China, Russia and India. The luxury industry has increased having a huge youth in demand. The luxury consumer have much choice in products, shopping channels and pricing of luxury products. It has possible relationship of age, gender, income and other demographic factors with purchasing intentions to influence the rational and emotional buying behavior regarding luxury fashion products.

(2) The second situation concerns the decision-making of make or female consumers are possible experience an emotional desires and cognitive (reasoning) mind in purchasing choice process. Their emotion includes negative or positive buying emotion and mood management and cognitive process components include cognitive deliberation, planning buying with the exception regard for the future.

University had been using analysis of variances tests, male and female students were found significantly different with respect

affective process components including positive buying emotion, and mood management and cognitive process components include planning buying.

Significant differences were also found between the following product categories: shirts/sweaters, skirts, coats, underwear, accessories, shoes, electronic hardware, computer software, music , CD or DVDs, sports, memorabilia, health /beauty products and magazines/books for pleasure reading. No differences were found in regard to suits/ business wear and entertainments.

The investigate proved that some products will have different emotion influence to cause female or male students whose final consumption decision to buy the kind of product. So, the difference od male and female students will have emotion influence to make purchase decision to buy the product in consuming choice process.

(3) The third situation concerns search advertising factor, e.g. online search to influence consumption behavior. Advertising is possible one method to persuade the consumer to choose to buy the product, even the consumer does not know the product exists. For example, proper cloth, a company based in New York, has a site on the social networking site Facebook.

Whenever the company posts a new photos of its clothes, all its face book " fans" automatically receive the information on their own face book pages. "We want to hear what our customers have to say." It seems online advertisement is a potential promotion method to promote any new attractive products to sell to let publicity to know to buy. Internet is one popular communication tool to be used by youth today. So, when one company can have one website to let any youth to find and enter to the website to discover any new things easily. It will cause many consumption chances to let online potential clients to attempt to choose any products to make purchase decision from online advertising tool easily.

How does the role of advertising influence the purchase decision process? Needs and motivations are the starting points of purchase decisions. In fact, advertising is a communication of photo image, sound image, and word advertisement image channel to persuade consumers to choose to buy the brand of product or consume the brand of service between the merchant and its consumers from television, radio, newspapers, magazine, movie etc. channels.

Why does advertisement influence consumer
choice? For this case example, when one buyer waits until more information is gathered before making a decision. The time, two types of cost are involved. First, there are psychological opportunity costs experienced by consumers who are deprived of the product who need and are consequently in a state of psychological tension.

As time elapses, this psychological tension becomes more frustration. Second, buyers experience costs with the information-gathering efforts. They must invest time and energy to visit several retailers, seek out and read advertisements, or inquire for other opinions about the best product to buy.

These delayed decision costs considerably increase as time elapses. The buyer must seek information until it is felt that a search for additional information will bring about more costs than benefits. So, an advertisement is reaching a potential buyer when who is seeking information will have a greater impact, since the buyer is spending time and effort needed to seek out this information himself and he is less likely to find other competing and advertisements to obtain the additional information.

In general, buyers are generally more responsive to different brand advertisements, when they are seeking information on these brands. This is why the becomes a choice target for the advertiser provided the advertiser can identify and locate them. Thus, a client has interested and is in an information-gathering stage is asked.

Then, the advertiser takes advantage of the consumer's having identified him or herself to send a series of informative and persuasive messages or to send a salesperson who will try to conclude a sale. Thus, advertisement gives a chance to let consumers to gather information to choose the best product to buy or the most excellent service to consume.

What of situations do merchants need advertisements promotion? The short purchase cycle markets are characterized by routine
purchase decision processes or by limited problem solving when a new brand is introduced on the market, e.g. coffee, bread , sugar, soft drinks, canned vegetables and household and beauty care products fall into this category. Another irregular purchase cycle markets are characterized by products that are purchased more or less regularly , e.g. cookies, cake mixes, wines, food products. Finally, long or unpredictable purchase cycle markets include all durable products, such as cars, household appliances and furniture (products from which occasions of purchase can't be predicted, which most consumers buy only occasionally). Hence, these kinds of products ought need advertisement promotion specially, due to advertisement can build brand image to let consumers to know. Especially , it is a new brand of product. In conclusion, advertisement will be one good channel to let new product to introduce its brand to let clients to remember in minds heart.

Consequently, future (AI) tool needs to learn how to design different kinds of advertisement to attract consumer attention to the product, needs to learn how to find what the bad factor(S) which cause(S) many consumers do not choose to buy the product, needs to learn when the product price needs to be raised up or fallen down in order to bring consumers' positive emotion to choose to buy the product immediately. SO, if (AI) tool can be invented to own itself effort to design different kinds of methods to predict consumer behavior in order to bring their positive emotion to the product successfully, then the manufacturer can earn positive consumer emotion advantage from the (AI) tool assistance for long term benefit to its product.

Psychological method predicts consumer behavior

CHAPTER FIVE

Psychological method predicts consumer behavior

Can apply economic models solve marketing changing challenges?

Economists indicate economic modeling can provide a logical, data to help organize the analyst's thoughts. The model helps the economist logically isolate and sort out complicated chains of cause and effect and influence between the numerous interacting elements in an economy. There are four types of models used in economic analysis: Visual models, mathematical models, empirical models and simulation models. Visual models are simply pictures of an abstract economy: graphs will lines and curves that tell an economic story. It is one kind of micro or macro-economic method to predict consumer behavioral change. Some visual models are diagrammatic such as which flow the income thought the economy from one sector to another (micro economic environment). It is mathematical model, when it is presented the mathematics are explained what the data analysis is or not. The model does not normally require a knowledge of mathematics, but still allow the presentation of complex relationship between economic variable.

For example, the common supply-and demand model is meant to show the effect of inflationary expectations upon price and output. In this application, an increase in inflationary expectations causes demand to shift, raising prices and outputs (macro-economic environment). For another example, a very simple micro-economic model would include a supply function (explaining the behavior of products or those who supply commodities to the market), a demand curve (explaining the behavior of purchasers) and an equilibrium equation, specifying the simple conditions that must be met if the model's equilibrium is to be satisfied. So, the variables in a model like this represent a type of economic activity (such as demand) or data (information) that either determines or is determined by that activity (such as a price or interest rate variable change activity).

Dynamic models, in contrast, directly incorporate time into their structure. This is usually done in economic modeling by this mathematical systems of difference of differential equations. For example, it can use a difference equation from a business cycle model, investment now depends upon changes in income in the past. Time is incorporated into the model. Dynamic models, when they can be used, sometimes better represent the business cycles, because certainly behavioral response and timing strongly shape the character of a cycle.

For another example, if there is a delay between the time income is received and when it is spent. A model that can capture the delay is likely to those higher consumption desire to the consumer. It is a micro-personal behavioral consumption predict method. So, the user can experiment with an endless variety of values and assumptions to see whether results obtained are realistic or insightful. Since computers are now powerful and cheaper, the importance of dynamic simulation models should follow the future prediction time, when the consumer income receive and when it is spent to predict how much degree of the consumer's consumption desire in micro-economic view point.

Another model to be applied to predict consumption behavior. It is expectations and enhanced model, it includes one or more variables based upon economic expectations about future values. For example, if consumers for whatever reason, expect the inflation rate to be much higher next year, then this year, they are said to have formed inflationary expectations. If numerical values are being used in a model and the current inflation rate is 9%, if they expect inflation to be higher next year, the variable for inflationary expectations might be given be a value if 12% or more.

Normally, though general models used for instruction or analysis, it assumes an expectation value to be high. Where it will have an impact on the models result or " low" or " mot existent" where it will have no impact. In the simple supply - and demand to model presented earlier, inflationary expectations were high, shifting the equilibrium and causing higher prices and output. Hence, expectations and enhanced model as well as demand and supply model is a good predictive tool to predict when inflationary rate rises to the general unacceptable level to consumers to influence their consumption desires in societies in micro and macro-economic both view point.

What factors can reduce social consumption desire in general. The theory of rational expectations presumes that expectations are formed when economic agents see new developments in the economy and they logically deduce expectations based upon the information they have. For example, if the country's government central reserve system were to suddenly increase the money supply, according to the theory of rational expectations, consumers would immediately form inflationary expectations, not because prices are actually rising, but become they deduce that excessive money supply growth is likely to cause inflation. It presumes that a relatively high degree of raising consumption desire to people or people have access to, or even care about, information on the economy, such as the money supply growth rate, the rate of taxation etc. So, it's the government micro or macro-economic policy to attempt to raise consumption desire, due to people feel more money supply to society. So, it causes the feel salary increase. Due to money is excessive supply, so they will accept to consume more. But in fact, their salaries growth, it is due money supply growth. Moreover, due to the social businessmen had not raise products price to sell, e.g. food price, entertainment price, school fee etc. Different kinds of consumption price. So, it makes consumers feel their salaries growth and social consumption expenditure have no growth to influence them to feel they have more extra income to accept to buy any more things to consume in society. So, the government inflationary policy (supply more money to society) is one example of macro-economic method to persuade people to accept more consumption behaviors in this inflationary (increasing money supply to society) period. It aims to assist social businessmen have more consumption in order to avoid businesses failure risk in society.

1.2 Micro and macro-economic analysis methods solve Starbucks coffee shop faces marketing change challenges

This Starbucks case indicates how Starbucks coffee drinking business applies micro and macro-economic analysis methods to predict consumer behavior. Today, Starbucks has become world famous and brings high quality coffee and beverages to its clients over the world daily. Their well-known mission statements is: to inspire and nurture the human spirit, one person, one cup and one neighborhood at a time.

How does it apply macro and micro economic analysis methods to predict consumers' coffee taste more accurate? According to the following statistics, coffee market is large market potential in the world for this particular coffee service and production. Starbucks along with many competitors, such as Costa coffee and Mc-cafe have seized this opportunity and continue to indicate within this coffee market. It is no doubt that this coffee market can be profitable in 2012 year, the CEO of Starbucks was classified as the 8th best -paid CEO in the United States of America making $ 103 million dollars of profit (Rushe, 2013). Hence, the question concerns that how Starbucks can predict its coffee customer fast accurate.

Micro and macro-economic marketing environment analysis: It is crucial to be aware and understand environment in which a company is operating in order to implement their strategies successfully. The micro environment strategies can be analyzed using in SWOT analysis and further completed with a macro environment study by doing a PEST analysis.

As Starbucks background, it can apply micro environment " a SWOT analysis" method, it must focus on the external factors since internal factors are rather analyzed in the core marketing strategy and extended marketing strategy and extended marketing mix. However, macro environment refers to everything external to the organization. So, it seems Starbucks can't necessarily fully control, only influence. Such as PEST analysis indicates political, economic, social and technological external environment factors. Such as certain political issues can raise since coffee beans are grown in developing countries and this could raise questions about the working conditions and child labor. Tariffs and import taxes could also influence the prices in stores as well as the country's economic recession or exchange rates change could threaten Starbuck's profits.

However, Starbucks internal strengths include that the development of new technologies and user friendly machines, such as home coffee machines, quality of beverages in other restaurants served are increasing and Starbucks should create Starbucks experience at home by manufacturing their own capsules machine with their coffee and tea. The emergence of social media is already used by Starbucks especially via Twitter where gift cards can be purchased and sent to friends (Starbucks, 2014). There are Starbucks internal strengths to win its competitors, although, it can not control external environment factors to threaten its business.

Coffee drinking sale industry is a service marketing, positioning has received little attention from marketers, but is very useful in defining and modifying the tangible characteristics of the different kind of taste coffee product and its intangible perceptions.

As Starbucks, customers are buying an expensive product high quality (tangible) every cup of different kind of taste coffee, but they also have the personalized in-store drinking experience enhanced by the trained employees, for example, the customer's name is written on the plastic cup their beverage will be served in (tangible), this helps Starbucks obtains the premium brand status and win competition.

Due to coffee drinking industry is a competitive business. In micro economy analysis strategy (supply and demand). Nowadays, different coffee drinking service stores supply numbers are increasing. Although, it has limited supply numbers growth. Also, coffee drinkers' taste demand is changed quickly , who need to drink different kind of good taste coffees and they also considerate coffee stores' staffs service performance when they can let them to feel enjoyable to sit down the coffee shops to drink its coffee. Hence, Starbuck considers its employees' service performance issue. It concentrates on training its staffs to let its every coffee drinking client has unforgettable drinking coffee enjoyable experience in its any one coffee shop. It implies Starbucks employees' service behavioral performance can influence every coffee drinkers' positive or negative emotion to decide to choose to go to Starbuck to drink coffee again or choose another coffee shops to drink coffee. Hence, Starbucks employees' service behaviors must have relationship to influence its future coffee drinking client growth number. If it's employees can provide kindly service attitude to every coffee drinker, adds it can produce any kinds of good taste coffees, adds it can let coffee drinkers to feel it's every cup of coffee price is reasonable. Sum of all the factors, they can influence why Starbucks can earn more sale of its coffee shops in global different countries in short term successfully.

I conclude that Starbucks still needs to find different kinds of new taste coffee to satisfy different coffee taste clients' needs. Because coffee drinking market will have many clients who like to drink different kinds of coffee. If Starbucks can not increase to provide different kinds of new taste coffee to satisfy client individual drinking new coffee taste demand. Otherwise, other coffee shops can provide new unique different kinds taste of coffees to satisfy their drinking new taste coffee demands. Then, due to Starbucks limited supply of new taste coffee factor, it will have possible to influence its competitive ability in this competitive coffee drinking market.

In conclusion, it needs to consider how many coffee supply number is not the main factor to influence its success. Otherwise, how much different kinds of coffee taste supply is the main factor to influence its success because coffee drinkers can either choose to go to supermarkets to buy different brands of coffee to drink at home or choose to go to other coffee ships to drink the kinds of coffee taste which Starbucks can not provide to them to drink. So, satisfying coffee clients' different kinds of coffee taste demand will be one main successful key to Starbucks, it is not how many coffee number supply (enough coffee number supply) factor to influence its success. It needs to find different kinds of new taste coffee to let clients to know and to have more coffee choice to drink to satisfy their drinking new taste of coffee needs. It reflects the new taste of coffee supply and the new taste of coffee demand micro economic theory to influence coffee consumers' drinking behavioral needs in this coffee drinking industry.

CHAPTER SIX

Micro economic assess the influence on location choices and growth performance consumption prediction.

Some economists indicate idea that seen central to the development of regional science at large and to economic geography and international trade theory. In this terms of economies of specialization increase returns to scale and in the case of regional science and economic geography, economies of localization and urbanization.

The questions concern: Can choose the best business location to attract consumption growth performance? Does the best destination attract consumption growth?

" Two cities attract trade from an intermediate town in the vicinity of the breaking point, approximately in direct proportion to the population of the two cities, and in inverse proportion to the squares of the distances of the intermediate town" (Reggiani, 1998).

It implies some economists believe that geographic location choice factor can influence consumption growth. It is possible due to the location has many people are living. So, it brings many business chance, or the location is one the country's main in economic development location, it can attract many travelers choose to go to the location to travel. So, it has many travelling clients to prefer to consumer.

However, a smaller region can still attract consumption growth, if it had good transportation system. For example, a small region may not have its own university, but inhabitants may still have access to higher education. Elsewhere accessibility measures are also need in activity location models, where access ability is the way through which the quality of the transport system influences the land use.

So, it seems although the regional land is small size and far from cities, but if it can have good transportation system to provide any people to travel the small size regional land from outside cities. It is possible to bring consumption growth. However, some economists believe that distance influence relations in economics and economic geography in two ways: first, natural resources are distributed unevenly across space and second, distance separates various activities from each other. They apply " law of demand" to support their reasons.

In regional sciences, accessibility plays an important role for analyzing the distribution of economic cities and regional development. Within regional science, the attempt to predict and explain the distribution of economic activity has become known as economic geography. Research in economic geography attempt to answer the question: What forces cause geographic behavioral consumption? Some economists support the production function and into the interaction between transportation cost and plant level scale economies, this geographical factor will bring much geographical behavioral consumption. For example, accessibility of population is an indicator of market size for suppliers of products and services, whereas successful ability to GDP could be an indicator of the market size for suppliers of high level business services (Spiekermannn and Wegener, 2007).

However, some economists argue that market potential is not necessarily the actual market. For example, since a person can't make the same purchase at two different locations. Hence, they believe that is one person has make purchase in one location far from whose home. Then, if he/she find another location which is close to whose home. The, he/she must not choose to buy the same purchase again, even he/she believe the seller's shop is close to whose home location. It implies that far location is not one factor to influence consumers to choose to buy the product if the consumer lines to buy the product. Even, the seller's shop is far away from whose home, he/she will still choose to drive whose car or catch transportation tool to go to the seller's shop to buy the product far away from whose home. Otherwise, if the consumer does not like the product, even the product seller's shop is close to whose home. Although he/she can walk to the shop to buy the product in short time. He/she won't choose to buy the product, due to who dislike the product. Hence, even close whose home, the seller product price is cheaper than the far away whose home, the another seller product price is higher than the similar or same product.

In conclusion, we have been downward trend of transportation costs of people, product and information to influence any geographical consumer behaviors. It implies that firms and people become less to restricted in their locational choices, it should lead to a greater homogeneity across regions. However, there are still great variation across geographical space in terms of incomes, cost of living, regional structure of production etc. different locational factors to influence regional consumption behavior in different countries.

2.1 Media economic methods to predict readers' behaviors in publishing industry

Media economics the application of economic theories, concepts and principles to study the macroeconomics and microeconomic aspects of most media consumption and industries, for academic lecturers, policymakers, and industry analysts. Media economics methods include how to apply variety of methodological approaches both qualitative and quantitative methods and statistical analysis, as well as studies using financial, historical and policy driven data.

Some economists define land, labor, and capital as the three factors of production and the major contributors to a nation's wealth. Can land, labor and capital be as three main factors of production any books, newspapers, magazines etc. reading products in publishing industry? Some economists believed price was determined by the costs of production, whereas marginal economists equated prices with the level of demand can be any books, magazines, newspapers etc. reading products prices is either determined by the cost of printing production or equated any one kind of these reading products with the level of reader' demand more.

The marginal economists contributed the basic analytic tools of demand and supply, consumer utility and the use of mathematics as analytical tools to develop microeconomics. Can apply the basic analytic tools of reader demand and the any one kind of these reading products supply and reading consumer individual reading need, utility and the use of mathematics as analytical tools to predict any kind of reading consumer numbers and reading interesting topic choice in media industry?

However, some economists also demonstrated that given a free market economy, such as in free publish industry, the factors of production (land, labor and capital) were important in understanding the economic system. Can apply the factor of production , e.g. publishing book sale location (land); publishing book salespeople sale experience (labor); and attractive book printing quality (capital printing expense) to influence the publishing industry reading consumer reading habit or purchase book activities?

However, some economists suggested two important contributions: Analysis of monopoly and price discrimination and the market for labor will influence consumer number. Such as publishing case: Can analysis of which famous royalty publishing book sale firm to the most monopoly and then following its different topic of books sale price to evaluate whether how much every different topic of its similar book topic sale price to be higher to avoid reduce reader numbers, due to the not famous royalty book seller which similar topic book to the famous royalty book seller's prices are too higher than the famous royalty publishers' book prices?

Book salespeople individual sale experience and sale ability and book knowledge (labor supply) influence the book publishing shop's reading clients buying decisions, such as the more experience book sellers can persuade many readers to buy the book store's books. Otherwise, the less sale experience book sellers can not persuade many readers to buy the store's books.

As the found in the field of economics, it became more refined, scholars began investigate many different economic concepts and principles to predict consumers behaviors, such as media reading customer. Nowadays, the media industries provides all of the elements required for studying the economic process. Content providers can offer information and entertainment, education etc. different topic books, magazine reading products which became the media publishing suppliers. Whereas, reading consumers and media advertisers formed the demand side of the media market.

The macroeconomic market conditions and the relationship among any media publishing reading product suppliers in various industries created microeconomic market conditions , e.g. publishing suppliers need logistic transportation service suppliers to help them to deliver books or magazines or newspapers etc. different kinds of reading products to book shops or magazine shops to sell every day. It can bring the logistic transportation service business to contribute social economic development.

Early media economists apply microeconomic concepts to examine newspaper competition and radio competition media industry. They predicted advertisement can help these both media industry to earn advertisement income to help other businesses to promote their products to let radio listeners and newspapers readers to know from these two media channel effectively. So, they believed that newspapers and radio extra income source can be provided advertisement service for other businesses, instead of radio audience income or newspapers reader normal income source. In addition to a number of book and edited volumes have contributed to the development of media economics to help them to predict consumer reading psychology.

How to apply media economic methods to predict media consumer's psychology? Some media economists believe the market structure-conduct performance model is as a tool for analysis, it has been widely used in the study of media markets and industries, such as book publishing industry. How to choose the attractive topic for every book product structure? They believe attractive book structure will help book structure firm to grow reader numbers. So, book topic and content factor is more influential to raise reader number more than cheaper book price sale factor.

In its most simply for the industries organizational model indicates that of the structure of the market is known, it allows explanation of the likely conduct and performance among firms. For example, in terms of market structure, the variables used for analysis include the numbers of sellers/buyers, e.g. US publishing book market number of US book reading publishers/number of US book publishing sellers every year in US book publishing market; product differentiation, e.g. US different topic and content of electronic book or paper book product ; barriers to entry, e.g. economic recession, tariff book import tax, limitation of import book number etc. different external barriers factors to influence overseas (foreign) book publishing import to US to sell their paper books ; cost structures, e.g. US book publishing firms need to spend how much printing expenditure to print high quality paper production of every paper book to sell and the degree of vertical integration, e.g. US book publishing firms how to choose middlemen to help them to sell books, e.g. themselves book publishing shops, other book retailers, themselves electronic book publishing website online platform sale channel or other book publishing sellers' websites online platform sale channel etc. different channels to sell the paper of electronic books to US readers. Hence, predicting the country' book market structure, it will have more confidence to evaluate book publishing competitors' effort and book sale price and how to design book content and topic to raise reading quality to let readers to feel much attractive to choose to buy the books from the book publishing shop.

Media economics research is in the sense that many different types of methods are used to answer research questions and investigate hypotheses. However, many economists accept to choose to apply any one of methods to predict media reader behavior, such as trend studies, financial analysis, econometrics and case studies.

Trend studies compare and contrast data over a time series. In assessing media concentration. Most trend studies use annual data as the unit of analysis. Trend studies are useful, due to their descriptive nature and ease of presentation and they aid in analyzing the performance of media companies and industries, e.g. study of changes in newspaper pricing and subscription costs.

Financial analysis is another common methodological tool used in media economics research. Financial analysis can take many different forms and use different types of data. The most common data include information derived from financial statements and the use of various types of financial ratio.

Econometrics involves the use of statistical and mathematical models to verify and develop economic research questions, hypotheses and theory.

Case studies represent another useful method in media economics research. Case studies are popular because they allow a researcher to gather different types of data as well as different methods. Case studies in media economics research tend to be very targeted and focused examinations.

What are forces to influence media industry development? There four forces consist of technology, regulation, globalization and sociocultural can influence media industry development. I shall indicate why these forces will influence media industry change in order media industry businesses need to consider s below:

Technology force: Because media industries are heavily dependent on technology for the creation, distribution and exhibition of various forms of media contents, changes in technology affect economic processes between and within the media industries. For example, many publishing book businesses choose to apply internet technology to help authors to publish electronic books sale. Due to it is popular to let online readers to study from internet, even they choose to pay visa card to buy electronic or paper books to read from internet sale channel. So, technology brings electronic book digital content and text and graphics digitally soon led to digital audio and video files to let authors to download their files to change to electronic books to publish to sell to electronic book readers to read from online channel. So, internet builds electronic book web sites to attract reading consumers to read from internet channel. They do not need to bring paper book to read. They only need to bring mobile phone or laptops to go to anywhere to read electronic books any time conveniently.

Regulation: If regulation is eliminated in publishing or media industry to any countries, the cross ownership rules would give publishing companies. The opportunity to acquire broadcast stations able cable systems within the markets, they serve, leading to the development of multi-media based companies offering content and advertising across multiple mediums.

Globalization can influence media industry development. Media products are often created with global audiences in mind, which is why so much content contains sex and violence. However, globalization of media content began with motion pictures and magazines, but then expanded into another media channels, e.g. television programming, VHS and DVD sales and rentals. These media publishing products' income are influenced by global audience entertainment choice.

Finally, it is socio-cultural force factor which can influence reader or media entertainment consumer industrial consumption behavior. Socio-cultural, such as the country's young people accept to like to read electronic books more than paper books reading behaviors. Then, it is the country's socio-cultural factor to influence the country's book buyers who prefer to pay visa card to buy electronic books to read from book store online website platform channel. It is electronic book reading cultural trend to influence the country young people reading behavior change . They will change their traditional reading habits to choose to buy electronic books to read from internet reading channel. So, online reading of electronic book method will be popular to the country and the country's paper book publishing shops ought consider to apply internet technology to develop their electronic book publishing business to let young people electronic book buyers to read electronic books from online channel conveniently.

Finally, all media industry players ought consider any technology development in order to predict readers‘ or media entertainment players’ whose consumption behavior changes to avoid themselves publishing media businesses encounter fail in future one day.

CHAPTER SEVEN

Can predict the real economic situation using liquidity of financial assets

How about alternative ways of measuring liquidity? Can liquidity predict turning points of a business cycles or predict whether customer number will grow or reduce in next year? Is it a good consumer number predictive tool for alternative macroeconomic predictive results? Can liquidity predict real economy variables in macro-economic view point, i.e. such macro-economic aggregate ass economic growth (changes in GDP), investments direction changes etc.?

There are some analysis to support its possibility , such as: Most of the predictability is coming from changes in the liquidity of small stocks (presumably the least liquid ones). How about alternative ways of measuring liquidity? IS it real liquidity? If so, which aspect concerns to the liquidity to the company? So, the conclusion of question concern: Can liquidity method predict macroeconomic variable?

Consumer changing expectation to consume any things will be possible to influence macroeconomic variable. If it is true, calculating how many of the kind of businesses liquidity data that can predict whether the year macroeconomic variable is better or worse to compare last year. Can it use the current and past year kind of businesses liquidity data to predict next year macroeconomic variable situation whether it is suitable

to any businessmen choose to do the kind of business or not to do next year.

The resulting trading decisions reflects changing expectations about whether business cycles and consumers' taste or consumption desires whether they are changing or not to cause the kind of most businesses choose to liquidity finally. So, if one foresees a deteriorating economy , one wants to shift the portfolio into assets better predicted in that case. For example, when one foresee an upturn one will shift into materials as the demand for that industry's products is likely to be high when investments are increasing. Using the sector as explanatory variable, one may catch this kind of behavior, since order flow is increasing in the desire for that particular sector.

So, if liquidity of asset method can be attempted to predict whether next year which kind of businesses will have risk. Then, it brings these questions:

Which liquidity measures are the best for forecasting?

How does liquidity measures relate to alternative forecasting variables?

I shall assumes that it has relationship between stock market liquidity and cost of trading shares, with macroeconomic conditions. For example is that liquidity levels of local stocks are higher (lower) , when the local economy has performed well (poorly). The relation is stronger when local financing constraints are more binding, the local information environment is more better or worse, and local businessmen ownership levels and trading intensity are higher. More liquidity seems temporary relationship, due to short time economic recession factor to influence some kind of businesses , but still, linking the country local stock liquidity with local business cycle, it is possible that the country's different kinds of businesses will liquidate more than one year if the country's economy is recession long time. So, predicting many kind different kind of businesses liquidity choice in the country in the year. It will predict how long time the country economic recession will occur or find what factors cause the country economic recession occurrence in possible.

In conclusion, it seems that gathering the country's any kind of businesses whose past liquidity of financial assets data, it will possible to predict whether what kind(s) of businesses has(have) risk to do the kind of businesses next year. What factor(s) cause(s) the country's economic recession, economic recession situation will remain how long time, This liquidity of financial assets data gathering method will give opinions to let the country's businessmen to choose whether it is right time to set up their new businesses next year or close down their old businesses to be better next year.

3.1 Micro solution methods solve macro-economic problem

Nowadays, global financial crisis cause a slowdown in world trade growth. The recent great recession has important impacts on international trade. The international trade has changed from three factors: The evolution of global imbalances, trends in globalization and the structure of trade negotiations.

For example, new technologies in manufacturing, connectivity and energy efficiency in particular, have the potential to transform the global economic risk. From macroeconomic perspective these new technologies increase potential growth, allowing the economy to grow faster and it may also put downward pressure on energy price. The US seems as a likely beneficiary, where its competitive advantage in the production and deployment of information technology is widely recognized. Otherwise, some countries' development could be threatened by the substitution of cheaper and more efficient capital for (labor and by the shortening of global supply chains).

I believe new technologies have the potential to solve global macro economic development challenges from micro economic (every country technological firms cooperation development) method. The reason as below:

(1) Recent advances in information and communications technology new innovations in methods of manufacturing and fresh ways of exploiting energy could bring significant growth benefits for the world global economic technological development from different countries themselves technological firms research new (undiscovered) technological products development to influence future human life, water energy, solar energy, nuclear energy,

vehicle battery energy new energy development technology. It aims to avoid global energy shortage challenge occurrence and new artificial intelligent cities development, it aims to let human feel to live in high technological development, artificial intelligent cities can let human to live more comfortable and more convenient in global cities from artificial intelligent assistance.

For another example, some of the new technologies allow companies earn higher quality of physical capital at lower prices. Enhanced energy storage, shale gas and oil techniques, and innovations in renewable energy are helping to drive down the price of energy relative to the trend that would have unfolded in their absence. In all cases, new energy development, these technologies have the potential to raise productivity growth sectors and countries, allowing faster, new energy supply growth and lower inflation, when human have different kind of energy to choose to use.

For another example, mobile communications technology can make the world economy more efficient and may also lead to significant dislocation. Mobile communications technology has the potential to bring 2 to 3 billion people into the world economy development. Additive manufacturing as 3 D printing, could remove up to 90% of the waste from some manufacturing processes. At the same time, advanced robots which can work as little as USD$4 per hour, may eventually display existing employment in manufacturing. So, on micro economic view point, technology will be one kind production of factor to global future manufacturing firms. Mckinsey Global Institute finds that our trend global growth could be 0.5 to 0.7 percentage points higher in 2025s than in the absence of technological change, it implies productivity gains comparable to apply only personal computer and internet revolutions of the 1990s.

(2) What is future these new technology? A new technology ought change the way the world economy operates in micro economic view point. A new technological change can shift the global economy's production function simply put, better technology allows the economy to produce more products and services at low prices. (production of factor). For example, potential efficiency gains include the widespread diffusion of mobile devices, easing access to the internet, artificial intelligence machine learning and voice recognition as well as the " internet of things", big of data gathering method to be applied to manage supply chains better in any factories (production of factor).

(3) In manufacturing efficiency gains include the deployment of more advanced robotics making it more practice and profitable to substitute capital for human labor. Low-cost robots can change manufacturing by increasing precision and productivity without higher costs. Further efficiencies can be exploited with the use of 3 D printing, which reduces waste in manufacturing, improves precision of design and shortens complex supply chains (production of factor).

(4) Finally, energy efficiency opportunities range from the extraction of oil and gas reserves from shale rock formations to enhanced energy storage. US storage team's work suggests that shale extraction techniques alone may add 0.5% points per year to US growth over the next 10 years (production of factor). New technologies may also put downward pressure on energy prices. Many of these technologies, such as waste -reducing , 3D printing, lower the energy intensity of global manufacturing and trade. By bringing product design and manufacturing closer to the end user, thus shortening supply chains, 3 D printing also reduces transport costs. The US department of energy

anticipates that 3 D printing could save more than 50% of energy use compared to today's existing manufacturing.

(5) What new technologies influence global economy. Some economists predict new technologies will bring benefits to global economy development. They have conducted model simulations suggesting that global GDP growth could be 0.5 to 0.7 percentage points per annum higher as a result of the adoption and diffusion of these new technologies. the models also suggest that global inflation levels could be one percentage point lower than would otherwise have been the case.

However new technology can also bring some countries; labor marker change. Labor markets in manufacturing could be materially affected as capital in the form of robotics and 3D printing replace low and semi-skilled jobs. For some new technological global manufacturing and trading system countries. For example, in South Asia, the Middle East, Africa and parts of Latin America development could be threatened by the shortening of global supply chains and by the substitution of cheaper and more efficient capital for labor.

Hence new technological manufacturing development will bring disadvantages to these without effort development of new technological manufacturing and trading system countries to influence themselves labor unemployment, if their employers choose to buy other countries‘ new technological manufacturing system, e.g. robots replace the human labor to help them to manufacture their products. Hence, it seems new manufacturing technology will have negative impact to the without effort development new technological manufacturing countries' manufacturing labor. Due to the robots can raise productivities to shorten manufacturing time and no salary expenditure and robots efficiency is higher than human labor.

However, if these countries‘ labor can learn how to apply robots knowledge to control robots to help their employer to manufacture products. It is possible that they won't be dismiss, even employers will need them to assist them to control the new robots manufacturing machines to manufacture their products in factories. It depends on whether they choose to attempt to control manufacturing robots or not.

In conclusion, new technology can be one important production factor to influence global macro-economic growth from micro new technological manufacturing sectors development. So global manufacturers will concern how to apply new technology to help them to manufacture any products.

3.2 Economic science or economic art methods predict consumer behavior

Economic is both a science and art. Economic is considered as science because systematic knowledge derived from observation, study and experimentation. An art is the practical application of knowledge for achieving definition ends. A science teaches us to know a phenomenon and art traches us to do a thing.

How to apply economic science or art method to predict consumer behavior? for example, there is a inflation US this year. This information is derived from positive science. The government takes certain fiscal and monetary measures to bring down to general level of prices in the country. The study of the monetary measures to bring down inflation makes the subject of economics as an art. Hence, as this case, if US government applies economic science or art method to predict this year will have inflation in US, then US government will attempt to avoid social general product prices to be raised, due to inflation influence. It aims to avoid US consumers reduce consumption desire in this year.

For another example, nothing could be more useful than water. But in much of the world waste is plentiful enough that another glass more or less matters little to a fresh water supply agent businessman. So, water is chap. But, if any offices buy bottle of glass fresh water to let employees to drink. It will bring advantages that they do not spend time to buy water to drink when they are working in the office time in any offices as well as employees do not need to heat water to drink to waste time to work in offices. So, the bottle of fresh drinking water supply agent is one kind of drinking water product monopoly fresh drinking water supplier to supply fresh drinking water to satisfy office employees who do not need to spend time to heat water to drink in offices. Hence, it is possible that replace other different kind taste of drink or office employees themselves heat water drink in offices. It is general office employees' drinking habits and drinking choice in offices popularly. So, the bottle of fresh drinking water supply agents will concentrate on selling their fresh drinking water to office employee customers only in global fresh drinking water consumption target market. The office employees must be fresh drinking water companies' main target consumers.

What is economic laws qualitative or quantitative method to predict consumer behavior? Law of economic are qualitative in nature. They are not exactly stated in quantitative terms. They tell the direction of change which is expected rather than the amount of change. For example, according to the law of consumer demand, the quantity demanded varies inversely with price, We don't say that 10% rise in price will lead to 30% fall in the customers' quantity demand.

What is economic merits of deduction method? This method is near to reality. It is less time consuming and less expensive. the use of mathematical techniques in deducing theories of economics brings exactness and clarity in economic analysis. The deductive method is highly abstract. It require a great deal of care to avoid bad logic or faulty economic reasoning. This method makes conclusions to predict consumer behavior, due to reliance on imperfect and correct assumptions.

It involves the process of reasoning from particular facts to general principle on the basic of experimentations, observations and statistical methods. In this method, data is collected about a certain economic phenomenon. There are systematically arranged and the general conclusions are drawn from them.

What are the advantages of inductive method to predict consumer behavior? It is based on facts as such the method is realistic. In order to test the economic principles, method makes statistical techniques. The inductive method is therefore more reliable, inductive method is dynamic. The changing economic phenomenon are analyzed and on the conclusions and solutions are drawn from them and this method also helps in future consumer behavioral investigations.

However, inductive method has weaknesses to predict consumer behavior, such as below:

It conclusions drawn from insufficient data, the generalizations obtained may be faulty. The collection of data itself is not easy task. The sources and methods employed in the collection of data differ from investigator to investigation. The result, therefore may differ even with the same problem and it is time-consuming and expensive to find data to predict consumer behavior changes.

How apply this method to predict general social consumer sources of income and consumption pattern when economic environment factor changes consumer behaviors? It should also be stressed that micro analysis plays other roles. First, it may serve to some macro data (any labor force by production sector or by skill category). Second, it can be used to estimate of key consumer behavioral consumption functions. For example, price and income elasticities can be estimated using data available in a typical householder budget survey. Third, in the case of tax reforms involving changes in exemptions or deductions is a model useful to estimate changes in effective tax rates changes how to influence consumer behavioral changes in society.

In conclusion, economists have proved macro and micro economic both methods have possible to be applied to predict consumer behavior when , how and why their consumption behavioral changing occurrence in order to manufacturers and product sellers or service providers can pre-make judgement to achieve the marketing strategies to avoid the number of client loss, due to marketing or economic environment changes to influence negative impact to consumer behavioral changes to influence the manufacturers‘ manufacturing products or the sellers’ products or the service providers' service provision which number to be decreased.

CHAPTER EIGHT

Marketing communication strategy predicts consumer behaviors

What are marketing communication strategy benefits?

Can marketing communication strategy help organizations to build brands, innovation, developing relationship, create good consumer service and communication benefit. Most marketing professionals believe effective communicaton strategy can help organizations to raise brand competition as well as to create and enhance relationship with consumers and other stakeholders. Marketing communication strategy is concept of communication through the promotional mix, with these better-educated, cost-conscious and demanding customers. Why do organizations need marketing communication strategies? Marketing communication strategy is concept used for sales promotion, product publicity, events sponsorships and direct marketing. It can help new brands to raise familiarity to let customers to know when the brand product plans to enter the marketing to sell in beginning.

Nowadays, organizations need promotional mix strategy to let consumers to familiar their new products, such as public relations, marketing, advertising, promotion and online media. Generally, organizations expect to achieve these aims. Otherwise, one effective marketing communication strategy can assist the organizations to drive forces for growth.

The driving forces include: Value of money means the organizations want to gain maximum value for money with maximum impact, resulting in raising value of money to different products in different departments and pressure on margins: Increasing pressure on organizations' bottom lines means organizations seek compensatory savings in all activities through saving, economic pressures and profitability, increasing client confidence means specially to understand retailers, cutomers and an increased confidence in using other marketing communication disciplines, a dissatisfaction with advertising means resulting in clients using other disciplines to improve consumer relations and sales, increasing mass media costs means where database costs decreased, mass-media costs (especially television, increased dramatically) and a reduction advertising agencies expenses in terms of strategic input and direction. Hence, one effective marketing communication strategy can be possible to assist the organizations to reduce advertising expense, raise brand familiarity, increase client number, raise product sale price for long term benefits.

Some marketing professional researches recommend marketing communication strategy ought have these several stages, they include as below:

Stage one is tactical coordination of marketing communication. It means to find what are the fails on function areas including advertising, promotion, direct response, public relation and special events. The tactical coordination of marketing communication strategy aims to find why a high degree of interpersonnal and cross-functional communications needed as formal policies and procedures are insufficient to achieve the organization marketing communication operation. It aims to find what the weaknesses are to cause the organization's internal communication between different departments and external communiation to its clients inefficience and ineffectiveness.

Stage two is refining the scope of marketing communication. The organization begins to examine communication from the consumer's viewpoint, include all contact and entry points between the organization and clients. The scope of communication activities also include internal marketing to employees, suppliers and other business partners.

The entensive information on consumers is gathered through primary and secondary market research as well as actual consumer behavior data and feedback channels are created to gather information about consumers. So, it aims to find what marketing communication challenges influence the organizations' internal and external communication difficulties to influence poor unsatisfactory customer behavior peformance to seek valuable solution to raise the organization's internal and external marketing communication more efficient and effective to raise customer communication success.

Then, third stage concerns how to improve and apply skill to build good marketing communication channel. Due to the marketing communication strategy implementation organization will need to learn how to use data obtained through IT skill to provide a basis for the identification of values and to monitor the impact of integrated internal and external marketing communication programmes over time. So, IT must be incorporated effectively into communication planning development and execution.

The final stage is financial and marketing communication strategic integraton. It emphasizes shifts from skills and data to driving corporate strategic planning using consumer information and insight. Financial measures should be adapted into the evaluation process based on return on consumer investment measures.

So, these stages will be the key compenent to raise or improve the external marketing communication efforts with the internal marketing communication efforts to raise the overall organizational corporate brand for long term effective and internal and external marketing communication channels to employees and consumers both stakeholders‘ benefits.

4.2 Marketing communication functions

Why do organizations need marketing communication? What are marketing communication functions to organizations? What kinds of challenges will encounter if the organization lacked an efficient marketing communication strategy? This chapter will be explained above these questions clearly.

Marketing communication seems to be gathered information and communication seems to be gathered information and communication technology, which will influence every aspect of consumer need in order to bring positive or negative emotions to the brand of product. Hence, if the organization had effective marketing communicaton tools and strategies, which will raise its competitive effort in nowadays business societies.

An effective marketing communication strategy or tool will help the brand of product to build good emotion to its consumers. The steps include: The organization needs have one good marketing plan. Then, it needs to design the right or suitable kind of marketing strategy to satisfy its products or services characteristics. Finally, if its marketing communication tools or methods are suitable to the organization to be used to promote. Then, it will either build good brand or remember or familiar as well as build either good (positive) or bad (negative) emotion to the customers. So, it seems an efficient and marketing communicatin tool or method will help the organization to increase customer familiarity and build positive emotion to its product or service. Otherwise, an inefficient marketing communication tool or method will not help the organization to increase customer familiarity build negative emotion to its product or service. So, it is one important function to any marketing communication strategy.

Why organizations ought need to spend time and human resource / communication tool resources to design the most right or the most suitable marketing communication strategy for its organization to promote its product or service? Before any organizatins design any communication strategy , they need to know what is this marketing suitation. In general, marketing is defined the establishment of mutually satisfying exchange relationships between the brand's product or/and service and its clients. It is managing profitable client relationships. It's goal of marketing is to attract new clients by promising superior value and to keep and grow current clients by delivering satisfaction.

Therefore, the marketing function is to identify client needs and to provide a product or service that meets some or all of those needs, accessibily and at an acceptable price to the target market. Hence, the organization's marketing communication strategy is only one part of its overall marketing strategy. A marketing strategy includes how to help the organization to promote its product or service, how to sell its product or provide its service, how to arrange the reasonable price strategy, how to help the organization to improve production and distribution efficiencies, how to focus on continue product improvement, how to focus on aggregive selling tactics, focuses on customer needs, applied on integrated marketing approach, how to give welfare of society.

How does the marketing communication strategy influence the overall marketing strategy success to the organization? An effective marketing communication strategy can create value for customers and build good customer relationship for the brand of product or service. It's function includes that is can let the organization understands markplaces and its customer needs and want more clearly, it can assist the organization how to design a customer-driven marketing strategy if the organization can build good relationship between them , it can also help the organization to construct a marketing communication strategy(program) that delivers superior value. Then, when the organization has an efficient marketing communication strategy, it can help the organization to build relationship and create customer delight in long term. Finally, it can help the organization to achieve a superior capture value from its clients to create profits and client quality more easily.

Why do organizations need have an efficient marketing communication strategy? The reasons include that as below: In fact, customers have much choices, usually different product or service marketing places will have (excess) oversupply of product or service to influence consumers to make careful choices to buy which brand of product or consume service in whose choice processes. So, if the brand of product or service cn build good communication relationship between itself and customers. It can influence customers to have positive emotion to choose to buy its product or consume its service. So, any organizations needs have good price, location (place), people (staff) strategies, it also need have good promotion (communication) strategy in order to learn how to communicate to its customers to keep close relationship and build positive emotion to let them to feel.

However, the marketing communication amix must include these several tools for any organizations to choose which kind(s) of communication tool(s) is (are) the best tool(s) in order to be used to promote its clients efficiently. They include: Advertising, it means that controlled paid for communication, it consists of communication messages, initiated by a specific communicator in the mass media to a defined target audience. Personal selling involves interpersonal communication between sellers and buyers through personal interactions. Sales promotion concerns the free and favorable exposure of a product's benefits or value in the media, public relations can establish and maintain favorable relations between an entity and its stakeholders. So, any organization needs to choose either only use one kind of communication tool or more than one kind of communication tools in order to achieve an efficient marketing communiation strategy to build positive emotion and good product or service image or familiar brand to let its potential customers to know by any above one media. Also, it implies that customers won't know or familiar to the brand more clearly if the organization had not implement any promotion tool(s) to promote its pooduct or service to letits clients to know whether its existing product or service can give what benefits to them.

How to achieve an efficient marketing communication strategy? To achieve an efficient marketing communication strategy to the organization. It includes this process: It needs to identify who are its target customers (main target customer) potential customer and prospects. Then, it needs to measure the valuation of its different groups of client (e.g. age, sex, shopping characteristics). Next, it needs to create and deliver the right or suitable or useful or persuasive messages and incentives to let its different group clients to know wha its product or service existing in its country or globale market places. Next, it needs to estimate how much it can earn return on its customer investment for its future possible reward. Because it if estimated that its marketing communication expenditure can not achieve its budget return in customer investment reward. Then, it needs revise its this (these) kind of marketing communication tool (s) whether it (they) is (are) useful to promote its product or service to let clients to know. Finally, it needs to implement its budgeting allocation and evaluation to review its every time marketing communication tool(s) whether is (are) achieved its original aim. If it believed or confirmed its slae result is not successful. Then, it needs to revise its marketing communication tool(S) whether they (it) is (are) the most suitable or useful one tool(s) t be used to promote to its clients in the future. Hence, the whole process of marketing communication strategy is very important to influence its sale number. Every product or service provider needs to spend enough time and human resource to marketing communication tool resources to decide how to design to implement in order to sell in failure finally.

For one integrated marketing communication model of brand contact delivery system case example: The brand;s customer (proposect exposure will include message and incentive both aspects. Message and incentive will bring promotin communication informations concern relevance and receptivity to the brand's product or service to let its customers to know or remember or familiar by these any one or more than one delivery systems , such as product/ use of the package product message tool or directed marketer channel or undirected member channel or traditional media tools (accesses or unintentional , such as TV, radio, magazine, signage outdoor direct marketing tool or electronic media tools (wired or wireless) such as website second intranet or mobile phone engins GPS or special events promotion methods (natural or sponsored) , such as holiday events or sport cultural trade events. All any one of these media delivery systems will be one choice tool to let the product/ service providers to be choosed to find which tool is the most efficient delivery tool. Hence, one marketing communication strategy elements include the marketing communication source is the company/brand or agency, the brand message concerns (planned , unplanned, product or/and service) and the channel includes newspapers, TV, radio, magazine, e-mails, salespeople sale service, customer service, internet and the receiver is the target audience in the whole marketing communication process. Finally, the delivery system will bring feedback to the company/brand, agency and the target audience both. The feedback includes that purchase/not purchase, request information, visit store, sample product, repeat visit/ purchase.

Consequently, any marketing communication strategy will bring feedback to let the product/service provider to know in order to judge or predict whether its potential customers will have positive or negative emotion (attitude) to choose to buy its product or consume its service. Thus, feeback affect will be one important factor to influence the product or service providers success. If the product / service providers and clients both feedback trends to more negative emotion to its potential customers, then it can attempt to follow whose ideas to find what internet weaknesses or external threats to cause whose potential customers feel negative emotion to its product or/and service. Then, it can attempt to find solutions to avoid whose negative emotion is caused more easily. Thus, an efficient marketing communication strategy can help the product/service provider how to raise its potential clients' emotion to be trended more positive emotion for their product or service choices.

4.3 The possible sale of relationship marketing and communication in public utility service

What are the function of marketing communication to public utility service ? If the public utility service orgnizaton lacks an efficient communication channel between internal staffs and utility consumers, what kinds of challenges who will encounter. How to they make solution ? What are the negative attitude of the utility consumers will be if it lacked an efficient communication service between them?

In fact, many countries' public utility service is monopoly market. Their governments ususally have a regulated prices to control their price to be charged to public utility consumers. Consumers have had affordable public utility access to these utility service, but they have been defenceless against the service providers . Hence , every government usually control utility service providers' price charged behavior in order to avoid their excess of charge. So, publis utility service providers have realized that those is a competition on the utility service market.

Hence, an effective and efficient marketing communication channel will bring those benefits ot advantages between the organization's internal staffs and every utility service consumer. I shall indicate the advantages as below:

Firstly, an efficient marketing communicatin channel can let utility service consumers to feel whether the public utility service is a real public service. Due to public utility service aims to provide any enough utility remains to consumers to use, such as electricity , water, gas, oil etc. is the field on non-business marketing because the public utility service providers do need aim on profit seeking . This is made characteristics as well by the fact that in many service field, e.g. higher education, public transport, public utility service. So , an efficient communication marketing channel can let the public service consumersm who can make easy to distinct between public and private as well as between profit and non profit , e.g. the students can judge whether their schools charge higher education fee or lower education fee in the general school fee charge level and judge whether the public transport charges higher or lower transport for general public transport service standard charge level and judge whether the gas, oil, water, electricity utility service charge is accepted to general public utility service charge standard level. Hence, an efficient marketing communication channel can let the public service consumers have more familiar and effort to judge whether the public service providers' charge is reasonable.

However, an efficient communication marketing channel is very important to assist the public utility service consumers to make a distinction as well . Every public utility service organization has responsibility to let public service consumers to know what are basic services to be provided to let them to judge whether the kind of possibility of public service substitution is small or large to let the publis service consumers to choose in the country 's current public service market to let them to judge whether the public service quality is good or bad and whether the price conditions are reasonable. Hence, an efficient marketing communication channel can build the good relationship between the public service organization and its public service consumers.

Do public utility services have important characteristics from marketing communication channel? It is agreed that efficient marketing communication channel is needed to any public utitlity service industries. It has chose marketing and communication relationship to any public utility service orgnizations. It is to think in terms of back office organizations in most person to person contact based services, but in the case of the utility services, the situation is unique different. In fact, the role of back office is significant different in the case of public utility services. In general , public utility consumers do not assess the work of background staff as they are unseen and are not usually part of the service providing process. However, the result of the servicing activity depends on the work of the back office. So, it explains that why efficient internal department communication is very important beween public utility service back office staffs. There is no effective public utility service without the tools, equipment and operating staff and the application of efficient and effective communication relationship marketing is challenges by this fact. For example, the role of power , heating, water and long distance telephone supply etc. customer service front office staff role is influential to their service efficiency by the back office staffs cooperation. If they have good communication channel to let them to work in order to achieve efficient communication effect. Then, the front office public utility service staffs can provide better consumer service to satisfy any public utility service consumer needs or build the high direct consumer service relationships between them.

Besides, efficient communication marketing strategy can assist the public utility service organization to promote its prices to let public utility service consumers to feel more acceptable to the price level chrge range. It is often difficult for service providers to apply differentiating price strategies and to use prices as promotional devices. Even, when price incentives are allowed public utility service providers rarely use. There effectively with elements of the marketing mix or with effective segmentation program to an efficient communication marketing strategy can help any public utility service organizations to solve any tangible and/or intangible communication challenges, such as back office and front office staffs communication challenges, fron toffice customer service staffs poor or inefficient service performance challenge, who causes utility service consumers to feel emotion unsatisfactory or do behavioral complains. So, effective communication marketing strategy is important tool to influence any public utility service organizations successes.

4.4 Understanding food industry marketing communication (pull marketing communication strategy)

In food industry , it needs have an efficient marketing communication strategy in order to the food providers can persuade their food consumers to choose to buy their food easily. Firstly, the food provider needs to understand the global consumer's prefence to find how any why to persuade they to choose to buy their food products. It is important to develop marketing communication strategies to solve challenges and find or seek opportunities in the communicaion process between the food providers (manufacturers) and its food retailers, food wholesalers (supermarkets , food stores). In its communication marketing strategy, it needs to consider two channels: The first channel is supply chain development and management channel. The food supplier (manufacturer) needs to learn how to manage its differene kinds of food supply chain, learn how to manage its food quality and food transportation logistics methods and learn how to communicate to its food retailers or food wholesalers how to help it to sell its different kinds of food to let consumers to buy attractively. The another channel is that it needs to learn how drive food consumer behavioral consumptionand learn hoe to predict why whose consumption behavioral change. Hence, the food supplier (manufacturer) needs to learn how to communicate with its food retailers and food wholesalers to know how any why its food consumers' choices to but its foods behavioral change. It concerns that it needs to communicate with them to learn how and why its old food consumers' taste change, researchs and builds new food product brand development as well as learns how to achieve efficient marketing communication strategy and point of sale strategies. Finally, the food supplier) manfacturer) will gather all data from there both channels to brings all data together to implement strategy revisited and revised the weaknesses and keep strengths in order to find the most useful solvable method to attract new potential food consumers to choose to buy to food or keep its old consumers to continue to choose to buy its food. Hence, one efficient marketing communication strategy which can represent the " PROMOTION" element of the marketing mix. Such on this food industry case, food marketing is all about food selling and communicating ideas be they to buy a good taste of food or good food salespeople service or take notice of a publis health apeal (e.g. eat fruit and vegetabl). None of this is possible without a good and effective communication strategy between the food supplier (manufacturer) and its food retailers or food wholesalers.

In many food and agricultural markets, the food and agriculture suppliers (producers and supply chain/ channel partners, it has become increasingly difficult to differentiate between food or agricultural product offerings. So, the number of available and visable positioning opportunities also diminishes. So, it implies that efficient communication strategy can assist them to create long-life marketing communication opportunities to promote their any agriculturl food success. Some of the key roles that promotion can play in food marketing include as below:

An efficient communication marketing strategy can help the agricultural food producers to build brand depth awareness. For example, when some food consumers ask the supermarket staffs concern which brands of chicken taste taht they can choose to buy in the supermarket chilled meat sections. If the chicken food supermarket staffs can speak some brands of chicken food, e.g. steggles, lillydale, ingham etc. brands. Then, the supermarket staffs can help those chicken brand producers to promote the different chicken taste food to let the supermarket consumers to know. So, it means that the brand of chicken food producers can build good communication relationship to the supermarket . Then, the supermarket staff's promotin behavior , it seems to advertise the chicken food producers to let the supermarket customers to know or be familiar the brand of chicken's different chicken tastes.

So, good food taste marketing communication strategy can achieve good or phycial availability , such as the food producers can arrange how much different food distribution to different wholesalers or retailers, such as supmarkets, food stores. Hence, if they had good communication relationship, whose middle sale agents, such as supermarkets or food stores will tell about how much different kinds of food will encounter food shortage or food excess perishable challenges in next month in order the food producers can predict who ought continue to increase supply the kind of food or reduce supply for every kind of food to the supermarkets or food stores to help them to sell next month. It aims to achieve all food will be fresh and good quality to provide to food buyers to eat. So, predicting food supply number will be one important solution to food perishable challenge.

In conclusion,an efficient marketing communication stragegy can assist the agricultural food producer to avoid to supply the excess of different kinds of food number or the shortage of different kindsof food number challenge. If the agricultural foos producers can build good marketing communication relationship between itelf and its food wholesalers/ food retailers, e.g. supermarkets, food stores. Then, the foor producers will have goos notice about its different kinds of food sale number data every month or every week ,even every day in order to decide whether it ought increase or decrease how much accurate predictive number of the kind of food to its food retailers or wholesalers to sell every day to avoid the different kinds of food excess or shortage challenges. So, efficient marketing communiation strategy is very serious to agriculturing food producers.

4.5 The role of marketing communication strategy in theatre management

Why does theatre industry need communication media, e.g. combination of advertisement, publicity, and public relation, plus other marketing tools in promotional activities of theatre management strategy. If the theatre performance provider neglected to achieve efficient marketing communication strategy , it will bring what kinds of challenges to influence performance entertainment consumers' entertainment desires.

Threatre industry can be explained to refer to any structure or group of people (even non professonal existing primarily for the preparation/presentation of theatrical performance, such as dance, music, song, movie, life show etc. performance for purpose of audience entertainment activities, such as movie is one kind of popular entertainment in threatre industry. It can provide entainment activity to entertain audience to satisf their visible enjoyable desires when they had bought tickets to choose any movies to watch in theatres.

What is the purpose of communication marketing management principles and strategies to threatrical procedures? Theatrical communication marketing management strategy consists planning, staffing, organizing , motivating, directing and controlling human and material resourcesin the arts of the theatre and their interaction in order to attain the predetermined objectives of guaranteeing satisfaction and maximizing profit. So , theatrical organization needs have efficient communication between its internal departments as well as itself and its any performance entertainment service providers . It aims to achieve every final entertainment performances which can be more attractive to let audiences enjoy to watch or listen any kinds of entertainment performances.

What role is a directing communication channel to threatre industry? Advertising is the structured and composed non-personal communication of information ususally paid for and usually persuasive in nature about products, services and ideas by identified sponsors through various media. Advertising can be explained the techniques and practices used to bring products , services , opinions or causes to public notice for the purpose of persuading the public to respond what is advertised. It seems theatre industry needs have efficient communication to let internal departments or entertainment performance service providers to communicate to them to achieve to prepare any attractive advertisments before any entertainment performance implementation. Because if one entertainment performance provider can provide attractive advertisements can persuade and notify potential audiences to choose to buy tickets to enter threatres to watch the entertainment performance service provider's any entertainment performance event more easily. So, the threatre service provider and its entertainment performance srvice providers need have good communication in order to advertise every different kind of entertainment performance event more attractive to let its audiences to feel. So, theatre provider needs to concern this internal and external communication issue in order to apply advertisement promotive channel to attract potential audiences.

Other kind of promotion channel to theatre providers. It is publicity , it is difference to public relations or even advertisement. Although, publicity seems a tool of public relations, but the aim of publicity is to create awareness through the media by placing news information about on organization, such as the threatre provider and its entetainment performance service providers. The major characteristic of publicity that differentiates it from other marketing tools is tat it is not be paid for by an identified sponor . Otherwise, public relation serves mainly the create an understanding between the threatre entertainment performance service provider and its publics (audiences) , thereby creating awareness for its entertainment performances. A public relations campaign takes various forms. It can be through the threatre provider's sponsorship of programmes beneficial to the audiences or through the award of scholarships is through any music, song, movie, dance, life show etc. different kinds of entertainment performance projects that attempt to build better understanding between the theatre provider and its audiences . So, having taken a critical look of advertising , publicity and public relations will be the important part of communication or promotion tools in theatre industry.

The aim of every well communiation methods to manag threatre , which can have much influential to impact audiences' emotions and their entertainment performance consumption desires to the theatre provider. However, the marketing communication channel of advertisement has weakness to theatre entertainment performance service provider, it depends on most printing spending times, as the printing of posters. This is not out of place because it has its role to play in marketing , but the fact, the electronic media advertisement does not need to print papers . Hence, this kind of promotion method will bring more economic benefit to the theatre service and entertainment performance service provider both.

A theatre entertainment performance provider will have different departments to cooperate efficiently in order to prodices theatrical performances, such as drama, dance, movie, opera, music , life show etc. entertainment performances. So, one department of any theatre provider needs t make uss of advertisement to create awareness about their any entretainment performance to any let audiences (entertainment consumers)to know. So, efficient communication is necessary between the threatre provider's departments.

In conclusion, in theatre entertainment performance industry, any theatre entertainment performance providers expect their every movie, song, mucis, dance, life show etc. art performances can be promoted from advertisement , publicity and public relations marketing tools successfully. In efficient marketing communication strategy is an essential facility available to every internal departments in order to strengthened cooperation how to design every advertisement, publicity and public relations channel to let every different kinds of art performance to be promoted to attract potential audiences to choose to bu admission tickets to watch or listen the theatre entertainment performances more easily.

4.6 Marketing communication function in clothing industry

What marketing communication tools are the most useful or suitable to clothing industry? I shall indicat mailings, telephones and personall interview marketing communicatiot ools to reflect the useful function to clothing industry. Nowadays, clothing fashion products total change of market had changed rapidly and its new trends which has changed too rapidly suddenly after 1950 year. So, the different brands of clothing products need to be designed unique to satisfy clothing buyer individual specific groups and / or lifestyle needs. Also, the different design of fashion clothing products can represent every different clothing brand's image. However, sufficient promotin will be one influential tool to help the clothing product designer to promote is any kinds of cloths to let potential cloth clients to know or help it to build familiar brand image in the clothing market.

Good fashion design can challenge conventional views. It should be recognized their consumers very in the conservation they have towards fashion styles and also speed and readiness with which change their opinions. So, an efficient marketing communication strategy will let the clothing products designer to gather whose cloth clients' opinions in order to predict how they ought to decide to design preferable fashion styles choices more easily in order to let it it follow general clothing product buyers' fashion styles design choice to design many attractive fashion styles of clothing products to let them to persuade them to choose to buy its clothing products more easily.

So, clothing buyer personal interviews or telephone individual contact or posting mail questionnaire enquiry promotion method will be one suitable to be used to promote in clothing industry. Because these markeing communication tools can gather any clothing buyer individual opinions in order to help the designers to understand. Then, clothing marekt can enhance the clothing design creating process and marketing personnel appreciate that within the fashion industry design can lead as well as respond to customer requirements progress can be made more easily. Thus, telephone, clothing buyers individual intervew or questionnaire researching or post mailing questionnaire researching marketing communication tools will have effort to help the bradn of clothing designer to predict how to design its cloths styles which can persuade potential clothing buyers to choose to buy its brands of any kinds of styles clothing products to wear more easily in possible. So, any clothing designer needs have a fashion marketing concept and have demonstrated equal concern for design, customers and profits. Thus, any clothing designer's marketing communication strategy needs to concentrate on fashion design promotion. It means that when the clothing product provider has good different styles of clothing design products and the suitable place(clothing stores) and the reasonable price setting , then it needs have good promotion (communication tool) e.g. telephone, TV, radio, magazine etc. to its target audience (e.g. child, young , old age , expensive or cheap clothing product buyer group, traditional design or popular fashion design style clothing product preference cloth buyers.

Nowadays, clothing communication medias include broadcast advertisement (TV and radio), print advertisement (magazines and newspapers), brochures and booklets, posters and packaging, motion pictures, directories, display signs and symbols and logoes. Any one of these communication medias can help any clothing designers to build its brand to be familiar to let its potential buyers to know. Instead of these communication media, sales promotion is usuall connect closely with adventing in clothing industry. The basic types of sales promotion include coupons, samplying , refunds and rebates, premiums and gifts , games, contexts. Any onf od these sale promotion will be one good communication method to persuade the clothing buyers to choose to attempt to buy the brand of any styles of clothing products tpo wear more easily. The primary communication objectives of these tools ususally are: stimulation of clothing consume trials, increase of rebuy rates and reward of loyal customers in order to fasten he selling process. However, promotion should bot be used as an ongoing program, as it is only a short term tastic. Otherwise, it can easily lower the price of the brand of clothing products.

The another kind communication tool is public relations, it means to build good relations with the clothing provider to public by obtaining favorable publicity. The " publics" are a the clothing provider's stakeholder, such as suppliers, employees, customers or governments, public relations activities can include press relationships, sponsorships, product placement, events management and crisis management. So, good public relation can help the clothing provider to build good brand image to let clothing buyers to know or familiar.

The final communication media is personal selling. It involves face-to-face activities, the clothing provider's clothing sales representatives of a particular clothing brand with the aim to inform, persuade or remind a clothing buyer to take appropriate action. The most common examples of personal selling include: sales presentations, sales meetings, incentive programs, samples, fairs and trade shows.

Consequently, any one of above communication medias will bring benefits to the clothing provider. However, the clothing provider needs to spend time and human resource and promotion communication tools resource to implement one effective marketing communication stragtegy to help its hw to promote its clothing products to let its potential clients to be familiar its different kinds of styles cloths more attractively. So, it seems on efficient communiation strategy can help the clothing provider to raise its different kinds of clothing design to attract its clothing buyers' consideration

APPLYING (AI) to business Environment

CHAPTER NINE

AI predicts Body shop facial product consumer behavior

1. Critically assess the extent to which whether AI can help Body Shop to predict facial product consumer behavior

Prediction method: AI can apply big data gather method to apply questionnaires method to enquiry different questions to let Body shop facial product consumers to answer what their emotion are after they use its any facial products.

So, AI can gather all different countries facial product consumer's positive or negative emotion data to analyze whether factors cause they feel negative emotions or negative emotions in order to concern how to solve the challenges to cause negative emotion and how to improve positive emotion.

So, AI big data questionnaire gather method can be possible to help Body shop facial product users to raise more positive emotions when it can find what factors cause they feel negative emotion and attempt to find methods to avoid as well as find what are the main positive factors to bring their positive emotion in order to keep them.

● Body Shop Background

The body shop international power line carrier (the body shop) was founded by Dame Anita Roddick in the England in 1976. It sold personal beauty care products, such as baby and child specific products, bath and shower and colour cosmetics, deodorants, skin care, hair care, fragrances, sun care etc skin health products to provide human body benefits. Nowadays, the body shop was skin and body care manufacturer and retailer operating in 55 countries with over 2,100 stores. It had 42 exclusive outlets in Hong Kong. It's missions were to dedicate to pursuit of social and environment change to meaningfully contribute to local, national and international communities in which trade to passionately campaign for the protection of the environment, human and civil rights and against animal testing and to make fun, passion and care part of our daily lives (Adrian, P. 2012).

● What is the difference between production orientation and societal marketing orientation and sales orientation

There are five main marketing orientations of which a company will adopt one. This will determine the way it interacts with the customer. Such as product orientation suggests that a company focuses inwards looking at what it is capable of, rather than the needs and wants of the client; sales orientation is based upon selling existing products with a turnover sale numbers relationship marketing orientation recognizes the value of repeat business over, not only with customers but suppliers as well; societal marketing orientation is relatively new in the scheme of things but suggests on top of meeting the needs and wants of the customer and the organization there is the societies interests to be looked and marketing orientation is based around the needs and wants of a customer to meet business objectives and it assumes that a sale depends on a customer's decision to purchase a product or provide a service.

● What is marketing two levels meaning ?

Marketing can be seen at two levels, the first level is such as a business philosophy, marketing puts customers at the center of an organization's consideration and which is reflected in basic values , such as the requirement to understand and respond to customers' needs and the necessary to search constantly for new market opportunity. In a truly marketing oriented organization, these values are instilled in all employees and should influence their behavior without any need for prompting. The personnel manager would have a selection policy that recruited staff who could fulfil the needs of customers rather than simply minimizing the wage bill in any marketing oriented organization. The other level is techniques of marketing also include pricing, the design of channels of distribution and new product development.

● What are the three components of market orientation ?

The assessing the nature and importance of market orientation for large firms, such as body shop. The three components of market orientation could be analytically separated. The components of market orientation organization include the first component is the customer orientation, it means an organization must have a thorough understanding of its target buyers, so that it can create a product of superior value to give client benefits ; the second component is the competitor orientation, it means any firm should look at how well its competitors are able to satisfy buyers' needs. It should understand the short term strengths and weaknesses and long term capabilities and strategies of current and potential competitors as well as the third component is to develop marketing plans that are not acted upon by people who are capable of delivering promises made to customers and a marketing orientation organization requires that the organization draws upon and integrates its human and physical resources effectively and adapts them to meet client's needs. Otherwise, a production and sales orientation may be appropriate to firms at certain stages in the evolution of markets. Where the dominant business environment is based on the need for good production planning above all, the company that does this best will achieve the greatest overall business success. It is either production orientation, it means organizations that produce what they imagined consumers wanted, rather than what they actually wanted. Planning for full utilization of capital equipment are often seen as more important than ensuring that equipment is used to provide goods and services that people actually wants. Production-oriented firms generally aim for efficiency in production rather than effectiveness in meeting customer's needs . It is either or selling orientation, it means advertising, sales promotion and personal selling techniques are used to emphasize product differentiation and brands and it does not focus on satisfying client needs or desire new product offerings and production led. Hence, one market orientation organization needs to focus on satisfying clients' needs profitably by these marketing mix, such as product, price, place, physical evidence, processed, people and promotion. Anyway ,Market orientation implied that body shop , which ought seek information about clients, such as current and future needs and took action based this information (client orientation); it ought seek information about competitors' current strengths and weaknesses and their long term strategies and took actions based on these information (competitor orientation) ; it ought coordinate the actions taken by sharing clients and competitors information internally (intra-firm communication).

- What is the three components of market orientation ?

The three components of market orientation meant social marketing and understanding boarder concerns and ethical environmental, legal and social context of marketing activities and programs. The cause and effects of marketing clearly beyond the company and the consumer to society as whole. New terms humanistic marketing and ecological marketing were suggested to societal marketing concept.

- What is the social marketing concept ?

The social marketing concept holds that the organization's task is to determine the needs, wants and interests of target markets and to deliver the desired satisfactions more effectively and efficiently than competitors and the society's welling being, such as body shop had achieved sales and profit gains by adopting and practicing a form of the societal marketing concept called cause related marketing.

- DISCUSSION

Body Shop is marketing orientation organization in 30 years.

Critically assess the extent to which I consider Body Shop to be a truly marketing oriented organization throughout its 30 years history . It seemed body shop had achieved cause-related marketing as an opportunity to enhance their corporate reputation, raised brand awareness, increased customer loyalty and built sales.

It's corporate values were composed of five core values. The first one was to oppose animal testing. The opposing animal testing for both cosmetic products and ingredients began in 1976 years.

In the 1980 year and 1990 year, who successfully campaigned with animal protection groups to change the UK and European laws to support the development products were tried on human volunteers. Along with the development of technology testing had played a leading role to protect the rights of both human and animals . The second one was to support community trade, it initiated the trade not aid objective of creating trade to help people in the third world utilizing their resources to their own needs. This reflects communities needed a fair price for natural ingredients who purchased from these often marginalized countries. The third one was to activate self esteem. Women were the main customers and employees in the body shop. The fourth one was to defend human rights. The body shop had long campaign on human rights, highlighting abuses and increasing the global awareness of issues by making full use of the geographic advantages of their shops and supporting other human rights organizations. The last one was protect our plant. In 2001 year, huge campaign against global warming was hosted by the body shop and green peace, who advocated the use of recyclable source and materials (Adrian, P. 2012). Although profits were an essential element of long run survival in body shop and it was likely to be overall corporate and marketing objectives, but body shop seemed more to be required level of profits rather than profit that there were many other objectives, which might pursue through its pricing strategies . For example, if body shop wanted to maximize market share or simply survive, a different set of prices would be delivered than if the objectives were to maximize profits. Hence, body shop ought to see viewpoint the marketing side of pricing and it ought not to see viewpoint the production / supply side of pricing if it was a truly marketing oriented organization. The key inputs for body shop to make pricing decision whether it was marketing oriented or productive / supply oriented included production objectives or marketing objectives, demand or supply numbers were considered cost or sale price and competitors or clients consideration factors, such as beauty skin care products in competitive markets demand, i.e. To decide the price whether customers are willing and able to pay is a major consideration in the selection of pricing strategies and levels of demands . Hence, body shop ought to consider demand numbers , it ought not consider production / supply numbers if it was a truly marketing oriented organization. For example, since most of the body shop's factories were still located in the UK, where wages and salaries were much higher than in Asia, so UK itself sale product prices were higher than that from Asia itself sale product prices.

I think Body Shop was a truly marketing oriented organization more than production/supply oriented organization throughout its 30 years history. In fact, Body Shop was experiencing market level growth. It could expand its sales market in Europe, America, Middle East, Asia and Africa etc different countries. It seemed that it had attempted to carry on marketing research to decide to choose which countries would have more client numbers to demand to buy its personal care products, then it would follow the countries' estimated client numbers to produce its products to sell to the countries. So, it was why some Asia countries sold its bath and shower and skin and hair care and colour cosmetics products more than its fragrances products, such as Hong Kong young people were more acceptable to use bath and show and color cosmetic and skin and hair care products more than fragrances products . It seemed that Hong Kong Body Shop sold fragrance products numbers were less than bath and shower and color cosmetics etc. products. Nowadays, I think the personal beauty care products new businesses which planned to entry this market was more difficult. It was possible than Body Shop was a famous personal beauty care products sale company, it had owned many clients too many years. So , it caused barriers to any new personal beauty care product competitors felt difficult to entry this market .Furthermore, Body Shop had build strong buyer and seller power to increase clients had more confident to use its products, it was possible that who felt its different kind of products could give more health to their skin or body more than other similar personal beauty care products. Moreover, I believe Body Shop had attempted to carry on technological experimenting to aim to build different countries' clients had more confident to use its products forever.

In conclusion, it seemed that Body Shop was truly marketing oriented organization more than productive/ supply oriented organization oriented organization throughout its 30 years history.

2. To what extent are the pursuits of profit and meeting the needs of wider groups of stakeholders incompatible?

Whether Body shop pursuits social responsibility aim or profit aim more.

Any companies need to consider the social responsibility during which are the pursuits of profit and meeting the needs of wider group of stakeholders incompatible. Without this self interest, there will be little motivation for firms to provide better services, workers couldn't earn better salaries and clients couldn't aspire for a high level of consumption. Hence, self interest which helps markets work more effectively for the benefits of all. Hence, companies should adopt a code of behavior and conduct and ethical behavior which would not influence any stakeholders groups' benefits to pursuit their profit honestly. Corporate social responsibility is a form of corporate self regulation integrated into a business model. It aims to give responsibility for corporate actions and to encourage a positive impact on the environment and stakeholders including consumers, employees, investors, communities and others and it is titled to aid an organization's mission as well as guide to what the company can give the best benefits to serve its customers. I shall use body shop company as one example to judge whether what extent are the pursuits of profit and meeting the needs of wider groups of stakeholders will be incompatible. Factually, body shop could adopt a code of behavior and conduct and ethical behavior which would not influence any stakeholders groups' benefits to pursuit their profit honestly. Such as, one of the major and most successful initiatives which body shop used an effective supply chain for their products and body shop made use of their sustainable chain supply strategy to ensure that there was the promotion and the maintenance of the social ethical behavior in its business. Hence, it seemed that body shop could be compatible to achieve an effective supply chain to deliver to different countries' stores to meet clients who had more need to buy different kinds of skin care products to provide them to choose to buy in the reasonable price choices in the short time. It is therefore in the best practices and interests for body shop to reach out to the communities in their businesses to provide raw materials to help the manufacturers of the beauty products. It also partook in the development of the market for such small scale suppliers. In many cases the body shop tried to outsource its raw materials to its customers. This had ensured the sustainability of its customer base this included it's sensitivity to its environment and the required standards of the labor practices of its partners. Hence, it seemed that body shop could be compatible to help its partners to earn profits and any countries' partners could provide more job chances to unemployed people to work from body shop's outsourcing strategy. Hence, this had been developed by the body shop by including strategies, such as third party logistic providers and intermediaries in which who had no ownership. The body shop was a multinational company also adopted trading to purchasing approach where it shifted from short term where focus of buying articles to long term focus of fewer suppliers. This was an attempt of it to develop quality products where prices were also fair and affordable to sell to different countries' clients. It seemed that body shop could be compatible to sell reasonable prices of products to it's clients. Moreover, it had included in its strategies the aspect of business promotion using catalogues. For the same reason, it had been involved in printing of catalogues which were given out to the clients with their purchases. It was important to note that it' catalogues always contained all it's information descriptions and any person who purchased it's products was bound to receive the explanation of all it's product. This was an attempt of it to develop quality products where prices were also fair and affordable to sell to different countries' clients. It seemed that body shop could be compatible to provide clear information description in catalogues to let whose clients to know what it's different kinds of style body skin care products ingredients and benefits were , then who could compare it's products to other competitors to decide to buy or not buy fairly.

In Oct. 2007 the campaign for safe cosmetic products, in which 25 multinational companies participated, tested 33 brand name lipsticks and found one-third of the sampled exceeded the limit of lead allowed in confectionery. The affected brands included L'Oreal and Christian Dior. A definite effect would be that consumers would be more concerned regarded the ingredients of products who used, which was likely to have an effect on cosmetics and skin care products were released to capture share. It seemed body shop needed to consider its beauty personal care products were the most ensure to own organic ingredients to let any countries clients (stakeholder) to meet their body health care needs (Adrian, P. 2012).

On the health and natural aspect, body shop had health and safe responsibility to consumers. Although, I felt who had considered this issue because it had 30 years history to operate this business and it had not received any serious negative complaints damage its health product image from clients before. However, with consumers were increasingly informed and were educated, who were now more demanding for more information regarding products and were becoming more aware of health issue. Products with organic ingredients and natural ingredients, such as tea and plants were gaining popular. Furthermore, consumers were looking for healthier substitutes to seemingly unhealthy products, such as color cosmetics. Hence, body shop began to sell the reducing numbers, it was possible due to clients compared it's body care products quality to the other competitors and who felt it's product's ingredients existed some poor ingredients to cause every one's body to be unhealthy. Hence, it's productive processing was very important. It seemed that body shop could be compatible to consider its individual client body skin health issue whether after who had used it's body skin care products to have skin hurt or skin pain feeling. In conclusion, to judge what extent are the pursuits of profit and meeting the needs of wider groups of stakeholders incompatible for any individual business, it is depended on whether the company's any stakeholders, such as employees, clients, suppliers, partners, society (communities) etc. who will have positive or negative influence from it. I feel that it will be incompatible if the company give negative influence to any one of its stakeholder. Hence, if any one company's at least one stakeholder who felt who had negative influence due to it did business to relate to whom unwillingly, then it's pursuit of profits aim would be incompatible to meet it's needs of its any one of stakeholder. Such as body shop will give positive influence to its all stakeholders. Hence, I feel it is compatible extent to pursuit of profit and meeting the needs of its wider groups of stakeholders definitely.

3. What companies, if any have managed to sustainable reconcile these two aims?

I feel that Nestle company has managed to sustainable reconcile to pursuit profits and meeting the needs of its wider groups of stakeholders two aims compatibly. Nestle was the world's largest food and beverage company. Nestle in the United States, which represented seven operating across the USA country and it was the first expanded effort in USA and achievement tied to Nestle 's global sustainability principle and commitment. Nowadays, It served 97% of American householders and Nestle 's mission was to lead the industry in nutrition, health and wellness and to create a more sustainable future. Instead of it's mission was to pursuit of profits aim, it had also achieved specific sustainability commitment and progress in the categories of nutrition, environmental impact and water use, social impact, rural development and responsible sourcing to meet the needs of it's wider of groups of stakeholders' aim. On the nutrition, health and wellness aspect, Nestle met the needs to its stakeholder (clients), such as, Nestle rolled out new portion guidance tools and launched an educational campaign and balance your plate to help consumers build nutritious and delicious and convenient meals that met the dietary guidelines for Americans; Nestle also reduced sodium content in many of its most popular brands, such as Stouffer's and DiGiorno and committed to further reduce sodium content by 10 percent in products that did not meet the Nestle; Nestle also reduced sugar content, such as ninety six percent of Nestle 's children's products met the Nestle criteria for low sugar and by the end of 2014 year, 100 percent of children's products would meet these criteria as well as Nestle also removed trans-fat content, such as Nestle committed to reach zero food and beverage products with trans-fat originating to use as functional ingredients by 2016 year. It seemed that Nestle had considered its food and beverage production content whether these content would have negative influence to its stakeholder (clients) nowadays (Adrian, P. 2012). On the environmental impact aspect, Nestle reduced waste during it's food and beverage products were producing. As part of its commitment to eliminate all forms of waste, Nestle reduced 44 percent of waste per ton of product since 2010 year in the USA five factory locations reached zero waste to landfill status by the end of 2013 year; Nestle also considered responsible packaging responsibility, such as Nestle Waters North America led the USA bottled water industry in light weighting packaging, in part by reducing the plastic content of its 1/2 liter bottles by 60 percent since 1994 year. Since 2003 year alone, more than 3.3 billion pounds of plastic had been saved by Nestle as well as Nestle also adopted responsible sourcing, such as Nestle Purina Pet Care implemented responsible sourcing guidelines for seafood that align with Nestle 's global responsible sourcing guidelines, working with experts to track suppliers and contribute to healthier ecosystem. In 2013 year, Nestle also reached an important target for palm oil, with 100 percent of palm oil now Round table on sustainable palm oil certified. It seemed that Nestle also considerate whether environment would have negative influence occurrence during it's production (Adrian, P. 2012). On social impact aspect, Nestle supported local communities, such as Nestle in USA donated more than $2.3 million dollars to support local United Way organizations; It also provided disaster relief, such as Nestle waters donated more than 685,000 bottled of water and Nestle Purina contributed more than 60,000 pounds of pet food and 41,000 pounds of cat little to local shelters across the USA for disaster relief as well as it grew supplier diversity, such as Nestle works with over 4,100 small, minority, women and veteran owned businesses to help to spur local economies. It seemed that Nestle also considerate social needs. Thus, it is seemed Nestle company have managed to sustainable reconcile these two aims to pursuit profit as well as it also could gave positive influence to its stakeholders. Such as consumer could feel safe to enjoy to eat Nestle company's health foods; societies could be reduced unemployment from its outsourced assistance job to partners; natural environment could be reduced pollution from its productive protection. Hence, it was not actually neglect its shareholders' benefits during it was doing business as the same time (Adrian, P. 2012).

4. What are basic lessons in marketing that the Body Shop might have taken on board in its early years in order to improve its chances of long term success?

The body shop is a global manufacturer and retailer of naturally inspired , ethically produced beauty and cosmetics products. Founded in the UK in 1976 year by Dame Anita Roddick, who now have 2,133 stores in 55 countries with a range of over 1,200 products in Europe, America, Middle East, Asia and Africa. However, the body shop has not entered the China market. It takes a strong position on activism, ethical business, human rights and environmentalism in a global perspective. The body shop is banned in China because cosmetics sold there have to be tested on animals, according to Roddick. In, 2006 when it was bought by the French cosmetics company L'Oreal which is a big player in China. China has launched scientific developing strategy for future the current policies of advocating. Hence, it is the perfect time for the body shop to enter China market. However, prior to that, as an independent member of the L'Oreal family, the body shop has to make decisions on differentiation marketing strategies, market segmentation and marketing position (Adrian, P. 2012). It might have taken two purposes to body shop marketing in its early years in order to improve its chances from short term to long term success. The short term objective was to generate more sales for the body shop. Through, the introduction of a new service, the market up class, it was hoped that clients could try and experience the body shop cosmetic products. Positive experience of using its products could then be developed through their trial using the market up class. It was estimated that this positive experience could push up the sales.

The long term objective was to educate the belief of the body shop to the young potential clients, so that who would become those who preferred natural cosmetic products and were loyal to the body shop in the future. Objectives could provide the starting point for marketing plans and strategies and should be specific targets that are obtained but also challenging. Specific, measurable, agreed, realistic and time related objectives might be taken to body shop to improve early years in chances in long term success. It seemed that Hong Kong was one good market for body shop to satisfy an unfulfilled customers needs to pursue body shop investment chance. Therefore, the objective were to push up sales and built a loyal customer basis for the future. For example, Hong Kong was one young student clients growth market to body shop. In the past, one cosmetic products market statistic was indicated that the colour cosmetic retail value had been increasing from 2002 year, HK$938.3 million dollars to 2007 year, HK$1,132,3 million dollars, so percentage was increased to 5.12% . (Adrian, P. 2012). It seemed Hong Kong might be one good skin cosmetic care products developed market to this body shop in early years. The another factor might improve body shop long term success factor was whether body shop had attempted to analyze direct competition. The body shop's direct competition was not from the name brand like Dior, Chanel or Olay, but rather the less well known brands, from Japan or Korea. Along with the great impact of Korean fashion, many Korean cosmetics brands like Missha and the Face shop had already established shops in China. These two brands also promoted their natural ingredients and target the young customer segment as what the body shop products competition concept could be offered to a market to satisfy a want or need and offered five levels, which were the core benefits, basic product, expected product, augmented product and potential product. Each level added more customer value and the five constitute client value hierarchy products of these three brands were all using natural ingredients and simple and natural in packaging. The body shop , however, differentiated itself at the top levels of the five product and transformations the products might undergo in the future.

Marketing management and planning was essential to body shop, it was the implementation of strategies to achieve long run profitability to body shop and growth. When body shop was looking at how it would achieve this in early years in order to improve the chances long term success, its two keys points to consider are: What was body shop man activity at a particular time? And how it would reach its goals? It might design a strategy that insured a consistent approach to offer its skin care products to raise competition in mind the skin care products changing market. These included product line, distribution methods, marketing communication and pricing. For example, achieving marketing research to Hong Kong and China skin care products market to analyze what were these factors to influence these country people who felt needs to buy its skin care products: Such as internal factors include personality, motivation, learning, perception and attitude; external factors included culture, social class, reference groups , family and personal influences and situational factors included time, income, mobility and availability. The reason was because due to consumers bought skin care products to protect whose skin (core benefits) and their expectations if who were willing to pay more basic product. To enhance the product level, body shop skin health product needed emphasize that skin products were natural. Products of the body shop offered the same effective and natural and flavor and unique corporate values. Body shop was mostly natural (augmented level). Far more than the visible products, the shop shop's unique corporate values create the potential value to fulfil customer's desire of making a better health world. It's good corporate desire citizenship went beyond supplying rational and emotional benefits. Body shop might enter China market to improve long term success. The body shop divided its markets to include overseas Pacific Europe, America , Australia and New Zealand, Middle East, Africa and local UK countries. Adrian, P.(2012) indicated that a sampling questionnaire survey was conducted among 200 consumers, ranging from 18 to 50 ages in May 2006, a total of 170 valid responses that were used for analysis. Among the 170 responses, 66% were females. The findings were:

(1) About 60 % hoped that cosmetics could be a symbol of being environmental friendly.

(2) 90% would choose products made of natural ingredients.

(3) 90% spent less than 300 RMB on cosmetics and skin care products quarterly.

(4) 83% Chinese youth (age range from 18 to 25 ages) were innovators and conscious of environment.

Hence, the body shop might take a share of potential market in China. It should launch its products among younger cosmetic industry were young females who chased beauty and were willing to spend money on it. So, packaging was one of the vital factors in attracting client. The body shop took a unique approach by choosing simple packaging. The package was not made for mature women. It was made for young female students, who could enjoy on international brand at an inexpensive cost. The body shop was not only to meet young people's demand for beauty , but the demand of being responsible to environment and human rights. Hence, the target market of the body shop should focus on young people ageing from 15 ages to 30 ages. Hence, body shop might take marketing

research in Hong Kong and China market to have more confident to invest in these market to improve more success. Next, Whether body shop might achieve price strategy to improve to raise success chance. An assumption is when the individual client is considering the price of any a body shop's beauty skin health product. Economic theory suggests that the customer will act in a totally rational economic manner, such that body shop's every client total utility (or satisfaction) is maximized. In deciding whether try or not try body shop's product, which totally rational consumer will carefully equate whether ought to buy or ought not buy body shop's product at the asking price set will maximizing whose utility. In making judgment, the economist assumes that the consumer has perfect information about both the prices and utility of all the other competitive products in the market and that price is the only consideration in choice. Clearly there are unrealistic assumptions. Price could be determined easily when a target market was identified. (Adrian, P. 2012) From survey indicated 64% of the 170 responses spent less than 1000 RMB on cosmetics and skin care every quarter and 24% of their expenditure was between 100 RMB and 300 RMB on cosmetics an skin care. This number could not be ignored if a cosmetics company wanted to enter this large market and be a leader. For the younger generation, the prices of the products could not be high. The price of these main competitors ranges from 10RMB to 200 RMB. The prices in Hong Kong have higher than that in the USA or the UK. And the consumer's purchasing power in mainland China is much lower than that of Hong Kong . Hence, body shop should adopt a price range in China which was similar to that of the USA or the UK rather than of Hong Kong. Once the body shop established greatly reduced and the capability of price adjustment would be achieved accordingly.
Further, body shop might have chain stores selling channel strategy to attempt to achieve long term success. Sample survey revealed that supermarket was for Chinese to purchase skin care and cosmetics. 120 out of the 170 responses hoped that who could choose products from the chain stores in the future, which suggested that the body shop should build up its own stores was regarded as cares about corporate culture and corporate image. It insisted on selling in its own stores rather than setting up counters in a shopping mall. The stores of body shop could be found easily worldwide because of stores were importance in this competitive buyer. Hence, in China, its appearance should be same as worldwide. Some housewives joined the body shop as sales agent and hold sales parties for other housewives. The sales channel allowed the body shop to reach out to more clients by bringing the store directly into client's homes. This would be a totally new method of marketing in China, but it offered a good opportunity for women to choose products and share feedback in a relaxed atmosphere. This fresh concept could attract female consumers. Nowadays, students in China could only obtain famous skin care products and cosmetics brands from campus agents, as who could not afford the products sold over the counters. It was a major problem that agents could not guarantee the ingredients and the quality of the goods. If the body shop could hold small parties to share products and opinions, that would be a good way to boost sales among students. Hence, body shop might take price strategy to Hong Kong and china market to predict whether what price who could accept to raise more confident to invest to this market to improve more success. Further, body shop might also have promotion strategy to attempt to achieve long term success. The body shop adopted environmental friendly manufacturing, opposed abuses of human rights and was accountable for its actions. The unique values attracted numbers of media groups in many countries. This results in

its establishing a good reputation without any advertisements. The body shop also joined numerous social causes, which substitute advertisements. In China, however, it was totally different. In this brand new market, most people were out aware of this company. If it carried on a marketing promotion of no commercials it was impossible to reach a high market share. Hence, commercial advertisements were needed in China. The body shop could use this advertisement to give on impression that women should care about their well being both mentally and physically and it had created a sexy grand with simple packaging and without objectifying women. Many brands reach customers directly by colorful commercials and show their products in movies and TV play series. For the sakes of brand image, some movies about human rights , environmental protection and animal protection could be chosen by the body shop as carriers for particular commercial as most of the audiences were well educated, well paid and environmentally concerned. The target consumers of the body shop aged from 20 to 40 ages were energetic , knowledgeable and environmentally concerned. The body shop could give some lectures on makeup or skin care on campuses to raise feeling among students. To reach brand awareness and high brand loyalty , some samples should be given to students by experience marketing approach. Hence, body shop might take promotion to Hong Kong and China schools to let many young people to know why who needed to buy skin care products to protect their body skin to persuade who felt more needs. In conclusion, the body shop was famous for creating a niche market sector for naturally inspired skin care and cosmetic products through it's unique corporate values worldwide. The significance of the body shop's early entry into China market were strongly proposed. Once the body shop decided to enter the China market, the relevant marketing strategies and management should be implemented, such as the market segmentation and market positioning with the proper consideration of Chinese consumers should be studied in order to win the mind share of potential Chinese customers with the right marketing strategies. Overall, the findings of market survey and theoretical analysis strategy support the feasibility of the body shop's early entry into China market.

5.2 AI predicts Walt Mark Supermarket food consumer behavior

1. AI can apply big data gathering method appropriate framework of analysis to find what are the main factors to cause the effects of change in the marketing environment on sales of ready meals to Walt Mark supermarket to influence its food consumers why choose to buy ready cooked meals more than not ready cooked meals. Thus, it needs to produce questionnaires to enquiry about these questions:

Why do you prefer to choose to buy ready cooked meals to change your traditional not ready cooked meals eating choice?

What are the main reason(s) to cause either your ready cooked meals purchase change or ready not cooked meals purchase change?

So, when AI gather all datas which concern the factors cause either their ready cooked meal purchase choice or their ready not cooked meal purchase choice. Then it can help Walt Mark supermarket to predict what factors to cause the different countries meal consumers why they choose to buy ready cooked meals to eat or they choose to buy not ready cooked meals to eat. Then, Walt Mark supermarket can predict what the factors cause the country meal consumers to choose to buy ready cooked meals or ready not cooked meals to eat.

Although, previously dismissed and a poor substitute for real cooking and ready meal sales have grown rapidly in recent years in many western developed countries, such as UK, France or Germany. But, Ready meal manufacturers ready to respond to a changing marketing environment. Due to one big change in recent year has been growing demand for ready prepared meals bought from a supermarket. An analysis of the reasons for the growth in the ready prepared meals markets indicates the effects of boards factors in the marketing environment on the size of a particular market. In fact, this food market is changing to drive the growth in the ready meals market, but there are differences in the food market potential between countries. The effect of change in the marketing environment on sales of ready meals, such as technology has played a big role in the growing take up of ready meals and new technologies have allowed companies to develop ready meals which preserve taste and texture, which still making them easy to use by the consumer. Furthermore, great advances in distribution management, in particular the use of information technology to control inventories, has allowed fresh, chilled ready meals to be effectively and efficiently distributed without the need for freezing or added preservatives. Ready meals particularly appeal to single householders, which individual family members tend to eat at different times, so family meals together remains stronger in many continental European countries than in the UK individual ready meals. Young people have lost the ability to cook creatively, as cookery has been reduced in importance in the school, so young clients group will rise to buy ready meals from supermarket. Marketing can be seen as a system that must respond to environmental change. A food market can be defined as a meeting place for stakeholder (consumers) and sellers. Food market can be set up in a supermarket or restaurants. A food market consists of the individual's target taste, such as older group, family group, young group or business clients who are actual or potential caters of a restaurant meals or supermarket package of foods. Grocery stores (supermarkets) have an influence of meals (fast cooked food) outlets in low income urban areas, which has contributed to the income in access to healthy foods. An organization's marketing environment means the individuals, organizations, and forces external to the marketing management's ability to develop and maintain successful exchanges with its customers. The marketing environment to ready meal manufacturers had three levels.

Firstly, it includes the micro environment, it describes those elements that impinge directly on the ready meal manufacturers themselves, so the micro environment of ready meal manufacturers which include business clients who have direct contact, such as restaurants, supermarkets and individual clients who have direct contact. Otherwise, supermarket shoppers, restaurant clients and food supply competitors who have no direct contract to ready meal manufacturers, so who won't include in food market micro environment to ready meal manufacturers. Secondly, it includes the macro environment, it describes things that are beyond the immediate environment but can nevertheless affect an organization, so the macro environment of ready meal manufacturers which include the export countries' economies forces, such as unemployment ratio, GDP; technological forces, such as the export countries' factories food productive technology; social/ cultural forces, such as the export countries' people taste acceptance; political/legal forces, such as the export countries' import food quota numbers. Thirdly, it includes the internal environment, it describes ready meal manufacturers' employees and equipment and finance and functional responsibilities. Environment means everything outside influences the person, in contrast with individual or personal variables . The effects of change in the marketing environment on sales of ready meals can be analyzed by creating healthy food and eating environment changing factor and supermarket technological changing factor as below:

The ready meal manufacturers could not ignore threats to the natural ecological environment change Due to the food companies could have technology to manufacture good taste cooked ready meals to provide to supermarkets to sell. Thus, it might influence the consumers to decide whether restaurants or supermarkets or ready meals suppliers who could provide the most reasonable price and taste to satisfy whose eating needs every day. Thus, it caused the growing demand for ready prepared cooked meals bought from supermarkets. Due to it was possible that consumers felt to eat ready cooked meals in expensive restaurants or who did not like to buy foods to cook from food suppliers or who could not feel which could supply more good food taste and health food quality to compare supermarkets specially. Otherwise, although, supermarkets could provide cheaper ready cooked meals to satisfy who to feel good food taste and health food quality. Due to ready meal manufacturers had new techniques to develop ready meals which preserve taste and texture, which still making them easy to use to eat by the consumers. Furthermore, great advances in distribution management, in particular the use of information technology to control inventories, has allowed fresh , chilled ready meals to be effectively and efficiently distributed to supermarkets or restaurants without the need for freezing or added preservatives. Creating healthy food and eating environments view describes an ecological framework for conceptualizing the many food environments and conditions that influence food choices, with an emphasis on current knowledge was been regarding the home, child care, school, work site, retail store and restaurant settings. The status of measurement and evaluation of nutrition environment and the need of action to improve health are highlighted in marketing environment. More processed and convenience foods are available in large portion sizes and which were supplied at relatively low prices at supermarkets. Parents are working larger hours, there are fewer family meals and more meals are eaten away from home. The school food environment is remarkably different. It seemed that it would be changed in the marketing environment on sales of ready cooked meals to supermarket more easily. Due to supermarkets' cooked meals should focus on selling high calorie and low nutrition foods are available in multiple venues throughout the school student client group target because it was possible that supermarkets could sell ready cooked ready meals prices were more cheaper to compare to restaurants or school canters' cooked meals provided prices.

The effects of change in the marketing environment on sales of ready meals which indicated that consumers chose prefer to buy ready cooked meals from supermarkets. It seemed that a restaurant market failure could be caused to arise. For example, there was poor information on the part of food (ready cooked meals) to provide to the restaurant about the foods that consumers in a location(place) would demand for a given price to compare to the supermarket sale prices. The restaurant would lose clients if which cooked the kind of meals to sell higher price to compare to the supermarket sale of the kind of cooked ready meals price possibly. Large size supermarkets could sell cheaper ready cooked meals to low income group clients. It could cause competition to constitute a market failure to small size supermarkets. If the small size supermarkets lacked good information on the true food (ready cooked meals) with concentrations to sell cheaper prices, then this ready cooked meal market failure was one potential reason why small size supermarkets did not locate to close to the large supermarkets. Due to supermarkets grew in size would influence clients' choice to buy the numbers of cooked foods (ready meals) products. Moreover, The advent of computerized logistics and inventory systems were integrated with the large size supermarkets themselves occurred between the 1980 years and 1990 years .

So large size supermarkets were reliance on their own distribution and cooked food (ready meals) inventory systems along with larger supermarket sizes to allow super center to change to sell ready cooked meals at lower prices. Supermarkets marketing can promote healthful eating by increasing availability, affordability or restricting / de-marketing unhealthy foods to sell cooked Food (ready meals) marketing strategy at supermarkets, including labelling, packaging, pricing and point of sale advertising. Consumers‘ cost saving efforts and income and ready cooked meals prices increasing or decreasing factors can drive the choice of supermarkets as well as cooked meal products use of coupons and loyalty cards bargain shopping is another factor to influence their choice. Private label or store (supermarket) brands are taking an increasing share of consumers shopping dollars as the importance of brands. Supermarket shoppers stated priorities are cooked food (ready meals) quality or taste and price and healthy cooked food (ready meals) choices. However, supermarket shoppers' buying behaviors don't always reflect on favor healthful foods. Due to demand for locally grown cooked food is increasing. Anyway, restaurant meals are changed to supermarket to sell, which decide what kinds of meals to stock and how many of different kinds of meals to stock and how much variety of kinds of meals to offer to any one supermarket as well as supermarket shoppers prefer fewer options, provided that their preferred brand or cooked food (ready meals) products are available. The designs of supermarket ready cooked meal products and packaging to supermarket to sell is the focus of unusual colors or shape which can be used to increase interest and is specially pervasive among fun foods to compare to restaurant meals. Package design, including where text and images are placed, which can influences cooked foods (supermarket ready meals repurchasing again).The influence of design differs by the type of display consumer segments seek (convenience, information or images) and ready cooked meals package sizes have a relatively strong influence on consumption; larger ready cooked meals packages might increase per-use consumption ,but smaller packages might not improve self regulation and might not actually increase total consumption. In conclusion, I suggest that this ready meal manufacturers need to give more attention to be paid to food sellers, such as supermarkets‘ competitive differentiation and understanding the way in which customers attribute value to its ready meal products choice. Moreover, many consumers have become increasingly concerned about the health implication of the food they eat, so ready meal manufacturers will need to continue responding to such concerns. For example, who have responded with a range of low calorie meals, and addressed specific, sometimes transient, health fads, with respect to trans-fatty acids and omega 3 supplements of these cooked meal ingredients. Many consumers have also become concerned about the ecological environment and some supermarket suppliers, such as Marks and Spencer have incorporated sustainability agendas into their ready meals, for example by reducing packaging and sourcing supplies from sustainable sources. Thus, it caused ready meal manufacturers why who needed to give more attention to concern how supermarkets helped them to sell cooked ready meals in this foods market.

2. Critically discuss the link between the economic environment and sales of ready meals in supermarket

The macro environment, it describes things that are beyond the immediate environment but can nevertheless affect the organization. Such as the ready meal manufacturers in its macro environment, including the economic environment which can cause the manufacturers sell ready meal numbers whether which can sell more or less to different exported countries due to the exported countries' unemployment ratios, GDP and Government policies etc factors influence. Economic theory can help to explain why it can influence consumer behavior. In food sale market, it can include consumer behavior and demand side as well as retailer behavior and supply side two issues. Consumer behavior and demand side issue, such as the exported countries‘ consumer whose knowledge of the nutritional benefits of foods whether which prices were raised to choose to buy reasonably as well as retailer behavior and supply side issues, such as investing for developing a restaurant or supermarket in an underserved area whether the types of meals choices which are valued or which are not valued to buy to offer to clients from imports. On the other hand, economic environment factor, individual income can influence who chooses the type, quantity and quality of food that is purchased for a house holder and it also influenced the cooking and storage facilities available in a household to influence food choice.

On the other way, economic environment variation factor can also influence food access across areas. It is important to understand the economic conditions that may contribute to food deserts, that is the costs that food retail businesses face and the choice available to consumers who want to buy foods. Economic environment factor considers the consumer and demand factors, business and supply factors and the market conditions that interact to create differences in the food retail environment across areas and subpopulations. In general, high income meal client group can accept to choose to go to supermarkets or restaurants to spend than low income meal client group. The impact of the economic environment on sales of ready meals is such as an individual get richer, who can afford to buy ready prepared foods, rather than spend time and effort to prepare to cook them at home. It seemed that low income consumers were decreasing to eat meals at expensive restaurant to the alternative of relatively cheap ready prepared meals at home. Research could also consider how consumer knowledge and preferences and the time cost tradeoffs affect consumer decisions of which foods to eat and whether to make or to buy prepared foods from supermarkets or to eat at restaurant meals . Travel costs and time costs of acquiring foods as well as the time costs of preparing foods (meals) are also likely to affect demand for particular foods. Research on price variation at the local level and demand models could also be used to help determine which factors contribute to differences in access to food retailers. Price is also major determinant of food (meal) demand. The higher, the price of a food(meal), the lower the meal quantity demanded. On the other hand, the higher the price of a substitute food (meal), the higher demand will be for that food (meal) item. Given the budget constraints of low income consumers and the price of some specific foods (meals), low income consumers may substitute higher priced foods (meals) with lower priced foods(e.g. hamburger for steak or canned fruits for fresh fruits). Considering restaurants foods purchasing choice, such as economies of scale, which is when the costs of operating a restaurant decreases as restaurant size increases and economies of scope, which is when the costs decrease as more meals variety increases, suggests that larger restaurants that offer greater variety can offer lower meal prices. Both factors may account for the ability of larger restaurants to survive more easily than smaller restaurants. Considering supermarkets foods purchasing choice, it is possible that food retailers (supermarkets) actually have some market power, especially in setting where there are few competitors to close. It would have an incentive to increase food (ready meal) price and restrict foods(ready meals) supply quantities to increase profit. Supply side conditions, such as economies of scale, it could lead to (ready meal) food retailers (supermarkets) to have more market power, if it was not close between supermarkets. Individual behavior to make healthy choices can occur only in a supportive economic environment with accessible and affordable healthy food choices. Hence, food environment and sale strategies is needed to consider to adopt the exported countries' economic change.

Food marketing client target groups can include home parents, students and working people groups mainly and marketing and economic environment factors would cause food choices and

these factors impact health and nutrition and the focus on the connections between people and their environments. In conclusion, macro level economic environmental factors play a more indirect role but have a substantial and powerful effect on what people eat. Macro level factors operate within the larger society, include food marketing, social norms, food production and distribution systems, agriculture policies and economic price structures as well as social environmental to influence within the home, such as model of healthful dietary intake by parents feeding style, frequent family meals may promote healthful food consumption among children.

3. Discuss the factors that might affect sales of ready meals in your country over the next five years.

Hong Kong people can choose to go to restaurants to eat or go to supermarkets to buy foods to cook to eat. Although, ready meal manufacturers had increased the sale numbersof the ready prepared meals in many western countries in recent years. However, there still had any factors to limit it's sale numbers to Hong Kong market over the next five years, so it needed to aware of what was changing in Hong Kong food market environment and appreciated how change in this Hong Kong food environment to lead to change patterns of eating cooked ready meals demand to attempt to win its similar food competitors in Hong Kong market next five years. Hong Kong food environment related to Hong Kong people eating behaviors, include social environments and physical environments and macro level environment. The cooked meal quality and quantity of available can influence food numbers to produce meal to supply to Hong Kong food market. Hence, Hong Kong natural climatic change can influence the overseas food supply numbers to be imported to cause meals prices to go up or go down. If next five years, Hong Kong climate was good to grow plants and feed animals e.g. pigs and cows etc. meats. The restaurant meals or supermarket meals sale prices can be cheaper due to farmers who have much foods and vegetables to supply , so who can sell cheaper price to these restaurants or supermarkets to cause whose production cost to be decreased next five years in my country. Hence, ready meals prices could not sell more higher than Hong Kong meals prices. Hong Kong people eating behaviors are often changed over a lifetime. In general, Hong Kong people want to eat to satisfy physical hunger and psychological desires and yet want to be healthy, which may enquire adopting eating patterns that conflict with these desires. My country people make decisions about food several times a day: when to eat, what to eat, with where to eat and how much per meal prices and how much per meal numbers .

In general, Hong Kong people like to eat Chinese foods , but who also like to go to restaurants to eat or supermarkets to buy western foods, such as liking of specific tastes are important influences. However, these can be modified by experience with food from various intrapersonal and interpersonal factors to influence Hong Kong people to choose to buy uncooked or cooked meals from Hong Kong supermarkets. The next five year, food retailer behavior and supply factors of food access might affect overseas sales of ready meals numbers imported to my country. In general, supply is driven by the costs of input foods. The land, materials, machines and labor costs are needed to build and operate a restaurant or supermarkets. If these costs are increased to these food suppliers in my county next five years, overseas food demand shall be caused to be decreased if Hong Kong economy had changed to be worse and the new restaurants and supermarkets which costs were changed to be higher to much as well as Hong Kong unemployment was caused to be raised and many people lost jobs to have efforts to go to supermarkets to buy higher prices ready meals or go to restaurants to eat higher price ready meals.

My country's social environment and physical environment which also might affect sales of ready meals numbers next five years. Social environment includes interactions, with family, friends, peers and others in the community to impact food choices through mechanisms as well as physical environment includes the different places where people eat or buy food, such as whether the supermarkets or restaurants locations which are close to the buyers, e.g. schools, offices, houses. Hence, food suppliers' locations choice can influence who (target client groups) choose to buy more or less ready meals numbers. Foods prepared at home factor there may be relatively greater time costs than those to buy cooked foods(ready meals) from supermarkets or takeout foods. Hong Kong consumers may value the convenience of a fast food or takeout cooked meal more because it doesn't require spending much time to prepare to cook at home. Hence, Hong Kong people whose taste is for different kind of cooked foods (ready meals) and who feel the food suppliers' locations whether are convenient and Hong Kong economy whether is better or worse to cause unemployment numbers next five years, these factors can affect sales of imported ready cooked or uncooked meal numbers to my country Hong Kong next five year.

5.3 AI predicts Ryanair airline & Easy Jet airline & budget airline traveller entertainment behavior

1. If you are the marketing manager of an airline, such as Ryanair & Easy Jet , You can apply AI to gather big data to find what reasons to cause its airline passengers to choose other airlines to replace it. It can produce questionnaires to enquire concerns: You do not choose my airline, what factor(s) are(is) the main influence to cause, e.g. feeling my airline pollutes air is serious , air ticket price is expensive, flight journey time is long, airline service staffs' attitudes are poor to let you feel unsatisfactory, food taste is poor etc. different factors. Then, AI can conclude what the main

factor(s) are(is) caused to influence your airline passengers feel unsatisfactory in order to improve easily.

In recent years, social, economic and environment pressures have pushed airlines to accept their social responsibility. Closely tied to this acceptance is a corporate policy that aims at raising social and environmental standards on a voluntary basis and that means beyond legal and contractual requirement. It means that corporate social responsibility is not just an optional
consideration to core airline business activities, such as airlines industry fuel consumption pollutes sky air to cause global warming problem. Rather, Ryanair airline needs to concern social responsibility because it's fuel emissions would cause negative influence to stakeholders. e.g. causing bad negative climate to influence farmers to grow rice and vegetables etc foods successfully, so global warming will make farmers stakeholder can not earn more income and food buyers stakeholder won't eat rice and vegetables etc. foods easily, even global warming will damage natural environment to cause strong wind or strong raining or water natural hazard to damage any countries' houses to make house owners stakeholder who lose their houses to live. Hence, in the long term, if Ryanair airline still continue consume too much fuels to use to fly to cause emissions to pollute air to any countries as well as other airlines do not achieve any actions to reduce to consume to use more fuels together efficiently. I believe that global warming will become very serious to influence human living and eating problem occurrence in our earth as soon as possibly. Hence, such as Ryanair airline is among of global airlines, which have responsibility to consider how to reduce fuel consumption to cause too much emissions to pollute air in our earth. Such as, I was Ryanair airline marketing manager , I ought need to let Ryanair airline to measure whether it ought only concern how to sell cheaper air fares and buy many airplanes and consume much fuels to fly to raise income or it ought concern it's fuel emissions to pollute environment to cause global warming to influence global human stakeholders encounter living and eating problem to face natural foods resource shortage to supply in the future.

The ecological concerns global warming problem is serious nowadays, it brings the possible long term harmful consequences of executive emissions to the atmosphere. The developed countries, such as Northern Europe and United States people needed often to play travel entertainment by airlines transportation choice. However, scientists proved airlines used fossil fuels to harm excessive emissions to natural environment which would cause global warming problem to cause devastation of low lying areas to influence natural environment danger, even the developing countries people life and their houses would also encountered to be hazarded in the long term. If I was the marketing manager of an airline, such as Ryanair, I must concern socially responsible needs to Ryanair airline. Although, Ryanair aircraft had become more efficient in use of fuel during 1990 years, but Ryanair airline's passengers were booming demand to cause to increase aeroplane numbers to supply to satisfy passengers' travel needs and to pursue raising profit aim every year.

In fact, Ryanair airline used fuels to give energy to push aeroplanes to fly and it also polluted sky air during it's aeroplanes often were flying to cause global warming. For example, Ryanair airline marketing strategy was low fare prices to attract to increase many passengers to choose to attract to increase many passengers to choose to sit it's aeroplanes and it designed a cheap weekend break by Mediterranean travel to increase the unknown and remote possibilities of global warming. Hence, Ryanair would increased many new airplanes to increase to use fossil fuels of excessive emissions to the atmosphere to cause the effects of aid rain, poor climate change , destructive winds, rising sea levels and devastation of low lying areas by global warming bad consequences. Hence, it seemed that Ryanair airline had responsibility to concern how to protect natural environment due to its airplanes numbers and passengers were increasing to cause to increase to use more fossil fuels to cause the possible long term harmful consequences of excessive emissions to the sky to bring global warming occurrence nowadays. As I was this Ryanair airline marketing manager, I shall recommend Ryanair airline needed to consider this global warming socially responsible issue due to its airplanes spent too much fossil fuels to cause harmful consequences of excessive emissions to the sky. It would bring threats to developing countries people life and houses by global warming, so it concerned only how to raise itself interest marketing behavior of performance, but it neglect the serious global warming to cause bad influence to any developing countries people life danger, it was possible that passengers would feel it was not a socially responsible airline company, so it could not build a good image to whom in this airline industry and its further passengers would choose its other competitors (socially responsible airline companies) to substitute its airline service provision.

- Discussion

If (AI) concludes that the main factor causes passenger number reduces, the reason is air pollution. Then , (AI) should suggest Ryanair airline needed to control fossil fuel numbers to reduce to harm excessive emissions to natural environment seriously and it could spend much expenditure to buy good quality of fossil fuels to active the reduction of too much emissions to damage natural environment aim and it could shorten the sky flying distance to fly to other countries' airports from its airport to aim to attempt to reduce to use much fuel to pollute sky air per day and it could cancel some long flight flying routes and increased short flight flying routes to reduce flight spending hours to attempt to reduce to use fossil fuels to provide every airplanes to fly to pollute sky air every day.

Although, these marketing strategies would be possible to reduce airline income, but it would also attract many further passengers to choose to sit to its airplanes to go to travel if it could build good image to prove it was a socially responsible airline to serve passengers to let them to like to choose to use its flying service to go to travel willingly, even it could lead other airlines to follow it to use its marketing strategic methods to reduce to spend too much fossil fuels to pollute sky air to raise global warming problem seriously together. Hence, if Ryanair airline could attempt to achieve to reduce the fossil fuel numbers to use to airplanes to fly , it was possible that the other airline companies should follow it to do the same behaviors to aim to do social responsible organizations to concern how to reduce the global warming problem to cause to harm to our natural environment seriously for long term in the future.

2. The case study refers to apparent hypocrisy of clients who may claim to be concerned about the environment, but nevertheless continue to fly what might bring about a narrowing of this gap between what consumers think and what they actually do?

(AI) can give opinions to solve the this gap between what consumers think and what they actually do if it concludes the factor causes its passengers to choose another airline is environment pollution factor. Then it can give opinions to solve as below:

In fact, some apparent hypocrisy of consumers who may claim to be concerned about the global warming harmful natural environment problem due to airline companies, e.g. Easy Jet,
Ryanair etc. western countries' airlines which allowed fossil fuels produced harmful consequences of excessive emissions to atmosphere, but nevertheless continue to fly. However, I might recommend these methods to bring about a narrowing of this gap between what consumers think and what they actually do.
I think to bring a narrowing of this gap between consumers were happy to carry on airplanes to fly and it would not influence them to concern about climate change problem at the same time.

There was certainly a possible that governments would intervene. Such as the UK government and European commission had floated the idea of taxing aviation fuel and brought aircraft emissions within scope of the European emission trading scheme. Thus, if these western countries governments raised to charge aviation fuel taxing, it would possible to threaten any western airlines to shorten any flight routes hours and flight flying distance to fly to destination of the countries' airports from these airline companies' every country's airport, so which would not need to use more fuels for its airplanes to use if it had shorten flight flying routes distance to arrive other countries' airports. Hence, the airlines did not want to pay higher aviation tax to government, so which would attempt to shorten some flight flying routes from long distance to be short distance when their airplanes needed to fly to some other countries' airport to aim to buy less fuel numbers or which would not buy more airplanes.

Due to they needed to pay high aviation tax expenditure to their countries governments every year. Thus, it was possible that high fuel tax expenditure would cause airlines to shorten flight routes time. The most important, when some airlines decided to buy less fuels. These airlines might bring about a narrowing of this gap between what consumers think and what they actually do and these airlines were possible to raise their competitive ability, due to which would possible to persuade the concerned environment protective passengers who would choose to buy these airlines air tickets to more than to buy the other airlines' air tickets. Due to some airlines could not reduce to buy more fuel numbers to provide their airplanes to fly and which would increase air pollution to sky seriously, those airlines' spending excessive long hours (time) of every flight flying routes to fly to different countries' airports which would use more fuel to fly to cause air pollution to harm natural environment seriously and which would let these clients to feel unhappy to choose to buy air tickets to sit their airplanes possibly. Hence, different governments raised aviation tax would cause many airlines to reduce to buy too much fuel numbers to use possibly. It seemed that airlines needed have a social responsible duty to concern they needed to buy more fuels if they increased airplanes numbers, then they would raise air pollution to cause global warming problem seriously. Hence, I think passengers would not buy air tickets to fly to travel by airplanes when who would have long days of holidays. Otherwise, who would choose to stay at home or who would choose to go to travel by cruises on water transportation on their holidays. However, in western developed economies, legislation to enforce environmentally sensitive methods of productive is increasing, so airlines might adopt environmentally sensitive flight service processes to gain a competitive advantages. The challenges of using fuels resources in more efficient and less polluting way has achieved research and development, e.g. wind power research, solar panels, heat pumps and carbon capture technology have presented opportunities for airlines to improve the efficiency of fuels and airline marketing to business and individual group passengers.

Legal actions to place control over the emission of air pollutants have been instituted in several ways, such as the form of a public nuisance low. This is when conditions cause discomfort, inconvenience, damage to property or injury from airlines fuels to cause air pollution. The governments have also intervened in the protection of the public to threaten the airlines‘ fuels emissions pollute air in the sky. As a result of much research, devices for pollution control have been developed, guidelines for air quality were established fuels tax increasing incentives were introduced to enforce ordinances for restricting the emission from airplanes' fuels. For example, governments can pass the clean air act, legislation to reduce air pollution in their countries. In conclusion, airlines can co-operate environmentally friendly management to prevent global warming, it is as a part of its corporate social responsibility and makes company wide efforts to do by saving energy and reducing aircraft fuel emissions. Hence, global airlines ought plan to achieve to reduce to consume excessive fuel emissions to reduce a narrowing of this gap between what consumers think and what they actually do concerned about the environment pollution was caused by airlines if which still wanted to make travelers who prefer to choose to go to travel by flying more than other water or ground transportation etc. methods.

3. How would a company , such as Easy Jet airline measure and monitor consumer's attitudes?

(AI) can give opinions to Easy jet airline how to measure and monitor consumer's attitude after it gather all data to analyze how to solve passengers‘ negative emotion challenge to it's flying service as below:

Easy Jet airline has created environment problems, e.g. harmful chemicals sift down from smoky trails of low-flying jets. The scream of Easy Jet airline engines is constantly heard by people who love near big city airports. It's aircrafts produce air pollution with consequent changes in climate.

It is a fact that many people prefer air travel rather than ground or water transportation, This has promoted a critical look at safety and quality control. Contributions to air pollution is a chief concern because of this revolutionary change in public transportation in the United States and around the world. The government must also establish standards for exhaust emissions. Thus, Easy Jet airline measure and monitor consumer's attitudes which needs to indicate to let them to believe that which suggests which airplane manufacturers are forced to develop low pollutant engines.

Due to the problem of air pollution from its airplanes involve a complex set of interactions among technical, social and economic factors. Hence, it also needs to measure it's emission from Easy Jet aircrafts, particularly on landing and take offs, are a source of bitter complaints from nearby residents. In a few airports visibility has been dangerously restricted by particulate emissions and photo chemical smog. Easy Jet airline also needed to have energy savings activities to its operations, ranging from procedural and flight plan improvement to reduce flight distance and attitude and weight management and it also needed to create energy through maintenance to achieve to continue to reduce co2 emissions by introducing high efficiency aircraft and through other measures to monitor consumers' attitudes . In line with its aim to be an environmentally friendly airline that harmonizes the needs of natural , humans and airline businesses. It aims to be respected by society , live up to its social responsibilities and make a contribution to society. Although emissions from aircraft are not included among greenhouse gas reduction targets, but it also needed to make systematic efforts to improve energy efficiency and reduce emissions by creating a road map to actively participate . Furthermore, Easy Jet airline also needed continually to pursue a management style that concerns nature, people and fellow corporations, even under the most severe conditions as a major practice toward implementing its environmental policy. Easy jet airline achieves environment goals to measure and monitor consumer's attitudes, such as minimizes energy and resource consumption and introduces up to date and fuel efficient fleet and engines and develops and apply energy efficient operation technique, it establish strict internal environmental standards to set internal standards that are stricter than general environment laws applied worldwide and minimize pollutants through systematic management and observance of standards. It systematically analyses the airlines' environmental impact and make the outcome to carry out reductions and evaluates the environmental impact of its aviation operations, maintenance and service and improves environmentally friendly processes and it continually improves environmental systems through feedback .

In conclusion, Easy Jet airline can increase the recycling of waste to reduce fuel consumption of resources and it can make systematic efforts to reduce emissions by creating a roadmap and actively participating in global warming by saving energy and reducing aircraft emissions through engine washing to aim to consume fuels efficiency and reduce emission to pollute air.

4. What might be the consequences for the marketing of a budget airline of Government policy measures which have the effect of doubling air fares in real terms?

(AI) can attempt to find the most method to decide the reasonable air fares measurement in order to win its competitors in different suitation.

If the country Government decided to raise higher flight fuel tax charge policy to budget airline. Due to the country Government hoped budget airline to reduce fuels consumption to provide to airplanes to use to reduce sky air pollution to cause global warning problem. In fact, budget airline needed to increase to use much fuels to provide to many flights to carry on passengers travel needs. Generally, budget airline would not like to choose to reduce to consume much fuels due to it's passenger numbers had been increasing. If budget airline decided to buy less fuels to reduce much fuels to consume for its flight needs. It would lose many passengers if it had not enough times of flights to provide airplanes to fly to different countries' airports to satisfy passengers' different flight route choices. However, the consequences for budget airline would also be passengers to choose to buy budget airline air tickets possibly if it decided to raise doubling air fares in real terms. Due to budget airline hoped to compensate its loss if it's country Government raised higher fuels tax to cause budget airline needed to pay high cost expenditure every year. Hence, budget airline needed to raise to spend two kinds of expenditure every year, such as purchasing more fuels expenditure and paying more fuels expenditure both. For long term, budget airline would choose to raise doubling or more air fairs in real terms in order to reduce to need to pay too much feel tax expenditure to compensate it's loss every year. In result, it's passengers would feel it's air tickets fares were not reasonable raised to compare it's other airline competitors, but it's flight services were not excellent to compare it's airline competitors specially. Hence, it's increasing air fares would cause many passengers to choose other airline competitors possibly.

5. Critically discuss how the marketing manager of a budget airline might respond.

(AI) can gather data to use cost benefit analysis method to help the airline to decide how to spend its expenditures n order to achieve the best beneficial effect.

Marketing manger might use cost benefit analysis to let budget airline to know how to invest in intangible asset, such as corporate social responsibility to give long term benefit to itself budget airline. I suggest this marketing manager needs to explain the reason why reducing fuel consumption is an investment in intangible asset to budget airline as below:

Airline transport has increasingly become a global technologically and dynamic growth industry. However, airline companies need to remain committed to satisfy the clients' growing demands in a sustainable manner when at the same time maintaining an optimal balance between economic progress, social development and environmental responsibility. The concept of corporate social responsibility is a challenge for who to face today's risky, competitive and complex airline business environment. There has been a need for airlines in the airline industry to develop an environment agenda and take measures to minimize the ever increasing environmental impacts created by their activities. The forms of corporate social responsibility in the airline sector includes working in partnership with local communities, socially sensitive investment as well as involvement in activities for conservation of the environment. The fact, airlines are spewing 20% more co2 into the environment then previously estimated and there is a tendency for amount to increase to 1.5 billion tons a year by 2025 year. So, airline industry must need to innovative, environmentally responsible industry that drives economic and social progress. It has risks (social, environmental, operational, threat, strategic and financial risks) that they have to deal with marketing managers airlines, such as budget airline marketing manager is responsible for the optional decision making about corporate risks in its daily business. Adrian, (P. 2012) indicated that the marketing manager of budget airline needs to indicate the benefits can be categorized into three namely to let budget airline to feel as below:

(a) Regarding the economic view, budget airline is essential for facilitating world business and tourism, it needs to create jobs and enables the expansion of trade across the global by opening
up new market opportunities. It also attracts businesses to locations all over the world, hence satisfying the mobility requirement of a growing portion of the world's population. It also aids in the movement of products and services quickly over long distance facilities economies and social participation by remote communities.

(b) From the social perspective, budget airline forms an unique global transport network that links people in different countries safely and efficiently. Air transport is increasingly accessible to a large number of people who can now afford to travel by air for pleasure and its business purpose.

(c) Lastly, in terms of the environmental perspective, there is a need for budget airline to minimize or contain the impact in its environment through the continuous improvement of its
fuel consumption, noise reduction and the introduction of new technologies. Budget airline marketing manager can enquire this question to whose company, such as how budget airline can quantify the benefits derived from such investments to do with how to quantify the benefits, so budget airline can be compared to the cost of investments. Through budget airline has be different over the years to value many intangibles, such as corporate social responsibilities. Budget airline marketing manager needs to make choices among several alternatives: it is important to adopt a tool that with allow choices to clearly weigh and distinguish between the options available. So, budget airline marketing manager needs to persuade whose company to believe to maximize the gain, which may be either economic or social and may be beneficial to an individual, a group or society at large, e.g. reducing fuel cost can maximize economic or social benefits for long term. The measurement of benefits from corporate social responsibility policy includes gains from additional income to an increased quality of life or a cleaner environment.

On the other hand, the costs are made up of the opportunities forgone, internal and external costs and externalities. For instance, increasing the flying route for budget airline, the noise and air pollution are the externality when the secondary effect could be an increase in the cost operations. In this case, the pollution creates the new cost (externality). The budge airline business cost is the increase in the cost of operating the additional route. The budget airline's fuel consumption causes air pollution will influence whose client stakeholders' powers of seeing and thinking, cultural setting, experience is from the past and motivation at the time of sensing to the airline image to be poor due to who will feel the budget airline is not a social responsible organization. It aims to earn profits from passengers, but it neglects to take care other stakeholders benefits due to its fuel consumption to pollute environment to cause global warming problem. It seems that budget airline needs to considerate to use more fuel consumption to cause global warming problem more than doubling air fares in real terms if Government decided to raise more fuel tax charging to it to reduce its income.

I suggest marketing manager of a budget airline to reduce to use more fuels to pollute air, so budget airline does not decide to increase double air fairs charges to clients due to Government raises fuel taxation expenditure. Because it will cause clients to cancel its air tickets if who feel its air fairs are not reasonable to raise prices to compare other airline competitors. The marketing manager of a budget airline might respond to promote this navigation system to persuade budget airline does not choose to double air fares if Government raised fuel taxing charge. Innovation of flight operation on the optimum routes using (RNAV) Area navigation, as conventional airways and routes between airports were built by connecting ground navigation aids to the destination, the budget airline often became rather inefficient. On the other hand, RNAV can build routes connected any points with almost straight line by confirming aircraft position by means of global positioning system etc in addition to radio navigation destination of fuel consumption and CO_2 emission through shortened flight time and distance. Other reducing fuel consumption include reduction of aircraft weight, use of new type point for aircraft painting to reduce emission of polluted to air . Hence, budget airline will spend less fuels to avoid to pay high fuels taxation expenditure to its Government and it does not need to charge double air fairs in real terms to cause many passengers who will choose to find other airlines to buy cheaper air tickets or who will cancel their budget airline air tickets due to who feel budget airline charges unreasonable air fairs. So, if budget airline did not achieve as above any methods to attempt to reduce fuel consumption, I believe that it will lose many passengers due to it decide to charge doubling air fares in real terms to compensate its fuel tax increasing expenditure .

5.4 AI predicts England wine bar different segmentation drinker behavior

1. Critically evaluate the bases that bars may use to segment their markets.

(AI) can help the England win bar to gather data concerns different win drinking segment consumer drinking wine taste choices, then it can predict what countries people will prefer to choose to drink the kind of wine taste in order to choose the preferable kinds of taste wine to satisfy different countries' wine drinkers.

The United Kingdom bars market is a mass marketing, it means a strategy that presumes these is one undifferentiated market and that the bars wine drinking service provision will appeal to all consumers in that similar bar market. Marketing matching strategy divides segmentation, it means act of dissecting the marketplace into submarkets (segments) that require different marketing mixes, then targeting, it is the process of reviewing market segments and deciding which one(s) to pursue finally positioning, it needs to establish a differentiating image for a product or service in relation to its competition. segmentation variables may divide geographic, demographic, psychographic and behavioral variables.

In general, marketers may use a single variable or two or more variables. Geographic segmentation is based on the location of the target market, people living in the same area have similar needs that differ from living in other areas, climate, population, taste and micromarketing. Demographic segmentation is based on factors, such as age, gender, marital status, income, occupation, education, ethnicity. Psychographic segmentation is based on lifestyle and personality characteristics. Behavioral segmentation is based on attitudes toward or reactions to a product/ service and to its promotional appeals, usage rate, benefits sought from a product/ a service and loyalty to a brand or a store.

There are three basic market targeting strategies, such as undifferentiated, differentiated and concentration. Undifferentiated strategy ignores differences between groups within a market and offers a single market mix to the entire market and it works when a product/service is new to the market and there is minimal or no competition. Differentiated strategy means targeting two or more segments with different marketing mixes for each, concentration strategy focuses on one sub-market. Most British towns would had many small bars, all looking fairly similar to each other, with relatively few point of differentiation. Thus, if the UK bars do not use to segment their markets. I believe these UK bars will face much competition between themselves. In general, the market for drinking in pubs was fairly homogenous, comprising mostly male, who went to the pub mainly to drink and only very rarely to eat.

Now, UK pubs, clubs and bars continues to be a popular leisure activity in UK and pubs have benefits from a growth in eating out.

But, pub operators face challenges , including taxes on alcohol, growing competition from supermarkets for off sales, a smoking bad introduced. Pub operators have had to focus the design of bars on meeting the needs of smaller and smaller market segments. No longer is the pub market dominated by males going out to drink-professional women and families are among many segments and the professional and families segments, who seems dislike loud music or big screen television, who like to drink good quality coffee served more than beer, who like to enjoy bright and airy decorative in bars, who like to drink served to the table rather than queuing at the bar. These may have been design features that were unsought or unwanted by the traditional male heavy drinker segment. Hence, it seems that UK female professionals and families shall be the popular segment in this UK bars market. However, segmentation can not be based simply on where people live, and must recognize their mobility and movement patterns. Therefore, for some sites located in town centers or on busy roads, an understanding of people's work patterns and commuting habits can be crucial. Being near a train station may be crucial for attracting a target market or urban professionals who want somewhere to stop off to meet friends before catching a train home. I think the UK bars may use to segment their market. Segmentation is essentially about identifying groups of buyers within a marketplace who have needs that are distinctive in the way who deviate from the average consumer. Some consumers may treat satisfaction of one particular needs as a seek to satisfy any of needs from a car purchase total market, the possible factor that might influence and individual's choice of car, car market segment targeted includes status, safety for families, a particular image, a cost effective transport, seeking environment by buying a green car and a company buyer saves tax client groups. Hence, British bars are fairly similar to each other, with relatively few points of differentiation. The market for drinking in bars was fairly homogenous and British supermarkets can sell wines and the comprising mostly males who went to the bar mainly to drink and only very rarely to eat. Today, the bar scene in any British town centre is much complex. Hence, I think British bars ought to segment their markets if which wanted raise their competition.

On the first hand , the UK bar owner can choose professional women and family segment, in upmarket local, low density housing areas, it is likely to offer high quality food, no loud music or big screen television, good quality coffee served more than beer, bright and airy bar environment, drinks served to the table, rather than queuing at the bar, due to the proportion of women using these bars is higher than most of the locals.

On the second hand, the UK bar owner can choose male segment, in basic or mid market locals, that were unsought or unwanted by the traditional male areas; trade is focused on regular drinkers and tend to be met lead with little food. Beer, cider and spirits are the big sellers. Most show televised most offer some sort of food. There may also be themed evenings, quizzes, darts or pool. Customers tend to use the bar to meet friend and relax.

On the third hand, the bar can choose young local customers aged 18 to 30 secondary and university students segment. Amusements including pool tables and machines with feature and chart music and video screen will be prevalent.

On the fourth hand, the bar owner can choose city local to workers and shoppers segment, such as non office labors and supermarket buyers clients, it will offer basic bar food and snacks as well as centrally located in town centers but offering high levels of food, city dry led bars target the same customers as city locals, but focus on office labor clients mainly and it tends to be large and it may have function rooms and restaurant areas.

On the fifth hand, the bar owner can choose office workers and shoppers both segments. It may locate in centrally city location, but it needs to change from day to night to attract different types of customers. It can provide coffee bar attract in the day serving office workers and shoppers, but provide wine attract to young people's bar with loud music by might.

On the sixth hand, the bar owner can choose bar is located on or near the young non student people's circuit. Expect loud music, possibly a dress code and door staff and food is less important.

On the seventh hand, the bar owner can choose adults no children targets, in more upmarket areas. Restaurant quality food served for whose premium dining aim.

On the eight hand, the bar owner can choose family with children target, it again focuses on food these bar offers good value for money dining during the weekend and early evening.

On the final hand, the bar owner can choose to meet point for a specific customer group for example bikers, sport client segment in bicycle areas. It may be live music or entertainers to drink whose wine after who ride bicycle to need to find restaurant to sit down to relax and eat food needs. Hence, UK bar market is such as car sale market to follow family life cycle, gender and household composition, age, ethnic group, social class, individual income, lifestyles, individual attitudes, values benefits sought, the bar loyalty, the bar geographic location etc. the client internal psychological factors or the external environmental factors to divide different segments to sell in the market. However, I suggest the UK bars market segment ought to analyze to target young adult wine drinkers mainly. Bar consumer segmentation in the wine industry takes on many forms: demographic, geographic, behavioral and others. For the bar wine industry, this group currently fits the legal drinking age range of 21 to 28 ages. With the recent oversupply of wine bars on the UK local market, so UK wine bars competitions are very high. Due to this situation, I recommend who need to focus efforts on finding new populations of wine existing consumers, rather than just redoubling efforts with existing clients.

I think wine bar marketers in the United Kingdom have primarily focused on the existing population of wine bar old consumers, which are the very large baby boomer young generation. This was an effective strategy for many years, when the wine supply and economic conditions were stable. Now, however, one of the most promising of the new wine bar consumer segments in the UK is that of the boomer generation. Generally viewed as children of the baby boomers. This segments group is considered whose consuming power and represented the future bars market for most wine brands drinking in UK bars. The children of the boomers who are young and who ought like to meet friends to go to bars to drink different kinds taste of wines and play entertainment in bars during who have school holidays. UK bars market segmentation means the process of dividing which different drinking wines taste into meaningful, relatively similar and identifiable segments or groups. In general, UK bars market segmentation is useful for two major reasons. First, it assists bars marketing searchers in analyzing the needs of a specific customer segment. Second, the resulting data, it allows bars marketing campaigns to be focused on these identifies needs. In the long run, this allows bars to spend their marketing and advertising budgets wisely when at the same time meeting the needs of the drinking wine customer. Ideally, this should result in efficient, effective and profitable bars marketing and sales efforts. There are multiple types and levels of segmentation used in various industries, but those used most frequently by the wine bar industry are those that also fall into for four classic marketing segmentation bases. There are geographic, which is based on where the customer lives, such as big cities or small cities, demographic, which is based on age, gender, income, social class, psychographic, which is based on lifestyle and personality and behavioral which is based on occasions, benefits, usage rate , readiness to purchase stage.

In bars business, the wine taste is main factor to influence the clients choose to come to the bar again. In general, there are five consumer segments, such as conservative, knowledgeable wine drinkers; image oriented, knowledge seeking wine drinkers, basic wine drinkers, experimental, highly knowledge wine drinkers and enjoyment oriented, social wine drinkers. Anyway, psychographic factor can influence people choose to go to bars, the psychographic wine segments identify five major wine lifestyle, such as relaxed lifestyle, dining ambience, fun and entertainment, social aspiration and travel lifestyle. Hence, psychographic factor and wine taste knowledge factor are reasons why people choose to go to bars to drink wines instead of who choose to go to supermarkets to buy wines to drink. Regarding geographic segments in the wine industry, it includes individual wine bars or organizational wine bars or supermarkets or stores wine sale methods in UK country. Regarding wine consumption behavior is another factor, it includes five segments: Super-core, who consume wine daily; core, who consume wine at least two or three times per month; marginal, who consume wine at least two or three times per quarter ; non adopters, who don't drink wine, but drink other alcoholic beverages and non drinkers who don't on the areas where are not close to supermarkets or stores and the living people who are super core to consume wine daily in the areas. The bar has more chance to increase client numbers, it is unconsidered whether the bar's wine taste can satisfy its clients needs. However, the young age market segment has very high consuming power. They don't only have a lot of money, but who influence family purchase. Many perform the grocery shopping for their families and have been given parent co-signed credit cards at a young age.

A key question in market segment analysis for this group is: What drives their purchasing behavior regarding wine? Young people can spend on average of 16.7 hours per week on the internet, excluding e-mail. They use it for shopping, in chat rooms, for research and to keep up is their primary source of information and who trust it. Because of this focus, wine bar marketers are urged to use integrated media to reach young people and not use only traditional channels. Online technology is a critical part of this,, but also offline locations where, such as music clubs, wine bars magazines, cable television and outdoor posters. E-mails targets at online interest groups and cell phone marketing are also useful. However, wine bars advertising that ought includes diversity of race and gender. In addition, young people are highly influenced by minority cultures in terms of music, sport, dress and language. The wine bars marketing implication is that advertising should show a variety of diversity in terms of race and gender. Another consideration is to emphasize values and focus on cultural values when targeting specific ethno-centric segments of young people population in UK. I believe why wine bars can attract more young people, it is due to their focus on wine brands and who like to attempt different new or old wine taste, young people are very wine brand conscious and seek wine brands that provide quality, but at a fair price. Anyway, young people market segment characteristics is their belief in fun and responsibility, who tend to believe that life should be fun and enjoyable, but at the same time who do want responsibility and challenge on the job, who want to make sure that who take time out to enjoy life and believe that certain activities, so I feel young people accept to drink wine in base , the possibility is more than old people or adult ages people.

In conclusion, I think this UK bar market is an undifferentiated mass marketing, due to any bars characteristics can only give places to provide similar tastes of wines or coffees drinking or foods and entertainment for clients to enjoy to single formulation of its food provided services, to bars have traditionally offer one standard of food service delivery to all of their domestic or foreign customers. Due to UK small, middle and large size bars and supermarkets and restaurants are increasing to cause competition seriously. Overtime, however, bar consumers' needs tend to fragment into segments of different needs. Where UK bar markets are competitive, a bar may no longer to able to ignore the bar clients whose special needs of small groups of its customers, because if bar owner sold similar taste of wines, coffees drinking and foods to its competitors of bars and restaurants and supermarkets, I believe the non segment bar will lose many clients to compare the segment bar in UK bar drinking wine restaurant industry.

2. In the context of bars, discuss the relative merits of quantitative and qualitative approaches to market segmentation.

(AI) can produce quantitative and qualitative questionnaires to gather data concerns what the wine tastes are their preferable choices, where are the wine bars locations preferable choice in England, what kinds of entertainments can attract to them to choose to visit its wine bars etc. questions in order to attract different countries wine drinkers choose to visit its wine bars in UK.

In UK bars market, I think it had the relative merits of quantitative and qualitative approaches to bars market segmentation. As UK bars market segmentation, the UK bar owners need to identify groups of bar customers who have similar needs and respond in a similar way to a given marketing stimulus to raise their bar competition. Hence, UK bar owner may use segmentation to measure whether whose bar ought to choose to locate where location (areas) to provide which kinds taste of wines, coffees, foods and entertainment to attract which kind of bar client group mainly, e.g. if the bar target client group is professional office female, it can locate at upmarket location in low density housing areas. It is likely to offer high quality food because there are many professional office female clients are in these low density housing living. However, bars market segmentation should be regarded as the bar wines and coffees drinking and entertainment service provision of critical thinking rather than as some pre-determined set of procedures.

It shall follow that to let the bar owner to know what is an appropriate basis for the bar segment and one client group market may not be appropriate to all bar client groups in the UK bars market. To aware of the criteria by which the effectiveness of any UK bars segmentation basis can be assessed. I shall indicate those four important criteria to measure the relative merits of quantitative and qualitative approaches to UK bar market segmentation which can earn. The four important criteria include the usefulness to the UK bars marketing planning; the size of the resulting to the UK bar segment; the UK bar measurability and the UK bar accessibility four criteria. On the usefulness to the UK bar's marketing planning criteria hand, it needs to ask this question before which chooses who is whose bar target client group and location and wine and food taste. Is the basis of bar market segmentation useful to the bar owner? It is easy to develop bases for market segmentation when losing sight of the purpose of the exercise. Essentially, the exercise is worthwhile only bar segmentation allows the UK bar owner profitably to penetrate a greater proportion of UK bars market then would have been the UK bar market case if the exercise had not been undertaken. UK bar market client groups identified as homogeneous bar market segments must be just that: Similar in terms of the needs of tastes of wines or coffees drinking and entertainment consumption behavior of the domestic or foreign individual client who contain. The UK bar shall fail in whose segmentation exercise because its assumptions about homogeneity within a bar segment, e.g. male or female or young student or young non student or family with children or family without children or bicycle sport client or office of non office segment, who overlooks some critical differences within the bar segment which leads to varied responses to the bar service offering that has been specifically targeted at the bar client segment. For example, a bar segment for the office workers target client group, instead of the bar owner needs to consider the location whether it is located to close to whose office, who also needs to consider these factors such as, what kinds of foods , wines, coffees drink taste and what kind of entertainment and service price charge and their habit consumption time. To be more effective, bar market segmentation must recognize the diversity of needs within this bar target client group. Hence, the bar can measure to quantify and quality its bar target client group to produce its bar market planning effectively.

On the size of the resulting to the UK bar segment criteria hand, the UK bar owner ought need to ask this question: Are the segments of an economic size to whose bar business? Any basic for bar segmentation should yield segments that are of a size that the bar can profitably exploit, because as the bar segments get smaller who get closer to achieving the marketing philosophy of satisfying each bar client's needs as though each one were the center of the bar's attention. The problem for the uneconomic to provide for what a reasonable size of bar segment is varies from one UK bar market to another and is constantly changing over time. In the bar market , it is possible to provide quite unique tastes of wines or foods to target very small segments of the UK bar market. For example, if the bar target client group is professional female office worker clients. I think it ought need to locate its bar in the office areas location and the office and the office can not be close to supermarkets because supermarkets will have different style of wines and coffees to sell and its provision of cup of wines and coffees drinking and foods tastes must be different to supermarkets wines and coffees and foods tastes and the bar needs to consider what the entertainment is the professional female worker clients who need to enjoy in the quiet or noise bar environment. Because this factors will influence the bar's female professional workers' psychological needs and satisfactory needs. If who feel the bar's drinking and food and entertainment service provision which can't satisfy whose demand, who can choose another bars to close to office areas to cause the bar female client numbers will reduce. On the UK bar measurability criteria hand, the UK bar owner needs to ask this question: Can the bar market segment be measured? Ideally UK bar should be able to know the precise size of its identified bar market segment(s).

This is imported in order that the bar segment(s) can be compared and its profit potentials assessed. Unfortunately, UK bars clients data are often not available to the UK bar quantity market segments. So the UK bar owner should believe the areas of bar clients exist but can't measure or the bar client numbers should define bar segments only on the basic of what it can accurately be measured, but the different areas (location) bar clients may have litter bearing on the homogeneity of bar consumers' needs and consumption aims or reasons. The UK bar market segments information have include, e.g. the age profile of an area, number of people per household etc. However, bar owner also needs to assess of individuals psychological subjectively factor, such as whose attitude and lifestyles, e.g. if the professional female worker who does not like to drink coffee or wine drinking, even the bar location is close to the professional female worker office client, it will not persuade who to enter the bar. Hence, the UK bar owner needs to find the areas where people whose lifestyles and attitudes to bar enjoyable feeling, then it may decide to measure whether the area (location) may have which bar target group(s) is/are the largest numbers to choose which kind taste of wines, coffees drinking and foods provision and which kind of entertainment to satisfy the bar's identified target client group(s) needs. Finally, on the UK bar accessibility criteria hand, the bar owner ought to ask this question: Are the segment(s) accessible to where bar business? There is little points to define the UK bar owner segment(s) of the UK bar market whose those bar segments are not accessible to the bar segments are not accessible to the bar owner or ever likely to be inaccessibility can come about for a number of reasons. Such as the UK bar owner may be prohibited by law from opening to locate whose bar in certain areas in UK geographic location (areas) or the UK law prohibits UK bar to sell some kind of taste of wines in whose country. Hence, the UK bar owner needs to know UK law prohibition to which kind of taste of wines drinking sold and where location (areas) to open its bars before who decides where to open its bar to sell wine to whose target clients segment(s) in British country. In conclusion, the UK bar owners can earn the relative merits of quantitative and qualitative approaches to market segmentation from these four criteria consideration.

5.5 AI predicts P&G (Procter & Gamble) body and skin daily product user behavior

1. How can use (AI) to explain the success of the fairly brand to P&G? (AI) can gather big data concerns why they choose to buy P&G any skin daily product, e.g. cheap price, good product quality, long business history and royalty, good customer service, convenient shopping location. Then, it can find which factor(S) are(is) the main influence to cause them to choose to buy its skin daily product to use.

P&G fairly brand which mainly sold low value consumer goods, such a household detergents from bar of soap washing products to sell in UK country supermarkets in the beginning. Then, it innovated to produce liquid soap washing products to sell in UK country supermarkets. Further, it continued to innovate to produce soap products, such as the power of four for price of one, launched this low bulk, high concentration soap product to sell more cost effective to sell in supermarkets, even overseas supermarkets. P&G predicted domestic dishwashing machines instead of liquid of soaps , so it innovated to produce dishwasher cleaning fluid detergents products to let housewives to clean their dishwasher after every family used dishwashers to clean their plates to aim to keep their dishwashers to feel more clean to compare to clean by hand washing. Even, P&G will continue to innovate to produce potential anti-bacterial food washes to satisfy consumers' increasing concern over resides on the surface of fruit and vegetables.

In fact, P&G can predict what the new washing products will sell in this washing market, who will be its direct competitors, which are generally similar in form and satisfy customers' needs in a similar way as well as who will be its indirect competitors, which may appear different in form, but satisfy a fundamentally similar need. Such as P&G sold bar soap washing products in the beginning, it aim to satisfy families wash body to feel more clean needs. But, P&G felt it's direct competitors can sell similar bar soap products, so it innovated to produce new liquid soap washing products to raise its washing unique products and was different to its body washing product competitors. On the other hand, P&G also predicted domestic dish washing machines instead of liquid of soaps , so dish washing machines shall be which indirect competitors. Due to housewives can use dish washing machines to wash plates, so who will not use hands to wash plates after eating, it will cause who reduce to use bar or liquid washing soaps to wash their hands. So, P&G innovated to produce dishwasher cleaning fluid detergents products to let housewives to clean their dishwashers after every family used dishwashers to clean their plates to aim to keep their dishwashers to feel more clean to compare to clean by hand washing.

Even, P&G will continue to innovate to produce potential anti-bacterial food washes to satisfy consumers' increasing concern over resides on the surface of fruit and vegetables. Hence, P&G had attempt to raise its competitive ability in fruit and vegetables food and dishwasher machines cleaning market instead of bar and liquid soaps human clean market. It seems P&G threats of new entrants and threats of substitute clean products. In fact, P&G considers it soaps or other washing products whether which will cause chemical harmful to human skin or foods or dish washers after consumers have used its washing products. In the absence of that safety relationship of P&G social responsibility, its brand can act as a substitute in managing buyers' exposure to risk. P&G branding simplifies the decision making process by providing a sense of security and consistency of buyers which may be absent outside of a relationship with a washing product supplier.

P&G brand addresses a number of dimensions of purchase risk which have been identified as: physical(Will it's soap or washing products cause consumer skin harm or foods harm or dish washers harm?); psychological (Will P&G soap products or washing products satisfy consumer's needs for safety of mind?); Performance (Do P&G soap products and washing products work in accordance with consumers' satisfactory requirement?); Financial (Will P&G soap and washing products provide adequate performance with consumers' budget?). Due to consumers will compare P&G soap and washing products to its competitors' risk level to choose which brand washing products can give the minimal risk to harm to their health to decide to buy from supermarkets. Hence, P&G brand needs be built objectively measured (bar or liquid soap products or washing products are such as unique shape and smell and reliability) and the subjective values that can be defined only in the minds of its consumers (such as perceived personality of P&G brand is unique compare to other washing products brands). It means that P&G will be recalled that its brand processes functional and emotional attributes. P&G brand has been variously described as having

personality that are ' fun', 'reliable ', 'traditional' and ' adventurous' and it needs to let consumers to feel it can give no harm to whose health after who use P&G soap or washing kind of products. In fact, P&G developed a single strong P&G brand strategy to sell different kinds of washing products, such as bar soaps, liquid soaps, dishwasher cleaning fluid and anti-bacterial food washes etc products, It aims to let consumers who choose to buy to use these kinds of washing products, then who must remember P&G brand. One approach to P&G branding is to apply the same brand name to every washing products which produces. The big advantage of this approach is the economic of scale in promotion. Instead of promoting many minor brands through small campaigns, it can concentrate all of its resources on one campaign for P&G one brand. But, the main disadvantage of this approach is that P&G can pose significant risks of confusing the values of it's brand. If P&G positioned its bar soaps, liquid soaps, dish washing fluid
and anti-bacterial food washes etc. products range as premium priced, top quality, confusion may arise in consumers' minds if it applied the same brand name to a budget version of its washing products. Does P&G brand still stand for top quality? This is a particular problem for P&G new washing product, such as anti-bacterial food washes and dish washer cleaning fluid products which are of unproven reliability. Hence, P&G sells in low price strategy in supermarkets to let many families can buy its different washing products to do trial test whether its innovative washing products which are better quality to compare to other brand washing products to satisfy who to choose to buy P&G brand washing products for every families to use long term.

In fact, UK soaps product is a imperfect competitive market. The different soap manufacturing companies produce similar color and shape bar or liquid soap products and they build different brands and they are targeted at specific segments, such as family group and they need promotion to promote their brands and soaps price is premium sustained. Hence, P&G needs a differentiated product may have significant monopoly power in that it is unique, but if it fails to satisfy customers' needs, its uniqueness has no commercial value. However, P&G had innovated it different bar soap products to liquid soap products, even it also launched dishwasher cleaning fluid detergents products, due to dish washer machines reduce housewives to use hands to wash plates to use soap to clean whose hands after eating as well as it launches
potential anti-bacterial food washes to satisfy consumers' increasing concern over resides on the surface of fruit and vegetables. Hence, P&G aims to be any new cleaning products leader to raise its cleaning market share effort.

The soap and other detergents manufacturing industry of Procter & Gamble (P&G) trends and characteristics who its primary intended is target client group(s). I think families (householders) or student individual daily consumption are P&G main target client groups. Soaps are personal care products. Consumers will compare different brands of soaps to decide which brand soaps ingredients can give health to them to wash their bodies and skins. The soap industry includes (P&G) and other soap manufacturing companies primarily engaged in making soap, synthetic organic detergents, inorganic detergents and crude vegetable and animal fats. In general, skin care soap sales include bar soap, body wash and liquid categories which can sell in supermarkets and discounting retailers and drug stores. Traditional , bar soaps, which are considered a mature category, exhibit very low growth, when newer products (shower gels and body washed) substitute products are launched. However, natural soaps still have opportunities for growth if which can be launched to raise care to skins and bodies health to human. The soap and personal products industry is being driven to a large extent by the changing age composition of the population, specifically, baby boomers have established anti-aging preparation as the chief benefit of health products aimed at correcting or improving the physiological condition of the skin. They have led the broad personal care sector of the economy to focus on the potential in aging consumers. Growth is occurring in a variety of age-sensitive product markets from soaps and skin creams to massagers and body fat analysis machines. As baby boomers lives get busier, stress relief soap products will become more important to carry on launching their skin care health quality for human benefits in daily washing. The group composed of 45 ages old to 54 ages old females is responsible for the highest amount of sales of body care and bath products in mass stores, who can influence householder families members spending effort in soaps consumption. P&G soaps are displayed to supermarkets to retail, the supermarkets' shelves are remained unaffected by the changing population in the personal care products sale areas. Even retailers like Brook stone and Sharper Image expanded their interest in branded personal care items. Not only was more retail dedicated to the personal care products, but they were often placed in specific "spa shops" within the store, with displays used extensively to merchandise the personal care category. Body boomers are not, however, the only group important to the growth of this personal care industry. The number of personal care products designed specifically for children is increasing. Health and beauty aids suppliers are using licensing to tap into the growing spending power of children. The traditional soaps manufacturers must carefully review their marketing and other business strategies in order to adapt to the transformed market. The changes also create better opportunities for new personal care product companies to enter particular market segments. The mass bath and body care category has made recent introductions reflective of several trends that department stores, salons and special boutiques have been offering for years. The world consumers are changing their personal care demand to cause a result of soap product innovation, so P&G also needs to replace older well known soap products with newer ones that contain special formulations. New product activity and the increasing popularity and liquid soap increase competition in this personal care market. A growing perception among consumers that who must deal with problem skin and rising levels of concern about germs are helping drive sales of personal soap. Although, traditional brands such as Dove, Dial and Irish Spring still hold the largest portion of the toilet soap market smaller special soap manufacturers are increasing their market shares. Hence, P&G needs to focus on concentrating who its specialty soaps. In general, consumers want a soap that fits their particular needs and specialty soaps, often made with natural ingredients to protect bath and hand skin health. However, some competitors choose to sell soap substitute products, such as oils, bath blends, perfumes and fragrances in supermarket. Hence, these personal care products can also influence P&G company liquid soap sales in overall soap retail market. In soap manufacturer industry, the naturals trends is also evident in the ethic segment of skin care.

Ethic consumers are seeking multi-functional products full of botanicals and vitamins butter natural ingredients. So, I think P&G needs to launch this kinds of new class of skin care product to raise its skin class of skin care product to raise its skin care health care to increase consumers‘ confidence. Due to personal care products market competition is increasing, such as one stop shopping stores can offer for a variety of health related items, healthy foods, dietary supplements, prescription and over the counter drugs, skin care products and other natural personal care products. In addition, smaller natural skin care manufacturers are staying competitive by targeting skin-related over the counter drug markets. Moreover, internet retailing of personal care products has grown rapidly. Web site can offer can be nearly limitless. One important advantage held by online sellers over stores with physical locations is the constraint caused by a lack of shelf space. The characteristics of online sellers allow them to stock a much wider variety of the products consumers want, if also provides an opportunity for small or large manufacturers audience of consumers. One of the greatest difficulties faced by a firm wishing to enter a consumer products market is persuading retailers that they will benefit by dedicating scare shelf space to the manufacturer's products to online selling reduces that problem.

A potentially important negative aspect of electronic commerce for personal products is that inability to feel and especially, smell the merchandise. Many personal care products list fragrance as an important characteristics. To the extent consumers are already familiar with a special products, this is not a problem, but such as P&G getting a new liquid soap products might be more difficult. Soap industry needs to launch to improve soap qualify to satisfy consumer need. It must need enough workers to help P&G to manufacture enough different kinds of soap to sell to different countries soap market. I think its workers include these kinds , such as packaging and filling machine operators, first line production supervisors, cleaning, picking equipment operators, hand packers and packagers, hand material movers and soap researchers because it needs these workers to help it to produce different kinds soaps in the manufacturing process in factory, so it needs to give training to raise whose proficient skills to prepare to produce any new kinds of soap efficiently and it needs to consider the labor supply to soap manufacturing market , e.g. who needs to know what the difference between chemicals and all natural ingredients to prepare to produce its soaps ethically. Because if they have errors in the manufacturing process to cause consumers feel to use P&G soaps to have chemical negative health response. These workers shall influence P&G health soap products image negatively. Hence, P&G needs to consider its workers' working attitude ethically. However, P&G was the largest soap maker and it did not own the most part maintain in house chemical manufacturing capabilities. P&G must therefore purchase new materials from other suppliers, so P&G needs to consider its raw materials suppliers market to measure whether who can give it the largest benefits and the cheapest costs both, Thus, giving the raw material suppliers global marker to choose who remain a greater incentive to provide superior service to P&G. I think P&G needs to spend time to choose who is its raw material suppliers who can provide the best natural health quality and the least chemical ingredients to cause consumers to use to feel uncomfortable response to their skins negative influence. Hence, I think P&G ought innovate its soap products quality to satisfy to avoid to use any cheap chemicals ingredients to produce its old or new kinds of soap products to sell to consumers unethically if it still wants to a sale leader in this personal care product market.

2. How do you think Procter & Gamble has been able to increase its market share at a time when competition from supermarkets' own-label brands has intensified?

(AI) can help it to gather data concerns that what are the factors to cause it's brand can build large market share in short time. Then, it can concentrate on keep it's internal strengths and attack it's internal weaknesses or attack it's external threats and keep it's external opportunities in ord ero keep its competitive effort in market long term.

Procter & Gamble operates mainly low value consume products, such as household detergents are among the most competitive and building successful brand is key to long term profitability. Differentiating one product from another in the minds of consumers can be extremely difficult, with one packet of detergent looking very much like another and performing similarly. It seems that it can not be unique to sell in supermarket. However, then it innovated new liquid soap products, it seemed to adopt to change in consumer preference, and maintaining consistent standards when exploiting new market opportunities. Adrian, P. 2012) showed that Fairy liquid was rated as Britain's number one cleaning brand by Marketing magazine and in 2010 accounted for 3 percent share of the UK washing up liquid category by value. The brand has been a regular household feature since the name first appeared in 1898 year on a bar of soap. P&G first launched Fairy liquid in the UK market I think Procter & Gamble (P&G) has this marketing strategy to supply its soap products to supermarket retailers. A supermarket is not only supply to likely to encounter a massive range of products, such as food , drink, homecare, personal care, luxury products etc. Consumers can see categories and see how much the offering changes, the range , the packaging , the branding and advertising or promotion of any brand products sale at shelves. Hence, such as P&G manufacturer in 1960 year. At the same time, the market for washing up products was still in its infancy, with most consumers using solid soaps, and only 17 per cent of households using liquid soap. But P&G gained most from a change in consumers' habits. It educated the public of the benefits of using washing up liquid. The launch of Fairy liquid soap products involved distributing 15 million trial bottles to about 85 per cent of household in the UK. Creating early awareness and trial of the Fairy liquid soap innovative products led to Fairy gaining a market share of 27 per cent by 1969 year. It had a proud positioning as a slightly more expensive product which is better value and worth. So, it created brand values of a soft, caring, homely image by advertisement promotion. It also attempted to adopt in response to changing attitudes, for example, a commercial in 1994 year for the first time used a father instead of a mother at the kitchen sink. During the first twenty years of the brand's life, product innovation had been relatively modest. However, an increasing competitive market, customers have forced P&G to innovate in order to maintain and strength its market share.

Adrian, P.(2012) showed that with emergence of many 'me-too' competitors from supermarkets, Fairy needed to offer additional unique advantages to raise its competition. In 1984 to 1985 years, P&G introduced a lemon variant of Fairy and its total market share increased to 32 per cent. By 1987 year the market share had increased to 34 per cent, with the newly introduced lemon variant accounting for one-third of sales. In 1988 year, a new formulation was launched , offering 15 per cent extra mileage, as well as more effective grease eradication. In 1992 year, the original Fairy Liquid was replaced with Fairy Excel, which claimed to be 50 per cent better at dealing with grease. This helped to increase the market share to 50 per cent . In the following year a concentrated version of Fairy Excel Plus was launched, with the slogan ' The power of four for the price of one'. P&G launched this low bulk, high concentration product to retailers, such as supermarkets, who were tiring of filling their valuable shelf space with more and more variants of basically low value products. Excel Plus offered supermarkets more cost effective and profitable use of their shelf space. Increasing ownership of domestic dish washing machines posed a threat and also an opportunity to Fairy. The threat came from a relative decline in sales of liquids used for hand washing of dished. The opportunity arose from increased demand for dishwasher cleaning fluid and the Fairy brand was extended to dishwashing detergents. In 2006 year, P&G introduced Fairy Active Bursts for dishwasher. Excel Plus was launched in the UK, Denmark, Finland, Germany, Holland, Ireland and Sweden etc western countries‘ supermarkets to help it to sell.

Innovation and reliability have been at the heart of Fairy's branding strategy, in a market which has been contested by other manufacturers' brands, and increasingly by supermarkets‘ own label brands. Preferences for new scents of detergent are continually emerging and provide an opportunity for innovation. Following a series of food safety scares, some observers of the market have pointed to a potential market for anti-bacterial food washes which would satisfy consumers' increasing concern over resides on the surface of fruit and vegetable.

Its innovative liquid soap products, it needs supermarkets where which compete with other soap product manufacturers for the attention and hopefully the purchases to shoppers choice. It's a soap products from bar soap to liquid soap kind of products. P&G brand have been a player in the household and consumer personal care products market for nearly 200 years. They started life making candles at a time when there were still a common source of domestic lightly. But they moved on from those to other related products, soaps and cleaning products. Today, P&G have around 300 brands, including Crest Oral Care brand, Pampers Nappies brand and Baby products, Tide and Arial brand washing powders, Tampax Sanitary products etc different brand in this personal care market. To keep a range as wide as this refreshed and to develop new and improved produce to feature on the supermarket stages around the world needs a powerful innovation engine. P&G had built a world wide research and development operation which involves some 7500 scientists and a spent of around USA$3 billion per year. It might be not as much as the high technology pharmaceutical industry, but still very impressive for its sector. P&G had some very effective systems and structures to ensure efficient soap products innovation project selection and progression . P&G had an impressive record on new product launches and many of their new categories billion dollars brands, products magic whose annual sales could be high as US$150 to US$200 million. But, in the late 1990 year, there were concerns about this approach to innovation. When if worked there were worries, not least the rapidly rising costs of carrying out research and development cost. However, I think P&G should not raise its new kinds of soap products sale price, such as liquid soap products. Even it had spent too much research and cost development expenditure. Hence, I think it still needs to keep competition to attract different countries consumers to buy from different countries consumers to buy from different countries supermarkets globally. Hence, low sale price is its major market strategy in supermarkets sale make. For long term, I suggest P&G chooses to outsource its research and development internal business department to one or more than more external technological research and development consultant company/companies to carry on researching any new soap products to avoid spending too much expenditure to raise soap products sale prices to

reduce its competition to sell in supermarkets. P&G 's pioneering use of advertising, direct distribution , marketing research , brand management and produce innovation strategies to raise it's growth throughout the 20th century. Diversification, globalization of it's brands, innovations in distribution and supply chain management and P&G 's technological and product innovation strategy continues to drive its success into the 21st century. P&G had pioneered a series of strategic innovations had sustained its competitive advantage in a number of highly competitive market and its primary focus was process innovations in many areas.
Firstly, background on P&G was from its origin to 2008 year briefly reviewed. Next five strategic innovations were each reviewed along with its competitive implications in the areas of direct to consumer advertising, direct product distribution, marketing research, brand management and technological and product innovation. Hence, P&G soap products innovation was divided to two stages of two different periods to aim to satisfy consumers' body and skin health needs of bar soaps choice to use liquid soaps choice in this personal bath and washing care market.

Adrian, P. (2012) showed that in 1915 year, P&G opened a facility in Canada representing its international operations. A chemical division was created during 1917 year and 1918 year which was responsible for research and development of new products. To sell these new products. P&G created a market department in 1924 year. The purpose of this department was to study consumer preference and purchasing inhabits (Data monitor, 2008:7). In 1926 year, a perfumed bar of soap was introduced. By the end of the 1920 year P&G had no longer produced candles, thereby signal a major shift in its core business . Then, 1933 year, the acquisition lead P&G into hair care products. In the early 1940 year, P&G established a drug products division which also developed and sold a variety of toiletry items.Then, P&G introduced new products and entering new markets, it had not stopped innovating on its established products , such as tide liquid soaps was launched in 1984 year. During this time P&G also purchased Blendax a popular tooth paste brand in Europe. As the 1980 year, P&G made a significant move in Asia by entering into a joint venture to produce products in China. In 2007 year, it invested US$35 to US$50 million in its Gillette manufacturing facilities in South Boston, USA. At the same time, it announced a restructuring whereby P&G. Beauty and health division would be managed under the P&G purchased HDS cosmetics laboratory skincare line that focuses on specific skin conditions that require more attention than general cosmetics. P&G 's history of marketing innovation began in 1980 year with Ivory soap on what had been promoted around the world as the floating soap (Dyer et al., 2004). Ivory represented P&G 's first attempt to brand a product through the use of advertising to connect with customers. Direct to consumer advertising was an innovation P&G pioneered with its customers and as such was a major innovation versus the traditional practice of advertising to wholesalers and practice of advertising to wholesalers and other distributors. During the 1800 year's soap was cut from huge soap slabs at the local grocer. Soap was a classic commodity with each manufacturer's product virtually indistinguishable from others. It is believed that P&G 's technological innovation was making Ivory out of Palm and Coconut oils, both less expensive than olive oil that was the basis of better soaps of the soaps to be mass produced and felt of finer higher quality soap (Dyer et al., 2004).Unlike other soaps of that, Ivory ingredient was lathered, easily and floated in water without melting. The unique blend of the soap meant that P&G could sell the soap in a premium market, such as supermarkets. However, since it used less expensive inputs, this led to higher margins. Those higher margins provided the mass to pay for advertising to raise the profile of the soap (Dyer et. al., 2004), thereby creating the brand and the beginning of a product differentiation strategy to sell in supermarkets.

3. To what extent can the principles and practices of brand management used for fairy liquid be applied to other goods and services, such as televisions and package holidays?

I think the brand management principle used for P&G brand, fairy liquid soap products sale which is more similar to apply to any television brands management products sale. Otherwise, the brand management principle uses for P&G brand, which is not more similar to apply to any package holidays travel services. Firstly, televisions and liquid soaps which have similar characteristics, such as they are products and it can be touched, seeing it existence and they are needed to launch to adopt consumers' taste, e.g. consumers link to accept to use liquid soaps more than bar soaps popularly as well as consumers like to watch colorful and clear image of televisions more than black and white image of televisions. Hence, any soaps and televisions companies which need to launch high technological televisions or more health ingredients of soaps to satisfy consumes' needs seriously if which wanted to build their brands famously and which wanted to retain old consumers and attract more consumers to buy their products in this skin care and television entertainment markets. Otherwise, if some companies did not continue to launch their television or soap products. I believe these companies brands will be not popular, even consumers will forget their brands existence due to other companies continue to launch their televisions or soaps to build strong brands in those skin care and television entertainment both product markets competitively.

Anyway, any one travel agent's package holidays travelling service is not similar to P&G brand fairy liquid soap products characteristics. Due to package holidays travelling services which can't be touched and can't be seen, the package holiday visitors who can only feel the travel agency whether whose travel journey itinerary arrangement, e.g. travelling destination, travelling date and time, travelling living apartments, hotels, restaurants, leisure activities, air tickets prices, airlines choice etc. whether this package holidays travelling is suitable to him/her only or whose family or whose friends with her/him together. The most importance, package holidays travel services are not similar to soap or television products which need to often launch whose skin care and seeing entertainment products to adopt consumers' needs. Although, the travel agencies sometimes need to reorganize new travel journal itinerary , e.g. seeking England, United States fresh and unique travelling places or cheap hotels who travelers choose popularly. But, travelling industry is seasonal period leisure business, it means that public holidays will have many consumers. Hence, basically, the seasonal periods are limited to travel agencies to build whose brand easily. It means that the client numbers are influenced by the seasonal periods, their numbers will not have much changing, even the travel agent often spend much effort and time to seek any new and unique travel journey itinerary holidays package. Although, travel agencies do not need to spend much money to invest to launch its package holidays travel arrangement service. But, they are existence in one competitive travel market. Every travel agent package holidays travel service price is controlled by the seasonal period whether the period is holiday or is not holiday and what the travelers' feeling to the country, e.g. safety extent, shopping places and prices extent, air ticket prices extent, accommodations and restaurants prices extent. These factors are controlled by the travelling countries. Agencies are difficult to differ their packages holiday travelling services to win other travelling agent competitors to build strong brand management famously. Due to which cannot control external factors to influence their price competition easily, such as airline companies air tickets prices, the destination (country) which hotels, restaurants, leisure services and transportation prices which are controlled by the travelling destination country's businessmen directly. It implies any travel agencies are difficult to build unique strong brands to attract many travelers who choose to find which to help them to arrange packages holiday travelling services to earn more commissions easily. However, if the travel agency had owned only concentrated on arranging packages holiday travelling services experiences and it had many prior packages holiday travelling consumers who feel that it can arrange the most suitable packages holiday travel arrangement services to let them to satisfy all different packages holiday services. I believe who will only choose this travel agent to help them to arrange any packages holiday travel arrangement services again, even who will introduce its packages holiday travel arrangement services to their friends to know the travel agency's brand by mouth speaking individually.

It seems that a new or an old travel packages holiday travel arrangement services agent who ought need more old customers who can speak to whose friends to know how it can give excellent travel packages holiday travel arrangement to them individually, so television or radio or newspapers media travelling advertisement channels do not need promote long time if whose old consumers feel which can provide excellent packages holiday travel arrangement services to make them to enjoy satisfactorily. Hence, it's old consumers' feeling whether who satisfy or who do not satisfy its packages holiday travel arrangement service which will influence the travel agent to build its brand successfully in this packages holiday travel arrangement market. Otherwise, a new or an old television products brand sale company needs more magazines, radios, televisions advertisement to promote which television products for long time due to every family who have different demand to choose to buy the television products, e.g. size, design, manufacturing history and manufacturing country's price. It implies the family can't influence to whose friends to decide to buy or not buy the television brand easily. Due to every family has different demand to choose which kinds of television company brand. The television brand's any different style of television products of the family to choose is not same to or influence to whose friends television brands, so the television brand's buyers speaking will not influence whose friends whether to choose or not choose to buy the television brand easily. Furthermore it will take a closer look at the motivational world of the travel agency staff and how both groups interact. These questions will be analyzed with regard to its significance and applicability in brand management. The results of a neuropsychological systems of package tourists and travel agents with a psychological test.

When investigating the travel market it must be taken into consideration that it is subject to considerable changes due to , for example new dynamic production processes, price comparing systems, the growth of online providers etc. Every travel agent needs to make each brand unique and distinguishable in its perception . The key issues discussed where: Why do package tourists buy? Which scopes and potentials are there ? When positioning style brands? How can potential customers be better addressed and won as a customer? Central question concerning travel agents where: What is there main motivation (commissions, incentives) ? How can travel agents be addressed more effectively? How can travel agents help to increase the sale? Sensing versus intuition concerns perception itself, thinking versus feeling are decision strategies based on perception and judging versus perceiving relate to the handling of these decision . Because individual travel agent needs explain why their choice of packages holiday arrangement is the best suitable to every consumer considerately when the consumer is the first time to contact the travel agent , so the travel consultants need have professional image to make whose visitors to believe whose packages holiday arrangement is the most right to satisfy them to travel in their journeys. Otherwise, one of television brand seller who does not need to build more professional image, due to who is only the television company brand representative, whose duties are needed to explain what the television features and functions to let whose customers to compare to other brand television products when who enquires any one of television brand seller. However, travel agent must need to seek any packages holiday travel informational to let any consumers to choose to let them to compare whether which packages holiday arrangement service is the most suitable to who from the travel agent immediately. Hence, a package holiday travel agent seems to be a travel economist, who needs to compare which packages holiday arrangement is the most right and the most reasonable price to follow travel data gathering to adopt to every customer needs after whose customer spends whose packages holiday arrangement to feel satisfactorily if who want to help whose travel company to build famous brand of providing excellent packages holiday arrangement successfully in this travel market. Hence, any packages holiday businesses which travel consultants seem to be individual mouth speaking advertising to every visitor when who enquire whose packages holiday arrangement ideas to achieve aim to let every visitor to feel travel consultant can suggest the useful packages holiday arrangement because who must not have confident to arrange their travel plan by himself or herself. It seems that a new or an old travel packages holiday arrangement service agent which needs more old customers who speak to whose friends to recognize its existence to build its brand for long term. So television or radio or newspapers travelling advertisement do not need to spend long term if whose old customers feel which can provide an excellent packages holiday arrangement service to them to enjoy satisfactorily. Hence, its old consumers' feeling whether who satisfy or who do not satisfy its packages holiday arrangement service from the first time, they shall influence whose friends or relatives who decide to attempt to enquire the travel agent successfully.

Otherwise, any one of television brand sale persons who do not need to build more professional image, due to the sale persons are only the television company brand sale representative, whose duties only need to explain what the television features and functions to let the customers to compare to compare to other brand television products to decide whether who ought to buy the brand television or ought not to buy the brand television. However, any travel agents must need to seek any packages holiday information about airline air tickets prices, itinerary journey and hotels, transportation, restaurant meals, leisure activities of the travel destination country to let any consumers to choose the different packages holiday arrangement programs to compare whether which packages holiday arrangement program is the most suitable to their travel needs immediately. So, their satisfactory extent to the packages holiday arrangement from the travel agent's consultant who can influence their friends or/and relatives to feel whether the travel agent can help them to arrange packages holiday satisfactory. Otherwise, a new or an old television product brand company needs more advertising from magazines, radios, televisions to promote which television products for long term, due to every family who have different demand to choose to buy the television products, e.g. television size, design, manufacturing history and manufacturing country and prices etc factors which can influence every family choice. It implies the family can't influence to whose friends or/and relatives to decide to buy or not buy the television brand easily. Due to every family members who have different demand to choose which kinds of television company brand. Furthermore, it will take a closer look at the motivational world of the travel agency staff and how both groups interact. These questions will be analyses with regard to its significance and applicability in brand management. The results of a neuropsychological study, which measured the implicit personality systems of package tourists and travel agents with a psychological test. When investigating the travel market , it must be taken into consideration that it is subject to considerable changes, due to , for example, new dynamic production processes , price comparison systems, the growth of online providers etc. Every travel agent needs to make each brand unique and distinguishable in its perception. The key issues discussed where: Why do package tourists buy? Which scopes and potentials are there? When positioning style brands? How can potential customers be better addressed and won as a customer? Central question concerning travel agents where: what is there main motivation (commissions, incentives)? How can travel agents be more effectively? How can travel agents help to increase the sale? Sensing versus intuition concerns perception itself, thinking versus feeling are decision strategies based on perception and judging versus perceiving relate to the handling of these decision. Because individual travel agent needs to explain why whose choice of packages holiday arrangement is the best suitable to every consumer considerably when the customer is the first time to contact the travel agent , so travel agent is needed more professional travel knowledge to arrange the best packages holiday to serve every visitor to enjoy their holidays satisfactory to build their brand. Otherwise, any television brand company sale representatives who only need to introduce what the style of television product which feature to let the visitor to know to decide to buy or not buy it. So, any television product brands which need more different kinds of advertising to help them to promote to build their brands long term.

In conclusion, P&G fairy liquid soap brand management principle, which is more similar to apply to television product brand management principle, which need to launch their different style products to satisfy clients needs. Such as P&G brand company needs to continue to change its product ingredient to let many customers to feel to use safely , e.g. it launches bar soap products to liquid soap products as well as any television product companies to launch how to change television images and colours to be more clear to attract many customers to choose to buy whose television brands products. Otherwise, packages of holiday arrangement tourism service, tourism consultants need to own professional travel knowledge to help whose visitors to arrange any the most reasonable price and the most safe and the most unique journeys to attract any visitors to choose whose packages of holiday services. In fact, travel agents who do not need to spend much money to invest to carry on launching their travel service to raise time to gather travel information to increase whose ideas to achieve to persuade every visitors to choose packages of holiday arrangement successfully. Hence, it seems P&G fairy liquid soap product brand management principle which can not apply to packages of holidays travel arrangement service clearly.

5.6 AI predicts Mobile phone company buyer behavior

1. Critically evaluate methods that mobile phone companies could use to assess buyer's likely response to new features, such as video on demand.

Can apply (AI) big data gather tool to help any mobile phone company to set up the most attractive and reasonable phone charge plan to every different mobile phone target clients?

Mobile phone is a product to satisfy customers' verbal communication needs during who leave home to need to communicate with anyone urgently . Mobile products are only bought for the verbal communication benefit. In other words, a mobile phone product is of value to someone only as long as it is perceived as satisfying some extra need, instead of verbal communication, such as watching video demand from internet when people are sitting on buses, or trains , or drive cars to watch video entertainment from their mobile phones. So, a mobile phone can be a material product, it can also provide an intangible service, such as verbal communication and watching video or sending email from internet by an 3G or 4G telecommunication fast speed internet service provision channel when who leave their home, who can also enjoy to watch video and call anyone and send email such as staying at home. However, mobile phone is a high level of emotional involvement communication product by the buyer due to there are many different and similar style of mobiles to provide to customers to choose to buy, so I think the mobile phone can provide watching video from internet feature is prefer to buyer to choose more than the mobile phone can not provide watching video from internet , even it's price is more than the non video watching mobile due to young people like to watch video instead of going to cinemas to see movies, it is possible who have no time or who feel movie tickets prices are expensive. Mobile phone is low level of accessible product, due to buyers can use home telephone when who stay at home or who can use any restaurant phone if who is walking on the street , it's location is near to restaurants. Mobile phones are shopping goods, due to consumers generally put a lot more effort into choosing shopping different style of mobiles to buy. Their evaluation include price, credit facilities, guarantees, after sale service, email or video entertainment from internet service.

Different brands of mobile products are distributed through fewer retail outlets and therefore there is likely to be a higher margin for the retailer. Customers are usually willing to travel to an outlet to find a brand style of mobile, rather than expecting it to be available on their doorstep. Large amounts of money may be spent on advertising to develop strong brands, such as 3G and 4G telecommunication provision service to watching video or sending email from mobile internet. In fact, mobile product needs to provide intangible service, such as verbal communication , watching video, sending email. Hence, many mobile users ought prefer to buy the brand of mobile company which can provide these kinds of services because who feel these services are whose basic needs, specially the students like to use mobiles to watch video entertainment or working people like to use mobiles to send email to their offices to keep communication when who need to leave offices to work outdoor. However, watching video on mobiles is one new idea to focus of whether who need this service, it can be unclear who the customer is and it can be difficult to conceptualize the exchange that takes place between the provision video watching service of mobile buyer and the mobile seller of the idea. Hence, mobile phone companies need to do market research to evaluate who are the preferable ages segment group and what factors which will cause who do not choose to buy their mobile brands of watching video mobile products. Mobile phone industry is a product innovation industry.

Nowadays, mobile phones have these features, such as cameras, MP3 players and web-browsing. The life cycle of mobile phones as a broad product category is now at the mature stage, some would say saturated. But when individual product formats are examined, a pattern of continual development, launch, growth and eventual decline is evident. Mobile phone companies vision is to affect people, process and technology by enhancing workflow, improving access to knowledge, increasing the speed of business transactions and providing better modes of video watching feature. Some mobile phone companies are already using mobile applications to deliver video image to increased client matching feeling satisfaction. The mobile phone video watching speed convenient availability and price is factor to influence individual client to choose the mobile phone company's style video mobile or chooses another mobile phone to buy.

Some mobile companies have complex products that need to be maintained at the client's premises. Photocopies are a good example. The quality of field service and support is an obvious factor is establishing customer satisfaction as well as in building the kind of customer loyalty that leads to repeat business. The mobile companies have leveraged the potential of wireless support tools are gaining ground in the marketplace. I think mobile phone is not seen simply as a way to communication function. It ought to spend on carrying on researching and development on internet to deliver email message communication and it also needs to provide on line video watching entertainment service new features when every individual client is using every mobile phone company's different style of mobile phone if the mobile phone companies still wanted their mobile phones can sell to clients in this global mobile phone competitive market. Today, mobile phone is popular communication tool to every family. Due to beyond the rapid consumer adoption and usage of mobile phone is the opportunity mobile phone companies offer for brands to connect more meaningful and personally with consumers. Considering it every individual direct line and immediate connection with audience when who is leaving at home to communicate easily.

Most brands spend less than one percent of their marketing budget on mobile. The argument is that the one percent spend level is too low, given the fact that most consumers devote about 10% of their media attention to their mobile device.

During the 20 century, marketers employed mass-market media channels-Television , radio. The result was that brands created marketing massages that out of necessity had to appeal to a broad spectrum of consumers. It implied that watching video had been every person's habitual behaviour everyday. If mobile phone can provide video watching feature to satisfy every client's seeing enjoyment. I think the individual client will choose to buy the mobile phone, which can provide video watching feature more than the mobile phone which can't provide video watching feature, even the individual client feels the owing video watching feature of mobile phone which price is higher than

the lacking video watching feature of mobile phone. Because there are many people like to bring their mobile phones to watch video when who are leaving at home.
I shall suggest to do one marketing research of open to close survey method to new features, such as video on demand by whose mobile phone.The survey questions can be conducted , such as whether the client will determine to buy mobile phone with video feature more or who will determine to buy mobile phone without video feature more when the client need to buy one mobile phone to use; whether the client shall compare all different style of mobile phone with video feature which price, size, design and functions before the client determine to buy one mobile phone with video feature; whether what the factor is the most importance to influence the client choose to buy the mobile phone style with video feature, such as function, design, price, colour, size, quality more durable use production of year; whether what factors influence the client to buy other companies' mobile phone with video feature, such as cheap price, unique indifferent design, attractive colour, smaller size or larger size, production of year, whose friends or family introduction, advertisement promotion, convenient availability more durable use and quality; what kind of mobile phone with video feature, the client won't accept to use, such as screen picture is small size, image lacks clear color, too big size or too small size mobile phone feeling difficult to control . Hence, after any mobile phone had gathered their questionnaire researchers idea, then which can analyze whose data to carry on evaluating to estimate whether video features on mobiles demand on the difficult countries' consumer numbers. For example, every country sample of 100 people whose ages were between 10 ages to 20 ages segmentation group, a sample of 100 people whose ages were between 21 ages to 30 ages segmentation group, a sample of 100 people whose ages were between 31 ages to 40 ages segmentation group, a sample of 100 people whose ages were between 41 ages to 50 ages segmentation group, a sample of 100 people whose ages are between 51 ages to 60 ages segmentation group etc. If the 10 ages to 20 ages segmentation group had 50 people out of 100 people who prefer to buy video feature on mobile. It can estimate the country's this age group whose people numbers whether how many population shall prefer to buy video feature on mobile in the country. Hence, market survey research method can identify to measure every country's different age segmentation of client numbers who prefer to buy video feature on mobile clearly.

2. In terms of a new product development process, how could the development and launch of Tele point services have been improved in order to avoid the problems that were experienced ? What lessons can be learnt for the development of 3G (or 4G services)?

Adrian, P.(2012) showed that Hutchison is not new to taking big risks in the mobile phone market. It was behind the Rabbit network of semi-mobile Tele point phones launches in the UK in the 1980 years. These allowed callers to use a compact handset to make outgoing calls only, when they were within 150 meters of a base station, these being located in public places such as railway stations, shops, petrol stations, etc. As in the case of many new markets that suddenly emerge, operators saw advantages of having an early market share lead. Customers who perceived that one network was more readily available than any other would all other things being equal be more likely to subscribe to that network. Operators saw that a bandwagon effect could be set up to gain entry to the market at a later stage could become a much more expensive market challenger exercise. Such was the speed of development that the Tele point concept was not test marketed. To many, the development was too much product led, with insufficient understanding of buyer behavior and competitive pressures. Each of the four companies forced through their own technologies, with litter inclination or time available to discuss industry standard handsets which could eventually have caused the market to grow at a faster rate and allowed the operations to cut their costs. The Rabbit network came with the announcement by the UK government of its proposal to issue licenses for a new generation of personal communication networks, these would have the additional benefits of allowing both incoming and outgoing calls, and would not be tied to a limited base station range. By 2006 year, the next generation of mobile phone services were under development, with Japanese trials of 4G faster than 3G telecommunication service. 3G phones were also challenged by the development of alternative wireless access services, notably Wi Fi. Many companies, such as T-Mobile had began offering mobile Wi Fi services, which allow users to log on a local access points and gain access to their email and browse internet. Subscribers to VOIP telephone services could also effectively make the free phone calls from a Wi Fi access point. For many business travelers, using their laptop, Wi Fi access seemed a more attractive and less expensive option than using a 3G phone connection to check for email. It was likely to become even more attractive, with development of longer range Wi Max services that extended beyond the very limited 50 meter or so range of Wi Fi. The pressure of 3G telecommunication services was intensified when the UK government announced in 2006 year that it would license the development of a national Wi Fi network.

It seems that 3G and 4G telecommunication service can be capable of speeds faster then Tele point Rabbit telecommunication in any places conveniently. It causes Tele point Rabbit telecommunication becomes obsolete to mobile to use. From 2003 year, mobile phones industry seemed that the new digital technology would be a third generation of mobile phones (3G). By 2008 year, work was well with the development of the next generation of fourth generation

mobile phone (4G) telecommunication service. In terms of a new product development process, the mobile companies need to consider the development and launch of Tele point services have been improved in order to avoid the problems that were experienced. The mobile product mix comprise range of mobiles that a company offers to the mobile market. Tele point service launching whether it is the individual mobile is with its core or secondary and augmented elements to influence consumers to buy mobiles essentially. I think the external factors, such as UK mobile phone companies whether which can sell the augmented mobiles or the secondary level mobiles or the core mobiles which can influence Tele point service demand, such as if the mobile company can only provide the core benefit, but it's style of mobiles which lacks the better characteristics in the secondary level to attract consumers, which shall reduce mobile sale numbers, features are such as mobile design, color, shape, reliability, texture, packaging , even if it lacks the augment level competitive effort, such as after sales service, brand name, credit facilities, speed of delivery and warranty. Thus, even Tele point service launching is useful to mobile buyers, if the consumers feel the mobile products prices are expensive and they are not valuable to attract them to buy mobiles. Tele point service is not the main factor to influence the buyers to choose to buy mobiles in UK mobile market when

this mobile phones are launched to
sell in the beginning. The another factor is that Tele Point was new telecommunication service in 1980 in UK mobile telecommunication service market. There is likely to be a lot
of promotional effort by Tele Point service to promote to mobile markets to secure sales.

It is likely that the network of semi-mobile Tele point phones telecommunication service needs have high costs in the development of its service, costs that in the early stages may not be covered by revenue. Potential customers for a new network of semi mobile Tele point phones telecommunication service may be few and far between and therefore sales in early stages may be quite slow. This stage is known as the introduction stage. However ,Tele point phones telecommunication network service had this limitation. It only allowed callers to use a compact handset to make outgoing calls only, when they were within 150 meters of a base station, these being located in public places ,such as railway stations, shops, petrol stations, etc. If it's service proved popular, more people will show an interest and start purchasing it. However, due to many other mobile network telecommunication competitors who copied Tele point network telecommunication service technology to launch more fast speed and no location limitation and they can make incoming and outgoing calls both functions, even 3G or 4G telecommunication internet service is provided to mobiles. Hence, Tele point telecommunication network can not adopt to consumers demands.

Although, Tele point is the first network telecommunication service to adopt to handset in UK, but it handset network innovation can't identified as a source to mobile users' long term competitive advantages in this mobile phone network competitive market. Due to other telecommunication network companies can improve or revise to Tele point network service to launch more advance telecommunication service to provide mobile users to use more conveniently. Tele communication network fails due to mobile consumers useful demands are raising, its existing telecommunication service may no longer satisfy their needs, telecommunication technological change may make Tele point existing network service obsolete, telecommunication network service competitors can provide more convenient telecommunication network to mobile phone users and the social and economic environment may have changed, creating new mobile users needs in the global mobile telecommunication network service market.

The development of information and communication technology (ICTS) with mobile can bring the benefits of within each of virtually all the world's people social communication, such as Japanese mobile phone focusing on 3G technology. Factors promoting it can be summarized as follows: Deregulations by government/ mobile number portability and collocation; competition among carriers, such as introduction of new change plans; technological development, such as connection speed and contents and applications. Dynamic models are based out only on the assumption, such that carriers don't instantaneously adjust to satisfy their long term demand but also on network externalities. The Japanese mobile market has shown a remarkable growth with more than 106.2 million 3G subscribers and 4.4 million 2G as of Dec. 2009. The 3G diffusion rate accounts for 90% followed by that of Korea and this implies the market is almost saturated. Another remarkable transformation is found in its usage: Data communication exceeded voice services. Japanese 3G(4G) mobile phone originally had much variety of functionality other than voice service, being based on supply and demand side of the services: The founder is 3G technology which enabled new services, such as m-commerce and e-entertainment while the latter is due to existence of consumers who are willing to utilize various services. Although, the global mobile phone market has reached to the saturation stage and the growth rate of subscribers has been slowing down. Moreover, the recent development is found in the fact that data communications exceeds traditional voice communication and being the first phenomenon in the world. However, the effects of price elasticity and product differentiation of various carriers and network externalities increase the demand for mobile phone. Hence the technological innovation , such as electronic payment, high speed access and consumers' attitude toward entertainment and m-commerce are important factors for the success of 4G telecommunication service need is more than 3G telecommunication service need to every mobile phone users popularly. Moreover, new business models including a flat rate charging plan can play an increasing important role. Operators under these circumstances are confronted with competition due to the short product life cycle and the pressure to differentiate. Although, 2 G networks are adequate for voice, there was a growing interest in shifting from 2G to 3G even 4G based on a number of important drivers. First, the higher speed of 3G technologies translates into added convenience, capacity and functionality for the user. Second, there is much excitement over adding internet protocol (IP) capability and hence internet access to the mobile phone. In developing 3G standards, international

telecommunication union worked with regional organizations and industry associates to reduce a large number of initial proposals to a smaller number of global standards.

In accordance with the development of mobile technology services already provided on 2G mobile phone , such as upgraded and consumers needed not feel difficult when using those services including email services (electronic mail, phone mail and video mail), web access and download music, movie and game. Moreover, carriers provide their customers more innovative functions, such as video mail, video-clips, video phone , broadcasting type video program, walk navigation, ringing tone songs, high speed internet connection, digital television broadcasting etc. via 3G mobile phone. In short, 3G services add multimedia facilities to 2 G phone by allowing video, audio and graphic application. Since 2G mobile had technological limitation of networks and handsets data transmitted via 2G was mainly text when due to development of networks and handsets, pictures and flash moving pictures are available and some handsets enables to view HPS for personal computer. Google and Yahoo started mobile search engines. Thus, 3G mobile becomes platform to use mobile contents, such as games and mapping services etc. Data communication , such as viewing web showed remarkable increase in 3G mobile phone, but monthly changes also increase and this became serious problem.

In case of the internet in fixed communications, the flat rate changes are already introduced.

In addition, mobile carriers don't adjust to satisfy clients' long term demands and than dynamic model approaches are available . Especially, network externality or network effect has to be considered in telecommunication. Mobile telephone is the most widely used form by communication in the world today. Mobile communication boost the earnings of many users change the local economy and even significantly, raise the GDP of many countries. The mobile phone has a number of benefits but there is a huge gap in 3G mobile phone why there is the case only two countries . Japan and Korean have more 3G than 2G subscribers. Similarly, why do leading nations like the USA, UK and Germany have 3G penetration rates of less than 30%?

The conclusion, we obtained technological innovation were achieved first, than based on this various service innovation were followed. It should stress that the former includes innovations in handsets as well as those relates to networks and IP technologies. The diffusion on new services depends on how they meet clients preference and needs, but behind services innovations those always technological innovations. On the other hand, some other social backgrounds, such as consumer's attitudes, economies and businesses systems are required. For example, the Japanese and later other service providers solved the first start up problem for mobile internet (mobile internet uses 3G with entertainment content that was supported by a micro-payment system) . In conclusion, Tele Point telecommunication service failure was due to it felt it was the telecommunication service provider to Unite Kingdom people to use mobile, it believed UK people, even any countries' people ought only chose to use its telecommunication service monopoly. So, in this mobiles market, it did not continue to develop and launch its telecommunication technological service. However, due to its telecommunication service had geographic location distance limitation and out calling only limitation to every mobile UK and overseas users in different countries. Hence, many mobile users who would feel inconveniently. However, then other telecommunication service providers copies it's telecommunication technology to launch and research to develop 2G, even, 3G and 4G telecommunication technology, its competitors can provide no geographic location distance limitation and in calling and out calling both to every mobile user who can use conveniently. Finally, Tele Point telecommunication service was not accept to choose to use to its old mobile customers popularly, even the new mobile customers would choose to use any telecommunication service providers, due to which telecommunication service could give more advantages to compare it's telecommunication service.

If Tele Point telecommunication could spend time and technology to continue to launch to improve its telecommunication communication time speed, raised incoming call function and reduced no geographical location distance limitation difficulties (weaknesses). I believe that Tele Point telecommunication ought attempt to continue to launch to improve its weaknesses of such as above weaknesses to adapt mobile consumers' demand easily, then it ought continue to keep its competitive position in this global telecommunication market till to nowadays.

3. Consider how the launch of 3G services in a less developed country with a less sophisticated telecommunications infrastructure may differ from a launch in a western developed county?

The growth has 3G telecommunication service in less developed country risk for the companies involved, especially where new technological displace the technology which went before them, calling for ever increasing capital investment, and no chance of a return from customers until long after the initial investment has been made in new capacity. Mobile phone companies need to predict the less developed countries, such as Africa country which has how many people who need mobile phone usage whether Africa has high businessmen who can support place, promotion, people and service to assist mobile phone companies to launch 3G or 4G telecommunication service.

I think mobile phone companies need to let Africa country people to know mobile phone 3G telecommunication service technology is as the key to a whole new world of mobile telephone in which the mobile phone would be positioned not just as a device for voice communication, but a vital business, leisure, and information tool. So, mobile phones can assist Africa people to communicate in any places conveniently. A less developed country is a planned economy, the government makes all decision for society. Producers only make what they are instructed to make. The main benefits are that most workers are employed and most people enjoy a similar basic lifestyle. The problems cause to launch 3G mobile telecommunication service include that a planned economy gives little capacity for development, so growth and investment is limited, the infrastructure is usually under-developed as government spends on other areas, such as defense, wages are state controlled, so people have less motivation to perform at higher levels, mobile charges are fixed by government, consumers often can't afford luxury products, such as computers or mobile pones which are taken for granted in developed countries. Otherwise, a western developed country is in market economies (also known as free enterprise), the government's role is limited to providing legislation to protect businesses and consumers and making sure or organization restricts competition. It also provides essential services (like policy defense) and ensures the developed country's money supply is stable .

Thus, businesses are motivated by profits to make products that clients will buy. Customers' demand for products and services affects the levels of supply and the pricing, if clients don't less be more efficient or produce on alternative product. For example, During 2003 year, the Hong Kong based Hutchison Whampoa became the first company to launch a 3G service in the UK, with its 3G telecommunication network. The launch was accompanied about the wireless internet and video capabilities. The world was going to be transformed by streaming of video and football matches live to customers' mobile phones and a whole new world of mobile advertising media would open up. However, launching 3G or 4G mobile telecommunication service to developed country , such as United Kingdom or less developed countries, such as Africa , I think the mobile phone companies need to consider what kinds of needs are the country people who prefer to get needs mostly. UK is a developed country, the people will need to get video entertainment, internet extra service from their mobile. Otherwise, Africa is a less developed country, the people live very far. It seems that location technology was value added data services. Even the emergency services stood to benefit from 3G's ability to precisely pinpoint a caller's location. By 2004 year, 60 per cent of calls to the UK emergency services were made mobile, but in instances callers did not know exactly where they were and ambulances and fire brigades only had very approximate locations. A less developed country is developing economy . It often face great difficulties in improving its economy. For example, in a planned economy, assets like land or property are owned by government. Individuals and businesses are not used to make decisions and operating to make a profit. Developing economy likes a less developed Africa country may also be market economy. But share features, such as the population lives on very low incomes, poor infrastructure , such as transport (roads or railways) or local government, poor communication systems, low levels of basic health and education and a low gross national product (GNP). Over 75% of the country's workforce is in agriculture which can be affected by the climate. Telephone landlines are scarce, expensive and difficult to install . It has less bank branches which are based in cities and tourist areas. Many Africa people are self employed business people, such as small farmers. The impact of mobile telecommunication technology on developing countries. The connectivity provided by mobile phone technology supports economic development. Its impact on a developing country likes Africa country has been extremely positive. Many families live in remote areas of the countryside . Installing landlines over those distances is expensive and difficult families are often separated as the main earners are forced to live in order to earn enough to keep their families. Many are self-employed small farmers or trades people such as plumbers and builders. For small business, better access to mobile technology means that who can advertise to a wider audience and don't have to rely for work on word of mouth. They can be sure that clients can contact them with ease. Due to far remote distance between houses and mobile phone companies, to launch in less developed county, any a mobile company must need a mobile network is quick and easy and secure to install and less expensive than landlines. For example, in a less developed country as Africa country, any mobile phone companies need to provide 3 G telecommunication service to any customers when who go to an accredited shop and in return for cash which has credit registered on their mobile to pay rather difficult than a pay as developed country mobile clients top up their mobile card.

So developed countries mobile clients must pay their charge more convenient to compare to developing country mobile clients. Hence, mobile phone companies need to locate mobile card payment stores in developing country, such as Africa country's petrol stations, supermarkets and retail bases stores places. Hence, any mobile phone companies ought need to spend more capital expenditure to launch rapid commoditization of 3G or 4G telecommunication equipment and rising separation of network and service provisioning are pushing the operators to adopt multiple strategies with network infrastructure sharing in the core and radio access networks to improve network costs to a less developed country, such as Africa country more than a developed country, such as Hong Kong country. However, Africa is a potential mobile phone market. Due to limited land line availability, the cell phone is becoming Africa's computer of choice. Never before has a technological innovation been adopted as quickly as the introduction of cell phones in developing countries. Africa county mobile market will be larger to compare to fixed telephone lines, broadband, computer in home telecommunication markets.

By international telecommunication union (2011) source indicated that global mobile usage, 2011 yr. of mobile subscriptions per 100 inhabitants statistic, Africa region had 53, Asia & pacific had 74, America had 103 and Europe had 120 inhabitant numbers. It implies Africa, less developed country had the least inhabitants to compare to any developed countries, so its mobile market will be large (Sullivan, 2007). In conclusion, extensive cell phone networks already are in place throughout the developing countries. These networks constitute and infrastructure providing clear solutions to many problems with building mobile transaction systems. These networks are not exist, but the majority of those in these nations, such as Africa country now uses cell phones for conventional voice communication and text messages to availability of inexpensive handsets and reasonable industry pricing structures. The features of mobile phones transaction systems in developing countries, include interface, network type, date, storage, power source for recharging cell phone, telecommunications provider, financial institution transactions of cash in/out receipt service.

5.7 AI predicts England NHS public hospital patient need behavior

England NHS public hospital patient price structure of marketing strategy case study

1. What do you understand by the concept of a pricing model? Critically discuss their relevance to a public sector service ,such as the NHS.

Can apply (AI) big data gather tool to help England NHS public hospital to judge whether how much patient price chrage is the most reasonable and the most attractive to persuade them to visit this hospital's medial service?

A price model reflects the fact that companies can generate revenue through a variety of combination of the basic price and prices charged for optional additional items. Some price models may be sustainable by giving away a product at very low price initially, but then charge higher prices for essential items that are needed to make the product function. Sometimes, the dominant pricing model in a market is challenged by a new entrant, with the result that consumers' expectations are changed. The price model can occur in perfectly competitive market or non perfectly competitive market. A perfectly competitive market characteristics include there are many producers supplying the market, each with similar cost structures and each producing an identical product. No single supplier on its own influence the market price because it is not monopoly, water and electricity is managed by government to control the public utility company which can not charge high fee to every householder user at the reasonable price ; both buyers and sellers are free to enter or leave the market and there are no barriers to entry or exit and there is a ready of information for buyers and sellers, for example about competing alternatives, e.g. oil products and stock markets where shares are bought and sold are exist in perfectly competitive market. In perfectly competitive markets, firms are price taker and their ability to set prices is limited by the level of demand and supply within the market they serve. If the total demand go up, all other things being equal, the going rate of prices in the market for their product will rise. Likewise, if there is a drop in total supply for whatever reason (e.g. because of bad weather, there will be further pressure for prices in the market to rise. The final price paid in the market will reflect the balance between supply side and demand side factors.

The model of perfect competition presented the forces of competition may be ideal for consumers because the tendency of market forces to minimize prices and/or maximize firms' outputs. But in such markets, suppliers are forced to be price takers rather than price makers. in a perfectly competitive market, firms are unable to use marketing strategies to affect the price at which they sell. At a higher price, buyers will immediately substitute identical products from other suppliers. Lower prices would be unsustainable in an industry where all firms had similar cost structures. Otherwise, an non perfectly competitive market, firms are able to use marketing strategies to affect the price at which they sell. Such as UK medical service market , private hospitals and public hospitals and clinics which can raise their service fee to their patients to follow their patients demand due to their doctors and nurses service performance, medicines quality and price and patient beds supplies factors to influence their service charges to their patients in UK. Hence, NHS needs to provide different and excellent medical service to its patients to make them to feel it's service is better to other private hospitals and clinics if it wanted to apply price model to its car parking or hospital phone system service charge to its patients because it is a public sector medical service organization. It ought not charge extra service fee to its patients in its hospitals. If it charged extra service fee, such as car parking and hospital phone system service which are same or higher or lower than other private hospitals or clinic , which need to ensure which medicine quality, doctors and nurses performance which are better than private hospitals and clinics and its patient beds need have enough supply to any patients when who feel need to sleep in its hospital. Because NHS image is a non profit medical organization to any UK poor patients, who choose NHS medical service are due to its medical service charge is cheaper than private hospitals and clinics and who feel it can provide free car parking and free hospital phone system service.

A market is defined here need not be a physical location where exchange takes place (as happens in retail and wholesale grocery markets). A market in the economist's sense refers to all individuals and firms who wish either to buy or sell a specific product. A market is defined in terms of products or service and geographic description, so the UK soft drinks market refers to all individuals in the UK who seek to buy soft drinks and the suppliers to that market. The UK medical service market structure can describe as the number of consumers, such as patients and medical providers , such as private hospitals and public hospital , such as NHS (National health service) and clinics; the barriers that exist to prevent new private hospitals or clinics or public assistance hospitals from entering the UK medical service market (or prevent UK patients do not prefer to choose NHS medical service); the extent to which the supply medical services is concentrated in the UK small number patients normally and the degree of collusion that occurs between patients and/or private or public hospitals or clinics medical service providers in the UK medical market. Governments often seek to regulate the prices of key products and service, such as electricity and telephones and public hospitals medical services, so it is important to understand how firms can reconcile the sometimes conflicting approaches of market forces and regulation, such as NHS public sector medical service in United Kingdom. Of course, if NHS public sector medical service planned to charge some non major service fees, such as car parking and hospital phone calling service to its patients and hospital visitors and staffs which are same to private hospitals, it needs to consider pricing model should never be seen as an isolated element of hospital's marketing decision making. It needed to consider its service performance of its doctors and nurses, its social responsibility of public medical service image whether it is better or worse than private hospitals that it had created and NHS 's distribution strategy whether it's patient beds supply numbers are enough to patients and whether it's medicine quality and supplies and prices which are reasonable to compare to private hospitals or clinics in this medical service market in United Kingdom. Private business organization with a broad range if products or services are often price different with their portfolio in quite different ways. They may have developed a price model, which describes the way that it uses pricing of its portfolio to maximize its overall revenue. Hence, one product or service may be charged at a very low price, on the assumption that it can raise higher price if many clients choose to buy its product or consume its service. In some sectors, a number of different pricing models co-exist. For example, in the emerging multi-channel television broadcasting market, some channels are provided free of charge to users, but make revenue from selling advertising space, when others charge to users, either on a monthly/annual basis or a pay to view basis. The idea of a pricing model is familiar to private sector organizations, but do they have a role to play in the public sector? In the UK, pricing models are increasingly being discussed and developed for services which have previously been considered a vital service and available freely to all.

Adrian, P.(2012) showed that the National Health Service (NHS) has a long and proud tradition of providing health service to all, according to an individual's need, paid for out of general taxation, according to individuals' means. Pricing has historically had very little role to play in the NHS. However, from the mid-1990 year, individual NHS trusts began exploiting charges for ancillary services as a means of boosting their revenue. One of the first targets for charging was users of hospitals' car parks. Trusts argued that providing car parks was not central to the mission of NHS trusts, and conveniently, government was encouraging more people to use public transport and leave their cars at home. Critics argued that patients were essentially captive and public transport was not a realistic alternative for most people. However, it showed that at one hospital in London, a patient who attended A&E on the advice of her GP, was charged UK$3.75 for the first two hours' use of the hospital car park and UK$7.5 thereafter. She was ten minutes over the two hour period and therefore had to pay higher charge. She also questioned the fact that charges were reduced to UK$1 per hour after 6:00 PM, when many hospital departments were closed. For private sector service, a lower evening price, when there is not much demand from customers, and plenty of spare capacity, it quite common. But is it right that a hospital should only charges lower prices at the not busy time when much of the hospital itself is closed? If lower prices are designed to stimulate additional demand, it this a realistic prospect when many hospital departments are only available between 9:00 AM to 5:00 PM? Another source of revenue exploited by many hospital trusts from the use of bedside telephones by patients. Many trusts entered agreements with private telephone service providers which allowed incoming and outgoing patient calls only through the officially appointed system, which used a premium rate number. A proportion of the revenue was retained by the hospital. Conveniently, hospital trusts pointed to evidence that mobile phones could harm sensitive medical equipment , and therefore used this to eliminate competitive pressure from patients' mobile phones, forcing them to use the hospital's own telephone system. The ethic of hospital telephone pricing was challenged by the House of Commons Health Select Committee, which accused some trusts of using excessively outgoing call, adding to patients' costs, and boosting hospital revenue. It cited a hospital in Essex where people wishing to telephone patients were being charges 49p per minute at peak time and 39p off peak. By comparison , a typical household rate for a long distance phone call was around 7p in the peak and 2p in the off peak. The select committee also expressed doubts about whether a ban on mobile phones in hospitals was actually a result of possible interference with medical equipment and recommend visitors should be able to use mobile phone within certain areas of hospitals. So, it seems that UK private hospitals patients phone calling service fee is below than householder phone calling service fee and it is not every patient must need to use phone when who stays in hospital as well as the visitors should able to use mobile phones and who should not use hospital phones within certain areas of hospital, who will not interference with medial equipment. Otherwise, by banning mobile phones, had private hospitals been more concerned about creating a monopoly environment for pricing their telephone service, than any possible risk to their equipment? However, I think National health service (NHS) which is one public government assistant hospital, it can not be same to private hospital to charge unreasonable car parking fee or hospital phone service fee to its patients, due to these ancillary services is not hospital main income source and it is one non profit hospital, it needs to provide the fair and non expensive medial charges to its poor patient segment because who are not rich, so who will prefer to choose NHS medical service to compare to choose private hospital services in United Kingdom.

National health service (NHS) is a privatization, fragmentation and market competition of health care provision supposedly to cut costs and improve the efficiency of the health service in England. The NHS was set up in 1948 year to be a free and accessible care, publicly owned and funded sector service in England. NHS needs to consider to redefine its relationship with health service, limiting the quality and quantity of care it can expect to receive, how it access that care, who is delivering if and even how it is paid for. The result will be poorer, fragmented services with larger differences in quality and access. Services/treatments will cost more and the public will increasingly have to pay for aspects of its care that used to be free at the time of treatment. Traditionally privatization has been through the sale of public assets and services to private owners through the mass sale of shares, e.g. the sale of telecoms, railways, energy or water services. These companies than own the services and are able to make profits from them like any other are able private businesses. In the NHS until now, this model of privatization is taking place through a combination of the reduction of the role of government in regulating health provision, the transfer of services to the private sector through commissioning from any qualified providers, such as independent sector treatment care centers, outsourcing of parts of services to the private sector, the creation of market mechanisms for the distribution of funding within the NHS (e.g. commissioning, payment by results mechanisms, the purchaser-provider split and so called patient choice policies). The use of private finance initiatives that use private money to build new buildings and infrastructure and then the state has to pay, the creation of foundation trusts that are run much more like private businesses and have the ability to raise funding through private patients that pay for services, allowing services to become not for profit organizations, such as social enterprises, cooperatives or mutual and thus leave public ownership, limiting access to certain services previously provided by the NHS. Provided healthcare tends to cost more. It requires a large bureaucracy to operate, with huge transaction costs that come with contracts, billing and litigation. In general, as the proportion of private spending on health care rises, so does the overall cost. The creation of healthcare market can also impact upon the continuity of care people receive. There is always the threat that the private sectors or other providers who take on a service that doesn't secure the expected financial returns may cut losses and withdraw from the provision of that service. NHS is under increasing financial pressure. For example, surgery like hip and knee replacements are more expensive areas of care, the results cause the loss of training opportunities for junior doctors expenditure spending and other health professionals as ever large shares of routine surgery and medical procedures are diverted away from the NHS. Centers for research and medical innovations are also threatened. This can lead to service being out. NHS hospitals will therefore fail financially and be pushed into greater debt. This could lead to hospital mergers, closure or the private sector coming in to run the service on profit making contracts. NHS will bring poor health care service if it will not increase its service charge price to patients. The poor service will be caused, such as permanent damage may have been inflicted on patients with serious conditions due to the lack of follow up care after treatments. In a second worrying example dangerous delays affected the patients of a privatized out of hours. A competitive market system leads to greater rationing and gradually drives patients to take on more responsibility for funding their own care. It seems this already in the privatization of long term care and dentistry. Patients may soon have to top up the cost of their hospital care in the same way that many already do for community health services. The concern is that the NHS will provide a less comprehensive range of treatments. For the private sector, the aim is to make a profit from every contracts, which is not the same as providing the best service . For example, Southern Cross, where the need to make profit lead to the rapid closure of care homes, leaving old people with no home. Hospital people with learning disabilities and challenging behavior were subject to physical and psychological abuse. Privatization will lead to fragmentation of the health services. This is a process on a commercial footing and redesigning the system along market lives. With different organizations delivering different service in different locations, it is also likely to lead a new health service with some area receiving much better care than others, hardest, leading to greater health inequalities. Fragmentation of services leads to worse clinical outcomes as staff have less opportunity to work in a fully integrated dynamic multi disciplinary team. Patients with complex needs can be particularly considerable. The impact of privatization on current NHS staff, who are transferred from NHS employment to non NHS organizations would be changed terms and conditions at the time of transfer. These terms and conditions could be changes at some time in the future, staff would no longer be covered by the national negotiating arrangement in the NHS, meaning they would not be entitled to any future pay uplifts or agreed charges to the change terms and conditions of service . If staff moved from this employer to another outsourced community service, who would lose their entitlement to access the NHS pension scheme and would be treated as new staff rather then former NHS staff, the new service provider could argue that the service who will be providing is so different that they will not be requiring staff to transfer. Those staff will than be made redundant. In conclusion, NHS is one public medical service non profit organization. It's pricing model ought be public service price model, such as no price discrimination and non competitor based pricing aim. It may be difficult or undesirable to implement a straightforward price-value relationship with individual of public services for a number of reasons: Such as NHS public sector medical service pricing can be actively used as a means of social policy, subsidized prices are often used to favor particular patient segment groups, such as car parking fee charges to visitors or hospital staffs only as well as hospital phone system service charges to visitors only or prescription medical service charges favor the very ill and unemployed patients and low income patients and students patients.

2. What factors should influence the level of charges at an NHS car park?

Principles for fair hospital car parking, such as NHS is important because its car park service represents the hospital reputation. Charging for car parking is often necessary, but needs to be fair, providing a travel plan for users of all types of transport, controlling parking fairly, with concession for those whose health conditions or work commitments mean they have to park frequently or at anti social hours, showing car park and transport costs and how charges are invested, thinking about the environment and how transport can reduce the NHS 's impact , being open and involve patients and the public. It is important to get car parking and transport policy and it is communication, right to ensure fair access, good patient and staff experience and to protect hospital organization , such as NHS reputation. Clinical and social changes as car ownership to patients, staff and visitors to hospital sites has increased. For services with rural or urban , as public transport infrastructure is less convenient and reliable . When for specialist treatment, some patients need to travel greater distance and modern hospitals have often been located on the edge of population centres.

Car parking is also a factor in patient's experience of using healthcare. When much progress has been achieves to improve the patient environment inside the hospital, including cleanliness and new buildings, patients frequently report dissatisfaction with transport and parking arrangement. Visitors concerns both cost of car parking and also the availability of space for people with an essential need, illustrating the competing demands that managers need to balance. Patient experience is an important objective for hospitals; poor experiences can undermine confidence in clinical quality and stress can be worsened by poor transport and parking policies. Car parking can have a major impact on the local and national reputation of the NHS hospital . As patient choice increases, reputation and loyalty will be key drivers for provider's commercial sustainability. It seems car parking is one important factor to influence patients who choose hospital more than location/ transport/ easy to get to/ reputation of consultants factors. Ensuring that patients can access hospital when they need to is an important part of healthcare delivery. Many patients who need to travel to hospital by car, either because of mobility or illness, a lock of alternatives or through choice. However, providing a car park is not the only component of a travel plan. Access to healthcare should be considered in terms of service planning, decisions on location of services, building design, access routes and the other transport modes. One of the factor of the current changes to the way that NHS hospital services are delivered is that healthcare should be localized where possible. In many cases, people who used to have to travel to hospital are being treated in community health centers. The NHS hospital can also ensure services are accessible. Most notably, ease of access has recently been improved by reducing waiting times and by enabling patients to choose and book their appointment at a time and location that is convenient to them. Another of factor is whether NHS hospital had or had not ran a bus service from a nearby park and ride car park that runs every 15 minutes. The service has proved popular and is now run by the UK country council. The hospital is been to extend the shuttle service to the other three park and ride car parks which serve the city. The other factor influences NHS hospital charge includes the control parking fairly with concessions for those whose health conditions or work

commitments mean they have to park frequently or at anti-social ours. In order to ensure that those patients who really need to access hospital by car are able to NHS often need to ensure that car parking space is available on site. Space is usually constrained, NHS hospital is in city or town center with high land costs and planning constraints. Charging some patients, visitors and staff to park can manage demand for space when ensuring that those who really need to park are able to access services. Where charging is required to manage demand, the overriding principle should be to ensure that where possible those patients who have the greatest need to park are prioritized. Where managing demand is a reason for charging for car parking, there may be scope for varying rates for different times of the day and the week, for example, increasing charges for non essential users in peak hours but applying a minimal charge at night when there is less reason to ration space. As well as prioritizing car access for those with greatest needs restrictions on car parking may also be required to deter non hospital traffic, particularly where NHS hospital is located in controlled parking zones, near shopping centers or other facilities that might need to illegitimate required use of NHS hospital grounds. In these cases , NHS hospital may be required to be charge the same as local car parks to avoid abuse by non visitors. However, alternative arrangement could also be explored, including day permits for people with appointment. NHS car parking fair policies should need to be fair application. This is often a cause of concern for patients and visitors. Concessionary schemes and season tickets should be well publicized and available, since a patient may not known in advance low frequently who will need to attend a clinic in the next month. Penalty charges, or towing away should only be applied extreme circumstances with a presumption of good faith that no patient or visitor chooses to stay in hospital longer than necessary and may how on arrival how long who will have to wait for treatment. Running a car park can be expensive. These are maintenance, security, insurance and running costs and the NHS hospital has to pay for the space the car park uses. Costs are particularly high where land prices are high or there is increased risk of crime. At the same time, patients and the public rightly don't expect healthcare to suffer to pay for parking. The transport costs of non car owners are not subsidized by the NHS budgets to provide subsidized free car parks . To make car parking fee would be to penalize those using public transport. Therefore, fair charging is often the most sensible answer to adopt these two demands. Climate charge and pollution and congestion factor also have health impacts. Reducing car dependency is also a public health objective in order to reduce traffic accidents and increase physical activity.

These NHS organizations have a number of environmental and health reasons to seek to encourage people to use other modes of transport. Parking charge together with the expansion of alternative bus an cycling options to encourage a modal shift from cars to alternative transport. Patients , visitors and staff need to be made aware of these aims. NHS hospital can achieve a travel plan to develop to its car parking with the aim of during a period of busy time reducing single occupancy car journeys by 15% over three years, ensuring tat patients and visitors do not have to search for a space for more than ten minutes at peak times, encouraging the number of direct bus routes to the site to increase reducing staff parking spaces per employee by 10% as staff numbers grow. Car parking charges were introduced as part of the plan with certain categories of staff on exempted from charges (night and weekend staff, disabled staff, volunteers, car sharers and tenants of residential accommodation. From an environmental perspective, NHS travel plan supposed to reduce numbers of cars arriving at the site and the numbers of bus car raise. It aims to improve bus services to cause air pollution at the busy car parking period and cycle parking spaces and improved cycle facilities have encouraged staff to commute by bike. Additionally, a park and ride scheme aims to reduce car traffic of the NHS hospital in the busy time.

Moreover, it is absolutely wrong to charge cancer patients regardless of income, for unavoidable parking costs. From a staff point of view, NHS hospital car parking is an indirect tax on healthcare. However, most unions also support the aim of reducing car usage, as long as policies are fair. Because NHS hospital needs to develop transport policies for patients requiring regular cancer treatment. This approach has potentially negative publicity into a positive image to public. These ought be free parking for the duration of a cancer patient treatment or as often as is needed.

3. If you are studying at a university or college, critically reflect on the pricing strategy that it has adopted for ancillary services.

The development of a costing and pricing strategy will provide an university staff with greater access to price information, thereby providing a more accessible platform from which to base negotiations with commercial organizations. As prices will be informed by cost, the university will be seeking to apply

pricing strategies that maximize university as opposed to maximizing income. In fact, any universities is education industry which is different to common businesses which provide service or product to raise price when client numbers are increasing easily. Due to if an university which planed to increase school fee to charge students, which needed have unique courses to attract students to choose to study and its lecturers educational experiences and education methods needed to make student to raise learning interest and feel the courses are useful to choose to study the university subjects, so who shall compare the university subjects to other universities subjects, then to evaluate their school fees and lectures educational experiences and qualifications to decide whether who ought to choose the university or another university to study. So, I believe that the university can not raise its school fee easily if it has no more confident its subjects and lecturers which can make students to study to feel more satisfactory till to graduate. Otherwise, it will reduce student admission numbers if it still increase school fees, due to it has not researched what the subject contents are students who like to learn. Hence, any universities can't increase its school fee easily.

However, university ancillary services have primary paths to reduce internal cost to raise competitive advantages, such as services differentiation, low internal cost or internal span structural advantage. I shall recommend these price strategy to

adopt to reflect some university ancillary service (non major) service. The pursuit of a service differentiation strategy to an university advantages. The university needs truly understanding its unique core service (value) and then focusing resources on its ancillary services. An implicit part of having a focused

price strategy is not only defining what the university is going to invest in, but is also clearly articulating what the university is no going to do. For example, if the university investigated its students did not like to eat some foods taste, which ought to change some foods taste which could satisfy its students eating needs in its university canteens. Even the university could charge cheaper student parking fee to compare outside public car parks when they park their cars in university parks from the morning to afternoon studying busy time. It could only permit students to park their cars in its students private car parks. Hence, university staffs and visitors could not permit to drive whose

cars to park in university private student car parks, so university staffs could park whose cars in university staffs car parks as well as visitors could park whose cars in university visitors car parks. However, who also needed to pay cheaper parking fee to compare outside public car parks to buy
car park tickets to park their cars in university staffs and visitors both car parks in any limited time. Even, the university book shop could sell lower second hand books and new books prices to compare other private book shops to attract students to choose to buy studying books from university bookshops. However, if the university tried to pursue too many areas of service differentiation, which was likely to invest too broadly and thus reduced the return on investment for previous capital possibly because it needed time to research whether which aspects of it needed to change to adopted students tastes to satisfy their needs, then it needed time to change its services and it also needed time to evaluate whether it's changed services which can satisfy its students demand to make decision to raise its service prices. Hence, it ought concentrate on changing one aspect of ancillary service to ensure it's changing was right to adopt students' taste to attempt to raise service price. Then, it could attempt to evaluate whether what ancillary services which needed to change to achieve price raising possibility. University recognizes that focusing on the core is hard to do, given the history and culture of university. But the worst case scenario for an university is to be relatively expensive and completely undifferentiated. Whether will who pay high school fee per year to go to an university that is completely undistinguished on any ancillary service?

An university looks to areas where which can make cuts and achieves efficiencies, an university should start farthest from the core of teaching and research ancillary services. Cutting from the outside in and building from the inside out. Growth in programs and research, increasing faculty and student demands and increasingly compliance requirements have all contributed to the growth of administrative costs. The reasons are often very legitimate. But as new programs are added, old programs often are closed down in some university ancillary services, e.g. unimportant administration internal service . The resulting breadth of campus activities creates too much complex it for staffs to manage with any efficiencies of scale in university. Units don't trust one another or the center to provide ancillary services. Data center management is a good example of fragmentation on campus. At the university, the central information technology group managed fewer than half of the servers on campus in its data center. For the servers located in the colleges, fewer than half were managed by college information technology groups, the rest were considered hidden at the department or faculty level. Despite the internet data and security risk of having too many unmanaged serves on campus in the university's central information technology department. In similar cases, outsourcing data centers would be a good solution. Third party data centers could provide more solutions, higher levels of securing, greater flexibility in capacity and lower cost than internal solution. Redundancy, an university is an many other campuses, it was managed at the department level, there were no product standards and each department negotiated its own vendor contracts. A sample of purchase order showed that the same item was being bought for as much as e.g. 36% more in some departments than in others. By centralizing end, standardizing more if its procurement to expect to save more expenditure. An university hierarchy, most campuses have too many middle managers. Before it reorganized , an university has average spans of control (the number of employment).

Campuses engage to save cost. An university campuses engage in too many activities that require to broad a skill set to effectively deliver in house. Take information technology application management for example, not only does it need to support classrooms and research needs across a diverse set of disciplines (history, music, law, engineering, biomedical science etc. different subjects), it also has to cover functions (finance, human resource, research, administration, student registrar, libraries and student services etc. functions). It weren't enough, information technology also has to serve industries beyond the core academics, including bookstores, retail food, debt cards, total museums, publishing houses. A single IT group would have a hard time managing all it that well, given the expertise required, leading to either poor service delivery, sub scale and costly delivery.

Outsourcing more of non core activities would reduce campus complexity and cost. Third party provides have greater scale capability and skill because the outsourced service is their core business, enabling them to deliver the same or better service at a lower cost. In order to reduce aministrative costs without diminishing service and perhaps even enhancing it's campuses will need to subscale operations by creating shared service or outsourcing improve processes by eliminating low value work and automating much. Better manage university assets to whether it is real estate, physical assets or intellectual property, a number of activities where partnership with third party providers would allow for financial relief and improved performance. Hence, an university can also invest its intellectual property to build its build to raise its market value for long term to raise its sale price for long term.

In conclusion, an university can attempt to use these two kinds of price strategies to adopt to reflect to its ancillary services. Such as the first is competitors price strategy, the university can set its students and visitors and staffs car parking fee by examining what its competitors such as, it's close public car parks are charging their car parking fee services whether they are similar in terms of the university car parking service characteristics fee to satisfy its parking car users' needs as well as the university can set its canteens meals price by examining what its competitors, such as it's close private outside restaurants meals price whether they are similar or different taste and low meal price to attract students or staffs or visitors to choose to eat their meals . The another is demand based pricing strategy, the students are prepared to pay represents the upper limit book numbers to the university's every year studying books. Such as the university book shops can decide every years different subject second hand or new teaching books price to follow the students demand. For example, if the subject second hand or new teaching books supply numbers is less than the student demand numbers, the university can raise the subject books sale price. Otherwise, if the subject second hand or new teaching books supply numbers is more than the student demand numbers, the university needs to reduce the subject books sale price, even it needs to reduce their prices to be lower than outside other private book shops marketing price to sell in the year. Hence, it seems that any universities can adapt price strategy to reflect to their services or products prices.

5.8 AI predicts a national chain of restaurant mobile advertising promotion behavior

A national chain of restaurant mobile advertising strategy

1. Critically assess the likely opportunities and problems
of mobile advertising for a national chain of restaurants from AI digital advertisement on mobile

Can apply (AI) digital advertisement technology to help any national chain or restaurant to advertise to overseas traveller' mobile phones in order to let they know where is its location and food taste and price? Future one day, (AI) digital advertisement promotion channel can be applied to mobiles to let any countries' target travellers to know any national chain of restaurants to attract them to choose to visit their restaurants to consume easily.

A global crisis in the advertising industry largely linked to the impact of the internet is transforming the business models of media industries, the content they create and distribute, and the audiences who consume that contents. Such as consumers can use whose mobiles to find where the chain of restaurants are located and meal and drink prices and meal and drink types and
restaurant opening and closing time etc. information for the national chain of restaurants from internet advertising when who leave at home conveniently. The opportunity to mobile advertising for a national chain of restaurants, it can expand its national chain of restaurants brand to different countries visitors and instead of its self country visitors to let them to know whether where its chain of restaurants can provide what kinds of food or drink to serve to them to eat before they prepare to go to any one of the national chain of restaurants immediately. Hence, when visitors travel to its country, it will be more easy to let them to remember where any one of the national chain restaurants are located in the nation when who enter the national chain restaurants website or enter yahoo website to type" national chain restaurants" word, then who can seek any one of the national chain restaurants from whose mobiles easily.

In fact, if a national chain of restaurants chose to use television advertising, due to the national chain of restaurants which locate at itself country locally. It is only concentrate on promoting it's country's domestic eating consumers target to know it's existence when its country's domestic eating consumers are watching television at homes. Usually, working people need to work and students need to go to school to study from morning 9:00AM to 6:00 PM at night. Hence, the national chain of restaurants can only advertise at night time. Furthermore, the overseas travelers watch the nation's television when who are staying in the nation's hotels at night time. Hence, the national chain of restaurants can only use television to advertise to attract the largest numbers of local and foreign visitors to watch its advertisement at night time possibly.

Due to mobile advertising exists, television advertising is more difficult to attract the durability of audience segmentation models to build upon demographic and it also lacks new opportunities to implement psychographic and behavioral models for understanding audiences. Such as, many young people who accept to use mobile to communicate, so it implies every family usually has a mobile to use and mobile advertising also have much opportunity to help any businesses to promote whose services or products to let many families to know whose advertising. In fact, mobile users can use mobile to watch movies or news, so who ought to link internet to watch during who are sitting on any transportations or walking, so when the nation's people who feel hungry, who can use their mobiles to link to internet to seek any restaurants to decide which restaurants are the most close to their locations to choose. As a national chain of restaurants, it is more effective to advertise it's different chain of restaurants' locations to let any it's different locations of national mobile users to seek its any one of chain restaurant conveniently when who are walking on the street if who feel hungry who can turn on mobile to find map to seek the national chain of restaurants immediately. In fact, the global households who the average viewing audience composition, the number of global households using the television set and the various times it is in use, the average audience (home viewing during an average minute of a

program) and the total audiences (homes viewing the program in excess of minutes) which are decreasing. Otherwise, the mobile phone users view mobile advertising numbers are increasing. Broadcast channels as well as whatever is available on their various devices, including computer, mobile devices, gaming devices, time-shifting devices or internet enables devices. As such, it is providing more and more difficult to track the audience and known who they are and the best way to target them. Additionally, the rise of social media adds another dimension to audience research. Social media provides new ways of segmenting audiences that currently can not be done on television. Hence, a national chain of restaurants can get better ways of segmenting its viewers from mobile advertising over a variety of platforms.

So mobile networks can be better

package to the nation chain of restaurants advertising programming and the national chain of restaurants advertiser can make a more effective to attract foreign visitors or domestic visitors to make them to enter its website to view its advertising from their mobiles. For example, car owners, such as those who own a BMW or Audi famous brands cars, which have very homogeneous demographic characteristics, but each car brand has a specific type of owner with a unique personality. A similar look as television audiences could allow advertising of those car brands (who attend the upfront presentations every year) to match their car buyers to specific television shows. Demographics have not caught up with these changes and presume that viewers are still watching in only the conventional way. For instance, there is not yet a way for the networks to get credit for online viewers and it is as more viewers more to online platforms, like a network in landing site.

Instead, a psychographic profile of the audience, one based on psychological segmentations , such as behaviors, attitudes, interests, values, opinions feelings which is a valid and valuable way of narrowing down the audience into segments for an advertiser. So, psychographic data can measure, such as peoples' activities how who spend whose time, their interests what they place importance on in their immediate surroundings, their opinions how their view of themselves and the world around them and some basic characteristics, such as their stage life cycle and income and education and residence location. The result of the research then provides a detailed profile that allows the marketer to be better visualize the target audience.

Psychographics start with people and reveal how the people feel client specific subjects, which can lead to be more effective marketing. When psychographic segmentations are used, the consumers are divided into group based on lifestyle and personality, often with all of this in mind, the research questions proposed here as follows: What psychographic measurements are being used right now to determine the television audience or mobile advertising ?

How are the various branches of the industry , such as restaurant industry adaptive to the new television landscape ,such as mobile advertising and what actions are they taking?
What are some challenges and resistances to psychographic measures between television advertising and mobile advertising?
What incentives or lack are there to change between television and mobile advertising?
What would be helpful for advertisers , such as a national chain of restaurants or networks , such as internet advertising to know or do in order to more towards wider use of psychographics?
A reason behind dividing audiences based on engagement can be illustrated with the Pod mobile phone, such as the national chain of restaurants organization has shown that audiences‘ attachment to specific the restaurants' brand corresponds directly to how much the audience will pay attention to the national restaurant brand's advertisements from mobile and how likely who are the actually to choose to go to the national chain of restaurants to eat lunch or dinner or breakfast more than its other restaurants.

The problem is how the national chain of restaurants to advertise it's foods taste, price and service and locations uniquely to win its other restaurant competitors from mobile specific program, providing the network to be best convenient that it's restaurant brand to advertise on that specific program. Another key problem is trend segments viewers based on domestic and foreign consumers‘ behavior are more specifically their viewing behavior mixed with their restaurants choosing eating behavior in whose countries, watching the national chain of restaurants television advertising from whose mobile , what who are watching to know its existence and on how to let them to know what their actual eating taste to the national chain of restaurants can provide. Hence, I suggest the national chain of restaurants can attempt to use surveys to carry on researching the different countries foreign visitors and domestic visitors whether what whose tastes are preferable to choose what kinds of foods and drinks who hope to eat in this national chain of restaurants from mobile advertising website. The problem is who may choose not to fill its surveys from its mobile website advertising. If they use computer to fill its surveys at home, it will have more opportunities to gather data from survey due to who can sit down to fill surveys in quiet environment. Hence, I suggest it ought use computer internet to do market research about what whose tastes are preferable to eat in its restaurants. When it estimates whether the foreign visitors and domestic visitors numbers, how many people choose to eat different kinds of foods and drinks to its identifications. After it can achieve mobile advertising to promote its restaurant brand more confidently in this mobile marketing advertising strategy.

2. Discuss methods that could be used to assess the effectiveness of (AI) digital mobile advertising.

Measuring social media marketing , such as mobile advertisement, effectiveness and identifying the target market. The use of social media sites as part of company's marketing strategy has increased significantly. Regardless its popularity, there is still very limited information to answer some of the key issues concerning the effectiveness of social media marketing , ways to measure its return on investment and its target market. The social media was started around ten years ago. It began with linked in, which was launched in 2003 year, followed by both My space and face book in 2004 year. You tube in 2005 year and Twitter in 2006 in year. The popularity of social media sites has also spread to companies as part of their strategies. Executives are concerned with their budget justification for a social media plan in computer or media online advertising, when there is lack of supporting materials to confirm the effectiveness of the social media platform , i.e. conversion rate, the relation between buyer-seller relationship and increase in sales and the rate of return investment that they can earn from this plan. Others also believe that their companies' performance are not affected by their lack of involvement in the social media sites.

Clearly, the fact that social media marketing is still relatively new among business practitioners has raised some major concerns , such as its effectiveness, the main purpose of including social media mobile advertising in a company's media platforms, it's relation to the existing platforms and the target audience of this strategy. The methods to assess effectiveness of mobile advertisement include that marketing research method is about target client segment of respondents' social media activities and buying decisions relationship survey. Survey questions can include whether how long time and how often who turn on mobile phone to use internet, such as a week is less than 20 hours average or a week is between 20 hours and 30 hours average or a week is between 30 hours and 50 hours or a week is more than 50 hours, why who like to use mobile to use internet and not use home computer to use internet, e.g. reducing to use home electricity, interesting, convenience, no computer at home, what who will seek to see from mobile advertisement, e.g. advertisement , news ,email , message, movie, whether who decide to buy products or consume services choice is from which kinds of channel advertisement influence mostly, such as television, radios, newspapers, magazines, computer internet, mobile internet. It aims to gather target client segment of respondents' social media activities and buying decision relationship to estimate whether there are how many numbers of target client will decide to buy the company's product or use it's service from mobile advertisement channel.

Hence, the survey result can indicate these five respondent groups, such as highly affected, somewhat affected, neutral somewhat not affected and not affected at all groups. Mobile phone advertisement is needed to any organizations to use internet to operate. Hence, to access the effectiveness of mobile advertising which may begin by using measures that were very easy to capture and understand, such as the number of website hits or percentage of users who clicked on an advertisement. These measures were very useful fro examining trends in traffic patterns, but the impact of this traffic on sale and other marketing objective was sales and other marketing objectives were little understand. Standardized approaches for capturing and summarizing websites behavior were eventually developed to help make sense of web traffic and patterns. Metrics, such as number of unique visitors and the amount of time who spent viewing web pages provided marketers with new insights into who was assessing the site and how who were using it. But even with a high level of detail about how customers were interacting with the company via the web, marketing manager often lacked the information how user behavior data translates into increased profits and business value. For example, organizations using websites primarily for after sales support have used exactly the same kinds of metrics as these selling directly from the site. This is not due to a lack of available data. Many organizations using web analytics gather and store vast amounts of information and develop large, complex databases to house it. But much of that information is never used. Because organizations who first began to market over the internet often lacked a clearly formulated strategy. In addition, the rapidly changing internet environment made it difficult for marketers to formulate clear expectation about the impact of activities. Both the amount of returns and amount of investments are difficult to measure. I suggest organizations may estimate the value of a visit to a particular web page by estimating the number of visitors who will become customers and then multiplying that number by the average value of all clients to estimate returns. What the 'clicks and hits' and 'measurement driven' approached have in common organization's strategic objectives and provide quantified models that plan and track internet marketing investments from intermediate outcomes to financial results. Hence, it can indicate how marketing expenditures in mobile internet advertising method to lead to increase shareholder value aim. I think investment in internet marketing , organizations will need follow these stages. In the beginning is inputs stage:

Organization and business unit strategy includes structures, systems, resources as well as marketing strategy includes structures, systems as well as information strategy includes structures, systems and market strategy transfers to websites, search marketing , advertisement and public relations, mobile marketing and marketing research. Next, it is outputs stage: It includes intermediate outputs, such as awareness and perceptions, attitudes and intentions, value provisions, channel optimization and market information as well as it includes final outputs, such as marketing assets: customer value, brand equity, knowledge as well as financial flows: increased revenue, cash flows, reduced revenue, lower cost, lower working capital, lower fixed capital and reduced risk. Finally, it is outcomes stage includes shareholder value, return on investment and corporate profitability. For example, Donald restaurant uses its website to promote lower calorie food and fruit options as well as its global campaign tied to the Olympics, nutrition (Business week 8-7-06). Each organization should carefully identify the outputs it seeks to achieve. How can process produce these outputs? Organization can attempt to enhance of website functional or initiation of an email campaign. The final question to organizations which will ask : How outputs contribute to the long term financial performance of the organization from mobile advertising ? Is critical for organizations seeking to enhance return on investment from mobile advertising? In addition, whether mobile advertising can give these benefits to any companies, such as market capitalization and shareholder value can be enhanced by increases in marketing assets (customer value, brand equity and knowledge base) that produce future corporate financial flows from mobile internet advertising method. Hence, marketing assets include customer value, such as using dynamic pricing to manage demand, supporting sales through online information sites, shipping directly to reduce need for inventory possession, shifting in store sales to online sales, eliminating clients with prior post sales problems from promotion lists; brand equity, such as additional revenue through brand premiums, using customer relationship to speed adoption of next generation products target marketing to loyal clients during predicted slow periods, reducing customer turnover and support costs, shifting responsibility and risk for inventory management to major suppliers, pool inventories with suppliers and clients to reduce warehouse space across the supply chain, using trust in brand to reduce unwarranted lawsuits, knowledge base, such as developing mass customization capability, reducing time to market through online concept trials, time promotions to smooth demand, eliminating product features that are not valuable to clients. Watching production timing to demand, direct in store sales to products that generate high contribution margin per square foot of fixed space and anticipating and respond to stakeholder concerns. Finally, customer value and brand equity and knowledge base shall transfer to financial flows aim, such as increased revenue, accelerated cash flow, reduced revenue volatility, lower cost, lower working capital requirement, lower fixed capital requirement and reduced risk.

However, Metrics can be used to access effectiveness of mobile advertising, both financial and non financial metrics are needed to effectively measure performance. Some non financial items , such as market research activities are difficult to measure and companies often avoid measuring those items. However, if the item plays a critical role in delivering organizational value. Measuring it, preferably in quantifiable terms, such as monetary changes or percentages. Even when such measures are difficult to obtain or depend a rough estimates, they provide a basis for examining trends over time and can provide useful information to managers. For example, two metrics for the output awareness are: The number of emails opened recipients and the number of clients that clicked on a promotional mobile advertising. Those two metrics can provide different perspectives on the meaning of awareness, thus the choice of metrics helps clarify the objectives, just as clear objectives can help in identifying specific and to be relevant must be specific and to be relevant they must be customized to meet the unique dynamics of the organization . It aims to achieve the best to capture and reflect the organization's unique sets of activities and results some may be relevant to all organizations and many can be readily adopted to be useful for decision making.

3. Discuss the relationship between (AI) digital mobile advertising and other elements of the promotion in campaign planning.

Mobile advertisement defines as the use of the mobile medium, it is as a communications and entertainment channel between a brand and an end user. In basic terms, it is the process of planning and execution conception, pricing, promotion and distribution of products and services through the mobile channel. Advertising is a form of communication intended to convince an audience (viewers, readers or listeners) to purchase or take some action upon products, information or services etc. The relationship between independent variables elements and mobile advertising which are environmental response and emotional response with behavioral aspect of consumer buying behavior with mobile advertising. It is time that people purchase those brands with which who are emotionally attached elements. Almost every one grows up in the world which is flooded with the mass media, e.g. television, films, videos, magazines, movies advertising and internet channel is either mobile advertising or computer advertising. Advertising is a subset of promotion mix which is one of the 4'p in the marketing mix, i.e. product, price, place and promotion. As a promotional strategy, advertising serve as a major tool in creating product awareness in the mind of a potential consumer to take eventual purchase decision. Advertising, sales promotion and public relations are mass communication tools available to marketers.

Telecommunication technology, such as mobile advertising enables business and industry to grow at a faster pace when contributing to the economic development and at the same time telecommunication infrastructure can be reliable. Cellular phone industry has been one of the profitable businesses in Asian. The country's growing population and huge demand potential have always been an attraction for many high-technological multinational companies. Societies used symbols and pictorial signs to attract their produce users. There elements were used for promotion of products. A company can't make dream to be a well known brand until which invests in their promotional activities for which consumer market have been dominating through advertisements. As the primary mission of advertiser is to reach prospective customers and influence their awareness, attitudes and buying behavior.

The major aim of advertising is to impact on buying behavior, however this impact about brand is changes or strengthened frequently in peoples' memories. Memories about the brand consist of their associations that are related to brand name in consumer mind. These brand cognition influence consideration, evaluation and finally purchases. The promotion in campaign planning to mobile advertising focuses on young people because who choose advertising information and characters as whose role models, who may not only identify with them but also intend to copy them in terms of how who dress and what who are going to buy. As the market is surplus with several products or services, so many companies make similar functional claim, so it has became extremely difficult for companies to differentiate their products or services based on functional attributes alone. Differentiations based on functional attributed, which are shown in advertisement, are never long lasting as the competitors could copy the same. Mobile advertising may differentiate companies‘ products or services promotion channel to attract client's attention, e.g. the company can use movable product images on internet video to show on mobile. However, mobile advertising time ought depend on the business nature, e.g. facial health products target segment is female, so it's mobile advertising time ought choose form 9:00 AM to 6:00 PM working time between Monday to Sunday, due to housewives or working women shall go back home to cook, who shall not turn on mobile phones at home. Hence, if the company had differentiated which brand and it had chose what time is the more popular to accept to let mobile users to turn on their mobile from mobile advertising. The company mobile advertising will have more promotion effort. For example, if the company sold toys, it's target segment would be 3 ages to 10 ages old. It's mobile advertising ought let every family to find its company website easily. If the family didn't know it's brand, but is was difficult to let the family to find what its toys sale from whose mobile phone because there are many toy companies were using internet advertising to promote which toys. So, it might let every family types " toy" word on yahoo, Google websites, then this toy company name would appear on their websites, the family only clicked its name on their mobile phone, it could show it' toys images, prices, which country manufacturing and which year manufacturing different kind of toys, sale payment and delivery method, e.g. visa card payment, air or land or shipping transportation flight delivery, toys manufacturing ingredients indication from website advertising and it's toys advertising time ought to choose family working time, such as between 9:00 and 6:00 PM , due to who shall bring their mobile to work usually. Hence, the toy company needs to consider family will choose what time to use mobile phone. It ought not choose night time to advertise its toy products from mobile due to family would not turn on whose mobile at home at night time usually. Economic theory has sought to establish relationships between selling prices, sales achieved and consumer's income, similarly before the company chooses to spend mobile advertising expenditure, it ought frequently compared it with sales actual income each month.

Social media marketing, such as mobile advertising effectiveness is highly influenced by three aspects: content quality, involvement and integration with the other media platforms methods to assess whether effectiveness of mobile advertising.

On the first aspect, content quality isn't quantity. It shows that managers should not totally reply on the monitoring software to measure and analyze their social media campaign. For example, the twitter website analysis show that some brands/companies, e.g. Microsoft used their Twitter account to connect and to
communicate with customers . Their Tweets were about communicating and connecting with their follows, through some personal conversations in subjects. That were relevant to their customers . As a results, Microsoft clients were able to
beat their main competitors in financial performances and Twitter activities. So, Microsoft can use twitter website to assess whether how many numbers of people use internet service to enter phone, then who decide to buy its software products . If Microsoft found the result of the number of buyers who decide to buy its software from mobile phone Twitter website advertisement channel which is more than mobile phone Yahoo or Google websites advertisement channel after who turn on mobile to see advertising. On the another aspect, building trust and long term relationship to mobile advertising to indicate to how to persuade to increase many shippers to decide to buy any products or seek service, e.g. travel tickets booking service after who use mobile to seek advertising habitually. Today, media marketing is about building relationship and trust through effective two way communications , e.g. talk about something that customers are interested in and creating products or service that will help to solve customers' problems from mobile advertising. Some of today's social media marketing campaigns are still driven by the old fashioned marketing and focus on short-term effect sales, which is also known as incentive induced behavior. To assess trust and genuine buyer/seller relationships achieved through consistent and engaging conversation will increase the messages (SMM) level of influence. Trust is the key factor to get the followers to actually to something , i.e. change in buying decisions influence their peers and turn it into revenue for the companies. It is crucial to build a strong relationship with customers and enhance brand loyalty. Hence, it implies mobile phone companies need to build trust relationship to let them to pay extract internet charges to aim to read email, news, watch movie habitually. Then, it will increase chance to let potential buyers to prefer to seek advertisement to choose to buy and products or consume service from mobile websites habitually. Hence, assessment of mobile internet habitual users who use mobile internet time per week from survey is one effective method. Also, firms should start their involvement by inviting their customers or prospects to join their social media community. For example, firms can post the icons of the social media main websites or giving some special deals to customers who become their fans or followers . In the online community, firms should start writing more effective posts. An effective post should reflect honesty and conciseness, it is as key elements of an effective post. It should also be informative to satisfy clients' need for information and experts; opinions. Effective contents should be able to actions from the audience (conversion) so that by the end of this process. Followers will place on order, subscribe newsletter or participate on online surveys. In the offline community, managers should share expertise with their speaker in the local community, which will help to attract more followers or fans and to strength connection with the community. A debate has been going on whether or not consumers are willing to receive mobile advertising. America consumers seem to willing to accept

mobile advertising to subsidize the cost of other mobile services , such as email and news services.

A study conducted by HRI Research on behalf of Nokia brand found that the core mobile phone subscriber market (16 to 45 year old) is not only receptive to experiencing mobile advertising, but also actively welcoming mobile advertising in the form of electronic coupons promotion. The relationship between mobile advertising and the four key elements contributing to mobile advertising's acceptance of the promotion in campaign planning. There were mobile advertising should allow users to decide whether or not to receive messages, users could bypass sales messages easily, users should be filter the message received and users want to get mutual benefits of something back. The SMA advertising campaigns of mobile advertising industry plays and consumers have been made afraid of the spam phenomenon deriving from negative email spamming experiences. The personal nature of the website phone markets spamming especially invasive compared to spam received via other channels and devices. Mobile advertising has the potential to be one of the most powerful one to one digital advertising mediums of utilized in the right manner. SMS trials across the would have show the power of mobile advertising in building direct one to one relationship. The online companies like AT&T, AOC wireless, Microsoft and Nokia to mention few companies that are focused on the potential of mobile marketing via mobile handsets. Factors contributing to the success of mobile advertising include that ability, setting up research. measurement, tracking systems, availability of specialist expertise in agency, service provide and establishing consistent rate mobile cards. Other factors impact of drivers on the development of mobile advertising include that personalized medium, users able to opt in , call to action , i.e. immediate response possible , location specific, interactive profiling, appeals to younger customers , one to many communication.

In conclusion, the relatively between mobile advertising and other elements of the promotion in campaign planning include as below: The first element is by utilizing mobile advertising, companies can run marketing campaigns targeted to tens of thousands of people with a fragment of the costs compared to other direct marketing mediums, such as direct mail or telephone and this in just few seconds of line. The advertising industry uses two types of cost calculation cost per thousand impressions (CPM) and cost per rating point (CPP). CPM is used for both print and electronic media when CPP is more popular for electronic media. For instance, if an advertising campaign costs US$5,000 and has an audience of 300,000 consumers, the CPM will be approximately to the initial CPM measure in media selection , such as quality of the audience, audience attention probability and believability of media selection when the CPM for direct mail is between UA$500 to US$700. For email the CPM ranges from US$5 to US$7. However when email marketing is losing its efficiency, mobile advertising offers new ways to promote products and services. A significant factor contributing to consumers‘ willingness to accept mobile advertisement is the capability of mobile handsets to service certain type of messages , such as multimedia messages. Evidently, most consumers in the future will carry on smart phone with them. The smart phones allow advertisers to reach consumers in different locations with personalize messages at a given time. Another element is the industry of SG or 4G network service is faster connection speed is a obvious enables users to receive digital photographs, moving wide images, high quality sound for their mobile handsets. From advertisers; perspective this opens various opportunities to plan and implement more advance m-advertising campaigns and integrate those with existing marketing channels. However, to develop and provide applications, for example, interfaces to the carrier's wireless network need to be provided in multiple areas: location, presence, billing, personalization, provisioning, packet network, transport and messaging systems. Next element is location awareness cab be seen as the driving force of many wireless applications and suits also well types of mobile advertising. When mobile phones are almost always carried with and intelligent location awareness technical solution are available. The final element is personalization means building customer loyalty by building a meaningful one to one relatively by understanding the needs to each individual and helping to satisfy a goal that efficiently and knowledgeably addresses each.

Personalization is about mapping and satisfying of client's goal in specific contest with a business's goal in its respective context. Personalization means understanding different kinds of individual preferences , needs, mindsets and lifestyles and cultural as well as geographical differences. Mobile are already equipment with a profiting options, e.g. silent, meeting, outdoors. For example, the utilization of time and location awareness as personalization variables has the benefit that mobile advertising is a marketing medium has features that other marketing channels lack. Hence, email advertising needs to keep every mobile users' personal information to be confidential, solicited message, relevance to users need and the right frequency.

CHAPTER TEN

Main barriers influence artificial intelligence consumer behavioral prediction

In future, it is possible that these barriers will influence how to apply (AI technology) to predict consumer behavior in success. The barriers may include: Lacking of a (AI) digital data gathering vision and strategy, lacking of efficient workforce readiness, (AI) technology constraints., non reaching (AI) consumer behavioral prediction mature stage, time and money and resource constraints, law and regulations prohibition to develop (AI) consumer behavioral prediction bug data gather technology.

However, the recommendation of solutions to attack the barriers to influence artificial intelligence consumer behavioral prediction not success, it may include gaining employee buy in to participate and develop (AI) consumer behavioral prediction technology, making customer experience to a concern (AI) big data gather questionnaire investigation, providing compensation, training to employees in order to achieve (AI) consumer behavioral big data questionnaire investigation research digital technological goals and strategy, task senior leaders manage any (AI) digital big data gather technology changes, putting policies and (AI) big data gather digital technology in place to support a fully remote, flexible workforce in any (AI) digital big data gather questionnaires research projects, teaching all employees how to code/understand (AI) big data gather consumer behavioral prediction software development, appointing a chief (AI) officer to manage any (AI) big data gather customer behavioral prediction projects and automate everything and encourage customers to attempt experience to self-service and (AI) big data gather questionnaire research to earn beneficial consumption aim after they gave feedback to any (AI) digital questionnaire researches. So, in the future, the (AI) digital big data questionnaire researches can include these industries surveyed, such as automat m financial services, public healthcare, private healthcare, technology, telecoms, insurance, life sciences, manufacturing, media and entertainment , oil and gas, retail and consumer products etc.

Hence, in the future, any of these industries can attempt to apply (AI) digital big data gather technology to predict how and why consumer behaviors will change in order to avoid reducing consumer number threat occurrence.

6.1 (AI) digital data gather technology predicts food consumer behavior's main barriers

What are the main barriers to food industry? When the food manufacturer applies (AI) big data gather technology to predict food consumer behavior? The barriers include that the food manufacturer / provider needs to decide whether when the right time is applied to the right (AI) digital big data prediction tool channel to find the right food consumers to be chose to full food consumption satisfactory questionnaires, how to gather multi-class food consumption classifiers on real-world food consumers transactional data from the food sale domain consistently to show the critical numbers of different kinds of food items at which the predictive performance most accurate? So, any food manufacturer / provider's advanced in (AI) digital data gather warehousing and management technologies can provide that opportunities for food business to enhance long term relationship with the food providers' clients.

However, food industry's (AI) digital data gather aims to improve food customer product targeting, increase food customer loyalty and food purchase probability to the food supplier. To effective identify, understand and satisfy the needs of their food customers, the food suppliers need to develop the right (AI) digital questionnaire questions and find the right food customers to fill every right questions from every digital questionnaire at the right time through the right channel.

Above of all these, they will be the barriers when one food supplier expects its (AI) digital data gather questionnaires which can conclude the most accurate prediction concerns any kinds of consumer food product choices. So, such as (AI) digital data prediction model, it is needed to incorporate into the food market segmentation, food customer targeting, and food challenging decisions with the goal of maximizing the total food customer lifetime. For example, (AI) big data gather transaction data is reasonable and accurate for building predictive models. Transaction data can be electronically collected and readily made available for data mining in lot quantity at minimum extra costs.

Suggestion to apply (AI) prototypes of food customer profiles method to predict food customer behavioral changes. Prototypes of food customer profiles mean to be extracted from the discovered bins and multi-class classifies models are built using those prototypes. The learned models can than be used to predict the class of food customer profiles (e.g. restaurants, school canteens, supermarkets etc. food suppliers) based on their food purchases. The approach is validated on the case study of a food retail and food service company operating in food and beverages market.

So, a food customer profile, it is a description (AI) data gather tool will record every of food customer using available information, which help in understanding their background and food consumption behavior. (AI) data gather tool can well develop every food customer profile, every food customer data is essential in food market analysis as they aid food suppliers in saving time and money by highlighting the real potential food consumers whose needs are to be met rather a range of individuals.

So, (AI) data gather tool can record every food consumer profile and every can be factual or behavioral food consumption. A factual food customer profile consists of a set of characteristics for (AI) big data gather record, e.g. demographic information , such as food customer name, gender, birth date, when a behavioral food customer profile consists of what the food customer is actually doing and is usually derived from (AI) digital transactional data gather record.

So, (AI) big data gather record's every behavioral food consumer profile can be much stronger predictor of the future food supplier consumption choice actions of a food customer. Furthermore, the food supplier's (AI) all past food consumer information that make up demographically based all past food customer profiles are expensive to acquire when the information for the food suppliers' past every food consumer food consumption behaviors. Moreover, food customer profile can be recorded to make real food purchase every time. So, when the food supplier finds the past food consumer's record from (AI) big data gather tool. Then, it can make more accurate judgement whether past every food consumer has chose to buy its food to eat how many times every year in order to predict whether its every past food consumer will choose to buy its foods how many times next year in possible. If the next year, its every past food consumer's consumption time to the food supplier is less than its current year consumption time. Then, the food supplier can attempt to find whether what factors to cause the past food consumers do not choose to increase food purchase times to the food supplier in current year. The factors may be possible be the food supplier's food prices are raised, food quality or taste is poor, the different kinds of food supply is shortage challenge, the food supplier's consumers lose confidence to buy the food supplier's foods to eat, when (AI) big data gather tool can help the food suppliers to find what the main factors to cause the past food consumer number to be reduced in order to predict how future food consumers' behavioral changes will be influenced from the food supplier's competitors in the global food supply market. Hence, (AI) big data gather tool can help every food supplier to attempt to find what the main factors to case the food supplier's food consumer number to be reduced as well as it can help the food supplier to predict how the food supplier's potential (past not every purchase its any food consumers) food consumers who can be persuaded to choose to buy its foods to eat by learning what the main factors influence.

In conclusion, (AI) big data gather tool can help the food supplier to find what the main factors influence its past food consumers do not choose to buy its food more times or find what the main factors will attract its potential (not ever buying its foods consumes) food consumers to choose to buy the food supplier's foods to eat.

6.2 The challenges of (AI) big data gather shaping the future of retail for consumer industries

Another challenge of (AI) big data gather is that how to shape the consumer behavior to let business owner to feel or know oe predict. It means that how it express it's conclusion or opinion for every consumer behavior after it had gather all big data in any data gather period, e.g. three months, half year or one year consumer shopping model data gather period.

Because every kind of industry, consumers will continue to demand price and quality change , with a wide range of convenient fulfilment options among of different kinds of products or services supply. Overall, the (AI) big data gather procedure gives opinion concerns every time retail experience will become more exciting, simple and convenient, depending on the consumer's ever-changing needs. So, I believe that (AI) big data gather every conclusion or result will be different, due to consumer's price and quality demand will often change to every kind of product or service supply in retail industry. So, how to shape (AI) big data gathering's analytical conclusion or result more clear. I shall recommend organizations need to build great understanding of and a stronger connection to increasingly empowered consumers before they plan and implement how to apply (AI) big data gather tool to predict consumer behavior as below:

Firstly, (AI) is empowered by technology, the consumer is redefining value. The traditional measures of cost, choice and convenience are still relevant, but not control and experience are also important. Globally, consumers have access to more than 2 billion different products choice by a wide range of traditional competitors and dynamic new entrants, all experimenting with new business models and methods of client engagement.

As choice increases, loyalty becomes more difficult familiarity and the consumer becomes more empowered. Businesses will have no choice and constantly innovate and disrupt themselves by meeting new technologies of high standards and expectations of consumers. So, (AI) data gather tool will need to follow different target group of consumers' needs to follow their different kinds of product design or style choice preferable to gather data in order to conclude the different target groups of consumer behavior to give opinion more clear and accurate to let businessmen to understand more clear how its customers' behavioral choice trend in the future half month, even to two years period.

Secondly, businessmen need to adopt changing technologies rapidly. Technology will be the key driver of this retail industry. Industry participants will only success if they have a clear prediction to focus on how to using technology to increase the value added to consumers. They must , however, do so will I realistic assessment of their costs and benefits. Hence, (AI) big data gather technological tools will need to design to help them to gather data efficiently by these ways, such as the internet of things (IOT), artificial intelligence (AI) machine learning, augmented reality (AR)/virtual reality (VR), digital traceability. So, future (AI) big data gather tool are predicted to be most influential customer behavioral positive emotion changing tool for retail , due to their widespread applications , ability to drive efficiencies and impact on labor in order to impact consumer behavior changing effort from negative emotion to positive.

Thirdly, (AI) big data gather tool is an advanced data science of consumer behavior predictive tool. Businesses will have to bring the journey from simply collecting consumer data to using it to scale and systematize enhanced decision making across the entire value chain. When focused on their business goals, industry players should not lose sight of the impact that future capabilities and transformative business models may have on society.

However, (AI) big data gather tool will encounter these challenges when any business plans and implements to apply it to predict consumer behavior in retail industry. The challenges include that as below:

1. The high cost and difficulty of implementing new technologies . The (AI) big data gather tool needs capital and capabilities to be designed to implement to be applied to different retail industry users. so, expensive barriers to innovation, an organization and the skillsets of its people to support a new design of (AI) big data gather tool, highly digital technology may be required.

2. Slow pace of cultural change. Consumers need to adapt or accept (AI) new technology consumption model in the traditional retail industry. The rate of change is outpacing the ability of businesses to keep up. (AI) big data gather tool needs to be designed to adopt in new or evolved business model requires, in most cases, a new level of customer behavioral predictive machine operation will impact to influence any retail businesses' consumer behavioral changes at a minimum, an organization's structure, capabilities, culture and decision making. If the retail business expects to apply (AI) big data gather tool to predict how to change its consumer behaviors and how their consumption behaviors will tend to change in order to achieve to change their positive emotion from negative emotion before they choose to buy its product or consume its service in success.

6.3 Challenge to using (AI) neural networks to predict customer behavior from big data gather tool

(AI) big data gather tool will encounter the challenge: How can predict customer behavior be represented as sequential data describing the interactions of the customer with a company or an (AI) data gather system through the time, e.g. these interactions are items that the customer purchase or views ? So, every customer data gather , (AI) needs to spend time to analyze how and why to cause whose consumption behavioral choice. It is too difficult matter or judgement for (AI) learning. So, (AI) needs to spend time to learn how to analyze every customer's shopping behavior or actin in order to gather all different consumers' past shopping action information in order to help business owners to predict future its potential customer shopping behavior how to change more clear and accurate prediction.

(AI) big data gather tool needs to learn to know that how to judge every customer interaction likes purchases over time can be represented with sequential data. Sequential data has the main property that the order of the information is important. Many (AI) machine learning models are not suited for sequential data, as they consider each input sample independent from previous ones. Therefore, at the end of the sequence, (AI) big data gather learn machines need to keep in their internal state of every customer purchase data, kind of product or service, price , whole year consumption times form all previous inputs, making them suitable for this type of data.

However, consumer behavior can be represented as sequential data describing the interactions through the time. Examples of these interactions are the items that the user purchases or views. Therefore, the history of interactions can be modeled as sequential data, which has the particular trial that an incorporate a temporal aspect. For example, if a user buys a new mobile phone, who might purchase accessories for this mobile phone in the near future or it the user buys a electronic book or paper book , he might be interested in books by the same author. Therefore, to make accurate predictions is important to model this temporal aspect correctly. To solve this predictive challenge of consumers to buy the product. One count the number of purchased products of a particular category in the last N days, or the number of days since the last purchase.

So, the (AI) big data gather designers can attempt to produce a feature vector which can be fed into a machine learning algorithm such as " logistic regression" will be the main feature and function to any (AI) big data gather machine to learn how to apply this " logistic regression" function or feature to predict any customer behavioral change for any product purchase or service consumption to the (AI) predictive consumer behavioral business users. Every different kinds of product purchases or services consumption will be needed to design " different model of logistic regression" in order to follow the kind of business to predict whose consumer purchase or service consumption behavior to predict more accurate.

6.4 Challenges of artificial intelligence, algorithms technology and machine learning impact to consumption market

Markets have played a key role in providing individuals and businesses with the opportunity to gain from trade. If (AI) big data gather tool can predict how to change potential customer behavior in success. The challenges to consumers will face that the overall market consumption model will be dominated by the businessmen only. So, it is not fair or reasonable to consumers, because (AI) big data gather tool has controlled or dominated all consumers' minds and it has predicted how and why every kind of product or service consumer shopping model or consumption behaviors how will change.

It will bring this questions: How can market designers learn the characteristics necessary to set optimal, or at least better, reserve prices after they had gather all data to conclude the analytical results of their consumers behaviors how will change? How can market designers better learn the environments of their markets?

In response to these challenges, artificial intelligence (AI) and machine learning are important tools for market design. For example, retailers and marketplaces , such as eBay, Amazon and many others are mining their vast amounts of data to identity patterns that help them create better shopping experiences for their clients and increase the efficiency of their markets. By having better prediction tools, these and their companies can predict and better manage dynamic consumption market environments. The improved forecasting that (AI) and machine learning algorithms provide help marketplaces and retailers better anticipate consumer demand and producer supply as well as help target products and activities for segmented markets. Another important application of (AI) 's strength in improving forecasting to help markets operate more efficiently is in electricity market example. To operate efficiently, electricity marker makers can attempt to apply (AI) machine learning tool to follow every household family electricity consumers' past electricity consumption record to judge (predict) how it will be every family's forecasting in the year.

An inaccurate forecast in the electricity supply and demand that can dramatically affect electricity market bad supply outcomes causing high variance in electricity charge prices or worse, blackouts. By better predicting every family's electricity demand and supply , electricity market makers can better allocate power generation to the most efficient power sources and maintain a more reasonable electricity stable charge market. Any example is design market, the application of (AI) algorithms to market design are already widespread and diverse.

(AI) algorithms technology , it is a safe that (AI) will play a growing role in the design and implementation of market over a wide range of applications. The challenges are that how (AI) can guarantee accurate to predict when and why and how consumer behavioral changes to any retail industries. In fact, retailers will need to discover the value that (AI) can bring to what benefits to influence their customer behaviors.

In the future, (AI) will bring their benefits to influence customers to build positive emotions to any retailers in these aspects as below:

1. Future (AI) big data gather tool will be an area of compute science that deals with giving machines , the ability to seem like they have human intelligence. In short, it is the power of a machine to copy intelligent human behavior. For examaple, machine learning algorithms are being integrated into analytics and customer relationship management platforms to uncover information on how to better serve customers, chat bots have been incorporated into websites to provide immediate service to customers.

2. (AI) adoption continue to rise with chat bots taking the lead. Due to increasing ease of deployment , instant availability and improved quality, chat bots will become more and more common to manage customer service queries and to make intelligent purchase recommendations. Also, retailers can engage this kind of technology to answer continue questions and supplement customer support with chat-based shopping experience. So, (AI) and declines personalized, customized and localized experiences to customers.

(AI) will be applied across the entire retail product and service cycle, firm manufacturing to post-sale customer service interactions. Hence, retailers can use (AI) to its fullest potential will be also to influence purchases in the moment and anticipate future purchases, guiding shoppers towards the right products in a regular and highly personalized manner.

3. (AI) technology can rise the conscious customers. Customers are demanding an increased interest in the ethical practice of the brands they buy from. Todays, customers have a well-developed sense of what is solely intended to drive sales. This has lead to a rise in consumers ho make values based judgements about what to buy and where to shop. These consumers believe their purchase habits have an impact on the world. To win customers, retailers need have good conscious to predict consumers' desire. Future, (AI) data gather technology will be a good consumer behavior predictive tool to predict about for years will now become customer expectations and will have drastically changed the path to purchase. So, (AI) data gather tool is the predictive consumer expectations tool on every interaction, they have these brands.

4. Future (AI) can be impacted to influence consumer behaviors by its potential to free up time, enhance, quality, and enhance personalization. The industries include: Healthcare industry can apply (AI) to support diagnosis by detecting variations in patient data, early identification of potential pandemics, imaging diagnostics; automat industry can apply (AI) to autonomous fleets to ride sharing, semi-autonomous features, such as driver assist, engine

monitoring and predictive, autonomous maintenance; financial service industry can apply (AI) to design the suitable personalized financial planning, fraud detection and anti-money laundering and automation of customer operation; transportation and logistics industry can apply (AI) to autonomous trucking and delivery, traffic control and reduced congestion and enhanced security; technology, media and telecommunications industry can apply (AI) to search media, and recommendation, customized content creation and personalized marketing and advertising to attract retailers to promote; retail and consumer industry can apply (AI) to design personalized production, anticipating customer demand, , inventory and delivery management; energy industry can apply (AI) to read and record smart metering , more efficient grid operation and storage and predictive maintenance; manufacturing industry can apply (AI) to enhance monitoring and auto-correction of processes, supply chain and production optimization and on-demand production.

Hence, future (AI) technology will impact consumer technology when any retailers apply it to assist its manufacturing processes or product sale or service provision processes to satisfy consumers‘ needs, it means that it can help any retailers to influence positive emotion to consumers in their whole sale or consumption or purchase proccesses.

5. (AI) and machine learning technologies make it possible to capture, process, and inter data on a massive scale effectively , then any human being could ever do. For example, Criteo's creative technology " Kinetic design" can apply insights from 1.2 billion monthly impressions to select and optimize individual branded advertisements components according to each shopper's preference and intent. This ensures more personalization and visually inspiring on brand ads. resulting in up to 12% more sales for (AI) technology advertiser clients.

Moreover, advertisers can now engage and inspire shoppers on a more personal level, rendering custom ads. it real-time for every impression. So, designer continues to learn from each design's success to make ads. more and more effective over time. Furthermore, brands are increasingly using paid search on retail sites to draw attention to their products on the crowded online shelf, e.g. Google shopping is a key growth area's more users are engaging with shopping ads. and across the globe. Google shopping has become essential to retailers' marketing strategies, but is a difficult channel to apply its tool to be promoted effectively . Thus, future (AI) and machine -learning technologies can dramatically improve digital commerce performance application to apply (AI) and machine learning to digital consumer. So, future (AI) technology can be applied to digital commerce aspect, it will fall into the categories of pattern recognition, classification, prediction and consumer behavior.

In conclusion, the benefits of using (AI) in digital commerce include: improved efficiency in discovering the relationships between datasets over traditional methods, which require complex modeling and coding, improved accuracy for clearly defined processes that involve a lot of manual processing, ability to deal with a large emotion of data with many attributes, for example: customer behavior data, multichannel and multi-device data , complex product data and fraud detection, more accurate analysis, such as customer segmentation sentiment, analysis and personalization frequent algorithum refreshes, such as several times a day, to capture the changes in customer and market behavior.

Finally, however, a lot of types predictive consumption behavior around (AI), in particulars that driven by vendors claiming their solutions are (AI) , ready and can deliver dramatic improvements over existing technologies. Application leaders for digital commerce can be misled into believing that (AI) can solve all their problems, which is not true for n in-depth discussion of the (AI) consumers and market behavioral predictive tool and machine -learning technologies bot. Thus, (AI) prediction consumer behavioral technology can give beneficial quantitative analysis for forecasting in business and market especially in consumer behavior and in the consumer decision-making process (consumer choice model) more effectively and efficiently.

Is Artificial Intelligent the most effective and accurate consumer behavioral tool?

Is (AI) the best and the most effective and accurate consumer behavioral prediction tool to compare other kinds of consumer behavioral prediction tools? Nowadays, retailing competitions are serious businessmen often find different kinds of methods to attempt to predict consumer changes. The consumer behavioral predictive methods can include as these below methods, instead of (AI) big data gathering tool.

Firstly, statistics is the popular mathematic method, it applies auto-regression, liner regression, structural equation modelling, logistic regression statistic techniques to be used to predict consumer behaviors. Secondly, it is classification method, it sis a support vector machine to assist businessmen to make consumer behavioral prediction, it also includes decision making tress diagram technique. Thirdly, it is rule mining method, it is algorithm, market base analytic etc. business marketing concept analytical tool, it also includes graph mining technique tool. Next, it is psychological prediction model tool, it is psychology prediction model too, it is a kind of psychological method to predict consumer behaviors. Finally, it is the most updated and potential artificial neural network (ANN) machine tool, it gathered big data, then it will carry on analyzing and applies psychological method to conclude the most accurate and reasonable solutions to give recommendation to businesses to predict when and how and why their consumer behaviors will change. So, it is one owned human mind's machine and owned psychological and analytical efforts to replace humans to make any judgement in order to make the most accurate predictive behavioral changes for consumers, instead of the traditional marketing concept and psychological and mathematic methods to predict consumer behavior, (AI) big data gathering tool will be another new tool.

What are the advantages of (AI) tool to be used to predict consumer behaviors as well as what are the different between it and other traditional consumer behavioral predictive tools? I shall explain as below:

Firstly, as above all case studies are explained to (AI) questionnaire design method benefit, I believe (AI) big data gathering tool can be applied to help human to analyze and design any the suitable valid questions to enquire any kinds of business consumers in order to gather the most meaning and useful opinions to conclude the most accurate consumer behavioral prediction for every questionnaire. So, future (AI)'s analytical effort and decision making effort most be exceed above human's judgement efforts. So, future (AI) can help human to design the most useful and meaning different kinds of valid questionnaire (survey) questions as well as assist humans to analyze and make accurate decision making and conclusions to give opinions to help businessmen to predict when consumer behaviors will change and how their consumption behaviors will change to influence their businesses in order to help them to make any efficient and effective and accurate solutions to avoid consumer number to be decreased and the most important benefit is that it can give opinions to help businessmen to explain why (what the factors) cause their consumer behaviors change suddenly. It will be human's efforts can not achieve to exceed (AI)'s efforts in the future.

Secondly, (AI) can make artificial machine judgement and analytical effort, without human misleading or unfair or unreasonable judgement. So, it can make more fair and reasonable and accurate conclusion to give opinions to predict when, how and why consumer behaviors will change suddenly to the kind of business in customer model building process and evaluating the results of customer relationship management –related investment more accurate.

Furthermore, (AI) big data gathering tool will help businesses to improve the success rate of acquiring customers, increasing sales and establishing competitiveness. (AI) big data gathering tool can give opinions how to build customer loyalty to be positive emotion impact and it can find solutions to avoid every client's negative emotion causes to bring complaints behavior to the businessman's product or service. For example, Telecom industry and aggressive research has been conducted in this by applying various data mining techniques to avoid long distance phone call users' complaints. If gathered any long distance phone call users' past complaint data to record what are their general complaint issues. Then, (AI) tool will analyze all these past complaint issues to conclude and give opinions to let Telecom knows whether which aspects encounter challenge that Telecom needs to improve it's long distance phone call services or functions in order to satisfy Telecom's long distance phone call users' needs for long term. After Telecom attempted to improve its services and/ or functions from (AI) opinions and solution methods, when it fell it's long distance phone call users have positive emotions to satisfy its service performance and function performance. Then, it can prove (AI) tool's opinions and solutions are useful. The consequence is that their complain numbers will be decreased and they won't plan to choose another long distance phone call telephone service company to replace Telecom long distance phone call service more easily.

So, (AI) big data gathering tool can concentrate on finding focus on components of customer relationship management method and datasets more accurate and efficient and effective than human's data gathering and analytical effort. It implies (AI) big data gathering tool has unique more efficient and effective and accurate dataset gathering and analytical and judgement and decision making effort, it is human can not achieve.

Thirdly, (AI) big data gathering tool has much customer loyalty predictive effort. It's effort is more easily subsequently selected, reviewed and classified to compare human's gathering data effort in whole data gathering and analytical process.

In (AI) big data gathering process, (AI) can organize whole big data gathering process and technique more easily in short time. It will include these four steps. The first stage is that customer identification stage, customer identification also known as acquisition has to do with targeting the population , who are most likely to become customer segmentation. So, (AI) can help different kinds of businesses to gather their competitors' consumer purchase behavior data in short time, it is human can not achieve. The second stage is that customer attraction stage, after (AI) maker has been segmented for the business when it has ensured to gather the businessman's global competitors' consumers data. Then it analyze these all data to find solutions / methods to give the best opinions to the organizations how to achieve the direct effort and resources into attracting the target customer segments. The third stage is that customer retention, it can be defined as the activity that an organization undertakes in order to reduce customer defections. TO be successful, customer retention starts with the first contact on organization has with a customer and continues throughout the entire lifetime of a relationship involves loyalty programs, one to one marketing and complaints management. SO, (AI) can consist the business to find the best or the most reasonable , efficient , effective solutions or methods and it will conclude all these solutions to find the most reasonable and useful opinions to achieve to the aim to help the business to reduce customer complain numbers and help the business to build confident loyalty relationship between it and its clients. SO, (AI)'s analytical effort and decision making effort can be more accurate than human's analytical effort and decision making effort. IT can achieve it's consumer behavioral predictive aim more accurate and efficient and effective in the shortest time to compare human.

Fourthly, (AI) big data gathering tool can design more accurate dataset program for questionnaire (survey) to compare human's questionnaire (survey) effort. It means that (AI) can spend less time to research and make judgement what are the most reasonable and meaning questions for different kinds of businesses' needs. This includes data conduction a questionnaire, survey or interview of the individual or environment researched, public data repository: This includes commercially available public data; organizational data; this contains data collected from an organizational database, organizational information system. For example, their website log details etc. It also includes company transactional data, data purchased from a company.

For example, one vehicle sale company expects to research all global vehicle sale companies' past the different kinds of vehicle styles, design sale number data, the different kinds of vehicle style, design sale price data, every country's vehicle consumer number to the vehicle purchase number data to the vehicle company in short time. (AI) big data gathering tool can help the vehicle sale company to gather all any one for these global vehicle sale competitors' past data in the short time. It is human effort, who can not achieve this efficient, effective and accurate data gathering aim for this vehicle sale company. Even, when (AI) had gathered all global it's vehicle competitors' past sale data, (AI) can make more accurate analytical and judgement and decision making effort to design different kinds of questionnaire (survey) questions to prepare to enquire it's different target segmentation vehicle potential clients in order to predict what are their needs to choose to buy any vehicles from the vehicle company. SO, (AI) tool can conclude more accurate conclusions and give the most reasonable and useful opinions to let the vehicle company to know in order to predict what are it's potential vehicle buyer's needs and manufacture the suitable vehicle styles or designs to raise their vehicle purchase desires.

Fifthly, (AI) tool is only one perfect tool for big data gathering in order to achieve accurate results and increased profit. What is (AI) big data gathering mean? The term " big data"gathering describes the accumulation and analytical of vast amounts of information, but big data is much more than a big amount of data. It is also the ability to extract meaning to sort through big volumes of numbers and find the hidden patterns, unexpected correlations and surprising connections that can be used in different industries like medical field, security and protection field or marketing that adopt " big data driven" decision making enjoy significantly greater productivity than those that do not. So, the benefits of (AI) is given to the company by using big data repaid complexity of implementation projects and hence project risks, when accelerating time to value. It is why that human's gathering effort can not replace (ＡＩ) data gathering effort.

All analysing above benefits to (AI) big data benefits to any organizations, it brinfs this question: How can (AI)apply big data gathering and analyzing to predict when and how any why consumer behavior will change suddenly? The purchase decision making process is consumers reducing purchase choice behaviors.

Consumers are being considered pure rational beings (consumer tried only to satisfy self-interest). Hence, due to future (AI) owns human's psychological , analytical , emotional predictive, purchasing decision making effort.

(ＡＩ) will be assumed to sees one customer how who will make purchase decisions. So, after the (AI) gathered all data concerns the find of business's past customer segmentation purchase activities, e.g. age, sex,. Income level, the product's style sale number, the product price variable sale etc. different kinds complex data.

It can makemore accurate psychological and analytical effort to predict when the business's consumer behaviors will change as behaviors will change as well as find what reasons their consumption behaviors will change and how trend of their consumer behaviors will change more accurate. For example, today there are a lot of industries that use big data: healthcare (treatment) becoming personalized and patient centric and predictive analysis are used to prevent diseases for example Angelina Jolie underevent a predictive double mastectomy after learning she had 87% rich to developing breast cancer, sports (by using sensors data are collected from players during a game in order to improve their playing schemes), weather(more than 60 years of global weather analysis are used to predict the risk of future extreme events), logistics (smart tucks and smart species, agriculture (monitoring weather and soil conditions for optimum point of harvesting).

Consequently, due to the evolving consumer demands, and the ever growing digitization, the world is digitally transforming which means the new technologies are needed to be used and driven significant business improvement. So, such as why (AI) tool will be our future main predictive tool to help businesses to predict when, how and why their potential customer behavioral will change. Big data is one of the our channels through digital transformation is made, together with cloud, mobile and networks. The challenges for digital transforming and therefore using ＡＩ big data gathering tool as main technology are: digital proficiency, legacy systems, security and jobs becoming absolute.

In the future, big data can use data from text to picture , sounds, movies, musics satellite coordinates or any other type of input or output data that type of input or uouput data that came from different influential aspect.

It is cloud solutions, bring big data will be for predict insight driven by business stategy, new product strategies and new consumer relationship, predictive consumer behavioral strategy. Using the right data in the right business decision will mean smart decisions, new opportunitites and utimately a big competitive advantage.Hence (AI) big data gathering tool is different is that (AI) can be one depth in-memeory database function, it can make real-time data analytics that provide meaningful information in short time, it is also the visualization tool , such as SAP Lumira, allow this exploration and understanding of the data, and ultimately supports the decision making process. All above these features, which will be human's data gathering effort who won't exceed (AI) big data gathering effort. Hence, future (AI)big data gathering will be the best choice to assist businesses to predict consumer behaviors successfully.

Reference

Adrian, P. (2012). Introduction to marketing theory & practice,
3 rd edition, London: Oxford press.

Ajzen, I (1991). The theory of planned behavior. Organizational behavior and human decision processes, 50(2), 179-211. doi: 10.1016/0749.5978 (91) 90020-7.

Alba, Joseph W. and J. Wesley Hutchinson (1987). " Dimensions Of Consumer Expertise", Journal of consumer research, 13 March, 411-454.

Bailey, L., Mokhtarian, P.L. Little, A. (2008). The broader Connection Between Public Transportation, Energy Conservation And Greenhouse Gas Reduction, Report Prepared As Part Of TCRP Project J-11/Tasks Transit Cooperative Research Program, Transportation Research Board Submitted To American Public Transportation Association in
http://www.apta.com/research/into/online/land_use.cfmi, accessed 17 April 2008.

Baucer, R,"Consumer Bhavior As Risk Taking , In Risk Taking And Information handling In Consumer Behavior", D. Coxceds Harvard University Press, Cambridge, Mass 1976.

Biederman, P. (2008). Travel and tourism, Pearson Prentice Hall, New Jersey.

Bogers, R. P., Brug, J. Van Assema, P., & Dagnetie, P.C.
(2004) , Explaining fruit and vegetable consumption: The theory of planned behavior and misconception of personal intake level. Appetite, 42,157-166.

Bolton, Ruth N. (1998), " A Dynamic Model Of The Duration Of The Customer's Relationship With A Continuous Service Provider: The Role Of Satisfaction", Marketing Science, 17 (1), 45-65.

B.Shiv and A. Fedorikhin, " Heart And Min In Conflict: The Interplay Of affect And Cognition In Consumer Decision Making", J. Consumer Res., vol. 26, pp. 278-292, Dec. 1999.

Brown, K.W., Ryan, R.M. Reswell , J.D. (2007). Mindfulness: Theoretical Foundatins And Evidence For Its Salutary Effects. Psychological Inquiry, 18, 211-237.

Burke, R.R. : Behavioral effects of digital signage, J. Advertising Res. 49(2), 180-185 (2009).

Cant, M., Brink , A. & Brijall, S., Consumer behavior, Cape Town, South Africa: Juta, 2006.

Conner, M. & Abraham, C. (2001). Conscientiousness and the theory of planned behavior: Toward a more complete model of the antecedents of intention and behavior. Social psychology bulletin, 27, 1547-1561.

Cooper C. Mallon, K, Leadbetter S, Pollack L, Peipins (2005) , cancer internet search activity on a major search engine, United States 2001 to 2003, J Med Internet Res. 7(3): e36.

Cope, R. R. Cope and H. Davis (2008). Disney's virtual Queues: A strategic opportunity to co-brand services ? Journal of Business & economics research, vol. 6 no10, 13-20.

Cornelia, B.F. (1999) Rural development news, the North Central Regional Center For Rural Development vol. no 24 , IOWA.

Couper, M.P. J. Blair and T. Triplet (1999). A Comparison Of Mail And E-mail For a Survey Of Employees In USA Statistical Agencies. Journal Of Official Statistics, 15, 39-56.

David J. Nowak & Gordon M. Melsler (2016) " Air quality effects of urban trees and parks." National recreation and park association, USA.

Data monitor (2008). The proctor and gamble company. Retrieved Nov. 15 2009 from http://www.datamonitor.com/

De Hollander, A. E. M., J.M. Melse, Elebret & P. G.N. Kramers (1999), " An Aggregate public health indicator to represent the impact of multiple environmental exposures" Epidemiology: 606-617.

De Visser, R.O., & McDonnell, E.J. (2013). " Man points": Masculine capital and young men's health. Health psychology, 32(1), 5-14. doi:10. 1037/a0029045.

Dunn, J & A Neumsister (2002). Knowledge management in the Information age. E. business review, Fall , 37-45. Jounral of service, spring 2011, vol. 4, no1, De Grovte (2009).

Dyer, D., F. Dalzell & R. Olegario (2004). Rising tide. Lessons learned from 165 years of brand building at Procter and Gamble. Boston, MA: Havard Business School Press.

Eysenbach G (2006) Infodemiology: Tracking flu- related searches on the web for syndromic surveillance. American Medical Informatics Associaion Annual Symposium Proceedings , Curran Associates, Red Hook, NY, pp. 244-248.

Ettredge M, Gerdes, J. Karuga , G (2005) Using web- based search data to predict macro-economic statistics. Commun ACM 48: 87-92.

Felce, D. and Perry, J. (1995). Quality of life: A contribution to its definition and measurement, vol. 16, no.1 pp: 51-74.

Feldman, Jack M. And John G. Lynch Jr. (1988), "Self-Generated Validity And Other Effects Of Measurement On Belife, Attitude, Intention And Behavior", Journal of applied psychology, 73(3),421-35.

Fiese, M, Hofmann, W., & Wanke, M (2009). The impulsive consumer. Predicting consumer behavior with implicit reaction time measurement. In M. Wanke (ed.) Social psychology of consumer behavior (pp.335-364). New York, NY: Psychology press.

Fitzsimons, Gavan, J. And Vicki G. Morwitz (1996), " The Effect Of Measuring Intent On Brand-Level Purchase Behavior", Journal of consumer research, 23 (1), 1-11.

Hallerman , D. (2008) video Advertising Online: Spending And Pricing , New York. E-Marketer.

Harriet Griffey. (2010) The art of concentration, enhance focus, Reduce, stress and achieve move. Macmillan publishers ltd,Basinastoke and Oxford, London UK.

Helleman, D. (2008) Video Advertising Online: Spending And Pricing , New York, E-Marketer.

Hensen, C. (2003). Kreuzfahrtourismus.www.christoph- hensen.de/Facharbeit.pdf.

Huang, H.I. (2012). An empirical analysis of the strategic Management of competitive advantage: a case study of higher technical and vocational education in Taiwan (Doctoral dissertation, Victoria University).

Jamieson, Linda F. And Frank M. Bass (1989), " Adjusting Stated Intention Measures To Predict Trial Purchase Of New Products: A Comparison Of Models And Methods," Journal of marketing research, 26 (August), 336-45.

Korea Ministry Of Environment. Public Organizations spend 2.2 Trillon Korean Won To Purchase green Products in 2014; Ministry Of Environment: Sejoung, Korea, 2015.

Kremers, S.P. J., De Bruijn, G.J., droomers, M., Van Lenthe, F. J., & Brug, J. (2005). Environmental interventions for selected dietary behaviors in adults. In J. Brug & F. J. Van Lenthe (eds.) , Environmental determinants and interventions for physical activity, nutrition and smoking: A review pp. 282-315. Rotterdam: Erasmus Medical Center.

Lee, D.; Kim, M. ; Lee, J. adoption of green electricity policies: Investigating the role of environmental attitudes via big data-driven search-queries. Energy policy 2016. 90, 187-201.

Lee, Terrence, " Tech in Asia-connecting Asia's startup system " Tech. in Asia- connecting Asia's startup ecosystem, N.p.,4 July 2016.

Los Angeles Country Department Of public Health (2016), Country Health Ranking Model, Retrieved From www.countryhealthrankgings.org/our-approach. USA.

Mayne, Lonnie. " Evolve of die in the age of the consumer". Entrepreneur, N.P. , 16 Apr. 2014. web of Oct. 2016.

McGregor, S.L. T., & Goldsmith, E.B. (1998). Expanding our understanding of quality of life, standard of living and well-being. Journal of family and consumer science, 90(2), 2-6, 22.

McMichael, A.J. M. Mckee, J. Shkolnikov and T. Valkanen (2004), " Morality trends and setbacks, global convergence or divergence?", Lancet 363, 1155-1159.

Melse, J.M. & A.E. M. De Hollander (2001). " Human Health And The Environment", background document for the OECD Environmental Outlook, OECD, Paris.

Moschis, George p. & Roy, L. Moore (1979), " Decision making among the young. A socialization perspective " Journal of consumer research , 6 (September).

Mulligan, M. Banerjee, T & Thomas, N. (2008) ,European Paid Content And Activity Forecast, (2008 to 2013), Jupiter Research.

Peter, J., Ryan, M, M, " An Investigation Of Perceived Risk At The Brand Level, " Journal of marketing research, 13 May 1976, pp. 184-188.

Pieters, R., & Wedel, M. (2007). Goal Control Of Visual Attention To Advertising: The Yarbus Implication. Journal Of Consumer Research, 34, 224-233 (August).

Parasuaman, and Leonard L. Berry (1985), " Problems And Strategies In Sevices Marketing", Journal of marketing, 49 (Spring), 33-46.

Priesnitz, W. (2007) Counting Our Food Miles. Natural Life, 1 July.

R.C. Oliver, " When is consumer loyalty?" J.Marketing vol. 63, pp.33-44.1999.

Reggiani, A . (ed). 1998, accessibility, trade and locational behavior, Ashgate publishing ltd, England.

Rushe, D. (2013) " The 10 best paid CEO in America". The Guardian , 22 Oct, (online). Available at: http://www.theguardian.com/business/2013/Oct22/best-paid-chief-executives-america (Accessed: 3 May 2014).

Spiekermann and Wegener (2007), update of selected potential accessibility indicators. Final report, urban and regional research (S&W), RRG spatial planning and geoinformation. ESPON. Available online at http:// <www.espon.eu/mmp/online/website/ contentprojects/947/1297/file_2724/ espon_accessibility_update-2006-fr_070207.pdf>, accessed on 1 July 2009.

Starbucks (2014) Our company available at http:// www. starbucks.com/about- us/company-information (accessed: 3 May 2014).

Shostack, G. Lynn (1984), " Designing Services That Deliver", Harvard Business Review, 62 (January-February), 133-9.

Shostack, G. Lynn (1985), " Planning The Service Encounter ,in the service encounter" , John A. Czepiel, Michael R. Solomon, and Carol F. Suprenant, eds. New York: Lexington Books, 243-54.

Shostack, G. Lynn (1987), " Service Positioning Through, Structural Change", Journal of marketing, 51 (Janurary), 34-43.

Soloman, Michael R. (1985), "Packaging The Service Provider", Service Industries Journal , 5(1), 64-71.

Stevens, C.W. (1980), "K-MartStores Try New Look To Invite More Spending" The Wall Street Journal, Nov. 26, 29-35.

Sullivan, Nicholas P(2007). You can hear me now: How Micro loans and cell phones are connecting the world, San Francisco, CA: John Wilsey & Sans, 2007.

T. Ambler, A. Ioannides, And S. Rose, " Brand s On The Brain : Neuroimages Of Advertising ", Business Strategy rev., vol. 11, 3. pp. 17-30. 2000.

Westbrook, Robert A. (1980), " Intrapersonal affective influences on consumer satisfaction with products, " Journal of consumer research , 7 (June) 49-54.

Wiig, k.(1993). Knowledge management foundations: Thinking About thinking. How people and organizations create, represent and use knowledge vol.1 , of knowledge management series schema press: Arlington, TX.

World Health Organization (2003). Diet, nutrition and the prevention of Chronic diseases report of a joint WHO/ FAO. expert consultation. Geneva: World Health Organization.

Wysocki, B. (1979), " Sight, Smell, Sound: They're all arms in retailer's arsenal" The Wall Street Journal, Nov. 17, 1979. 1-35.

Yale Center For Environmental Law And Policy (2006). Environmental Performance Index. Data available on-line at http://epi.yale.edu

9 798886 410488

Printed by Libri Plureos GmbH in Hamburg,
Germany